Drafting the EU Charter

Palgrave Studies in European Union Politics

Edited by: **Michelle Egan**, American University, USA, **Neill Nugent**, Manchester Metropolitan University, UK, **William Paterson**, University of Birmingham, UK

Editorial Board: **Christopher Hill**, Cambridge, UK, **Simon Hix**, London School of Economics, UK, **Mark Pollack**, Temple University, USA, **Kalypso Nicolaïdis**, Oxford, UK, **Morton Egeberg**, Oslo University, Norway, **Amy Verdun**, University of Victoria, Canada

Palgrave Macmillan is delighted to announce the launch of a new book series on the European Union. Following on the sustained success of the acclaimed *European Union Series*, which essentially publishes research-based textbooks, *Palgrave Studies in European Union Politics* will publish research-driven monographs.

The remit of the series is broadly defined, both in terms of subject and academic discipline. All topics of significance concerning the nature and operation of the European Union potentially fall within the scope of the series. The series is multidisciplinary to reflect the growing importance of the EU as a political and social phenomenon. We will welcome submissions from the areas of political studies, international relations, political economy, public and social policy and sociology.

Titles include:

Justus Schönlau
DRAFTING THE EU CHARTER
Rights, Legitimacy and Process

Forthcoming titles in the series include:

Heather Grabbe
THE EU'S TRANSFORMATIVE POWER

Ian Bache and Andrew Jordan *(editors)*
THE EUROPEANIZATION OF BRITISH POLITICS

Lauren McLaren
IDENTITY INTERESTS AND ATTITUDES TO EUROPEAN INTEGRATION

Karen Smith and Katie Verlin Laatikainen *(editors)*
THE EUROPEAN UNION AND THE UNITED NATIONS

Morten Egeberg *(editor)*
MULTILEVEL COMMUNITY ADMINISTRATION

Palgrave Studies in European Union Politics
Series Standing Order ISBN 1–4039–9511–7 (hardback) and ISBN 1–4039–9512–5 (paperback)

You can receive future titles in this series as they are published by placing a standing order. Please contact your bookseller or, in case of difficulty, write to us at the address below with your name and address, the title of the series and one of the ISBNs quoted above.

Customer Services Department, Macmillan Distribution Ltd, Houndmills, Basingstoke, Hampshire RG21 6XS, England

Drafting the EU Charter

Rights, Legitimacy and Process

Justus Schönlau
Researcher, European Parliament
Brussels, Belgium

macmillan

First published 2005 by
PALGRAVE MACMILLAN
Houndmills, Basingstoke, Hampshire RG21 6XS and
175 Fifth Avenue, New York, N.Y. 10010
Companies and representatives throughout the world

PALGRAVE MACMILLAN is the global academic imprint of the Palgrave Macmillan division of St. Martin's Press, LLC and of Palgrave Macmillan Ltd. Macmillan® is a registered trademark in the United States, United Kingdom and other countries. Palgrave is a registered trademark in the European Union and other countries.

ISBN-13: 978–1–4039–9373–1 hardback
ISBN-10: 1–4039–9373–4   hardback

This book is printed on paper suitable for recycling and made from fully managed and sustained forest sources.

A catalogue record for this book is available from the British Library.

Library of Congress Cataloging-in-Publication Data

Schönlau, Justus, 1971–
    Drafting the EU Charter : rights, legitimacy, and process / Justus Schönlau.
        p.   cm. – (Palgrave studies in European Union politics)
    Includes bibliographical references and index.
    ISBN 1–4039–9373–4 (cloth)
    1. Civil rights – European Union countries – History.   2 Constitu-
tional history – European Union countries.   3. Legitimacy of
governments – European Union countries.   1. Title.   II. Series.

KJE5132.S366   2005
342.2408′5 – dc22

                                                            2005050074

10   9   8   7   6   5   4   3   2   1
14   13   12   11   10   09   08   07   06   05

Printed and bound in Great Britain by
Antony Rowe Ltd, Chippenham and Eastbourne

Meinen Eltern
és Krisztának

Contents

Abbreviations

AG	Advocate General
BVG	Bundesverfassungsgericht (German Constitutional Court)
CDA	Christen Democratisch Appèl (Christian Democratic Appeal, Netherlands)
CDU	Christlich Demokratische Union Deutschlands (German Christian Democratic Union, Germany)
COREPER	Committee of Permanent Representatives of the EU member states
CSU	Christlich-Soziale Union in Bayern (Christian Social Union in Bavaria, Germany)
DS	Democratici di Sinistra (Democrats of the Left, Italy)
ECHR	European Convention on Human Rights and Fundamental Freedoms
ECJ	European Court of Justice
EDD	Group for a Europe of Democracies and Diversities
ELDR	Group of the European Liberal, Democratic and Reform Party
EP	European Parliament
EUCFR	European Union Charter of Fundamental Rights
GRÜNE	Die Grünen (Greens, Austria & Germany)
GUE/NGL	Confederal Group of the European United Left/Nordic Green Left
MEP	Member of the European Parliament
NI	Non-Inscrits, non-alligned members of the European Parliament
NGO	Non-Governmental Organisation
ÖVP	Österreichische Volkspartei (Austrian People's Party)
PDS	Partei des Demokratischen Sozialismus (Party of Democratic Socialism, Germany)
PP	Partido Popular (People's Party, Spain)
PPE	Group of the European People's Party (Christian-Democratic Group)
PS	Partie Socialiste (Socialist Party, France)
PSD	Partido Social Democrata (Social Democratic Party, Portugal)
PSE	Group of the Party of European Socialists

RPF	Rassemblement pour la France (Movement for France)
SAP	Socialdemokratiska arbetarepartiet (Socialdemocratic Workers' Party, Sweden)
SFP	Svenska Folkspartiet (Swedish People's Party, Finland)
SPD	Sozialdemokratische Partei Deutschlands (German Social Democratic Party)
SPÖ	Sozialdemokratische Partei Österreichs (Austrian Social Democratic Party)
TEU	Treaty on European Union
UEN	Union for a Europe of Nations Group
Verts/ALE	Group of the Greens/European Free Alliance
VVD	Volkspartij voor Vrijheid en Democratie (People's Party for Freedom and Democracy, Netherlands)

Preface

Since the 'first' EU Convention drafted the EU Charter of Fundamental Rights in 1999/2001, both the European Union and the world around it have changed considerably. Enlargement to include ten new member states, which was at the time an important, but rather distant prospect has happened, and a second Convention has been and gone, proposing a 'Constitution' to the Union which was subsequently rejected during the ratification phase in two national referenda and then 'put on ice', raising a number of fundamental questions about the Union and its future. At the same time, the challenges which the Union is facing seem ever greater, and the pace of change sometimes risks obscuring the significance of individual steps in the process. Therefore going back to my own writing about the Charter Convention, after having followed closely also the Constitutional Convention, has been an interesting journey of 'rediscovery'.

Even though the Charter and its drafting process have been recognised as an important reference point for all those involved in the following stages of EU constitution-making, it was and is striking, just how much of the debates in the 2002–2003 Convention had already been anticipated by the exchanges about the Charter. Not only the working method of a Convention embarked on the search for consensus, but also many questions about the contents, meaning and legitimate scope of the European Union's legal, moral, historical and political dimensions, including the controversy about Europe's religious heritage and its role for current-day EU politics, already featured in the 1999–2000 Charter process. It therefore seems appropriate to present this analysis of an important piece of 'EU history' now, while the issues discussed resonate strongly in the debate about the EU again, and to keep it 'on record' for the future.

The original research for this book would not have been possible without the friendship and support of Valerie and Malcolm Boddington, and of my friends and family. For understanding and patience during the final phase of this project I am particularly indebted to Kriszta.

J.S.
Brussels, Summer 2005

Acknowledgements

This book is based on original research at the University of Reading which was supported by a one-year ambassadorial scholarship of the Rotary Foundation International, and a two-year studentship at the Faculty of Letters and Social Sciences of the University of Reading. I am indebted to both institutions, as well as to Richard Bellamy and Alex Warleigh, for their guidance and support, and to Christopher Lord who encouraged me to publish my work.

The collection of data during the work of the Convention drafting the EU Charter was greatly helped by the support of Jo Leinen (MEP) and by the openness to share information of many members of the Convention and those working with them. I would like to thank all those who agreed to be interviewed or who provided information otherwise.

Further work on this book was undertaken in the framework of the project 'Citizenship and Democratic Legitimacy in the European Union' (CIDEL) within the 5th framework programme, and I am grateful to colleagues and friends within the EurCit and CIDEL research networks, in particular to Dario Castiglione, John Erik Fossum, Chris Longman and Augustin Menéndez.

1
The EU Charter of Fundamental Rights: Legitimating the European Union

EU legitimacy and fundamental rights

The European Union has a legitimacy problem because some people think it has one, and react accordingly. Like any form of political organisation, the European Union has to find a balance between the growing diversity of its constituent elements and the unity which is necessary for their co-existence, between the flexibility to continuously adapt to change, and the stability which provides security. Only if such balances are found, adapted when necessary, and maintained over time, and if they are seen and accepted to be so, can the EU be legitimate. The current debate about the 'future of Europe' and the *finalité* of European integration is part of the ongoing search for these balances, and it is significant because it acknowledges more clearly than previous rounds of the same political process that the legitimacy of the EU as a political order is a 'make-or-break' issue for the integration project. Not only its further development, but its very existence are potentially at risk if the problem of legitimacy continues to grow. The challenge is more tangible now because of successive enlargements which disturb delicate balances within the polity. Yet, the problem of legitimacy is not new: political actors in the EU have tried to address it in a variety of different ways over the years. At the same time, the opening phrase of this paragraph also alerts us to a number of essential difficulties in responding to the legitimacy problem with political action: the legitimacy of a political order is in large parts a subjective issue, it forms part of a highly complex pattern of social relations, it usually becomes visible only when there already is a problem, and it cannot be measured.

Despite these problems, the 'quest for legitimacy' is an important element of political action, in particular of the European Union.[1]

Especially since the problems surrounding the ratification of the Treaty on European Union in 1991/92, and more recently in the process of reforming the EU to prepare for its biggest ever enlargement in 2004, the issue of legitimacy is of growing concern to the actors in the European integration project.[2] The aim of this book is therefore to understand how the drafting of an EU Charter of Fundamental Rights (EUCFR) in 1999–2000 addressed the perceived legitimacy problem of the European Union and which role it played in preparing for the subsequent steps in the EU's constitutional process. In this, the volume wants to make a contribution to the ongoing debate about the Union's legitimacy, both by refining the theoretical concept of legitimacy itself, and by testing it against the effect of the drafting of a Charter of Fundamental Rights. The central question which guides this work is therefore: *What contribution has the EU Charter of Fundamental Rights, and the process by which it was drafted, made to a more legitimate European Union?*

The rationale for such an investigation is the shortage to date, within the general debate about the EU's legitimacy, and in the emerging literature on particular aspects of it, of research which critically evaluates the relationship between the normative premises on which the debate is based, and concrete political action by European level actors. There is a substantial, and rapidly growing body of mainly theoretical literature concerned with the concept of legitimacy, its normative foundations, and its particular complexities in the EU context.[3] At the same time, there is of course a vast number of political and/or legal analyses of European integration, its institutional development, its mechanisms, and its impact on the legitimacy of existing frameworks of political organisation. Yet, so far, much less attention has been focused on how the legitimacy issue itself has directly influenced political action. Even though it will be argued that there are distinct examples of EU-level 'legitimacy policy' since at least the early 1970s, it is quite clear that with the drafting of the EU Charter of Fundamental Rights in 1999/2000, the issue of how to legitimate the European Union acquired a political visibility until then unknown.

Why draft a Charter for the EU?

This investigation maps in detail how the empirical reality of drafting a catalogue of fundamental rights for the European Union was shaped by, interacted with, and possibly promoted the development of a more thorough understanding of the normative foundations on which the legitimacy of the integration project must rest. The Charter process is used here as a 'case-study' of EU legitimation policy because it offered a great possibility to combine empirical data from the debates on the EU Charter of Fundamental Rights with a critical assessment of the concepts underlying, and rationale supposedly validating the initiative which aimed at endowing the EU with its own fundamental rights document and which paved the way for the wider project of drafting an EU Constitution in 2003–2004.

The starting point for looking at the Charter process in this perspective is the link, postulated by the Cologne mandate (see below), between the legitimacy of the EU, a list of fundamental rights, and the decision by the European Council to draft a Charter of Fundamental Rights for the European Union through a particular kind of process. The European Council decided, at its summit meeting in Cologne in June 1999, to commission a special body to draft a catalogue of fundamental rights. The particular arrangements for this exercise were spelled out at the summit meeting in Tampere in October 1999, and the 'Body' met for the first time in December that year. It consisted of 62 titular members, including two representatives from each national parliament, one representative of each national head of state or government, sixteen members of the European Parliament, and a representative of the Commission. The 'Body' named itself 'Convention' in its second meeting in January 2000, and elected Roman Herzog, former president of Germany and before that of the German constitutional court, as its president by acclamation.[4]

The decision at the June 1999 summit to draft a Charter became known as the 'Cologne mandate'. It states that the '[p]rotection of fundamental rights is a founding principle of the European Union and an indispensable prerequisite for its legitimacy.'[5] This statement became the guiding light for the work of the Convention. It suggests a strong conditional link between the protection of fundamental rights and the EU's legitimacy. As became clear from this statement, and was reaffirmed in the subsequent text of the mandate, the rights in this equation were taken as given. According to the Cologne mandate, the Charter was supposed to contain rights which are already protected elsewhere. By merely listing these rights and making them 'visible' to Europe's citizens, the Cologne text suggests, the European Union as a whole would become more legitimate. In the following a critical approach is taken to this statement because the link between rights and legitimacy is not as straightforward as it appears in the formula of the Cologne mandate, at neither a theoretical nor an empirical level.

Rights fulfil a dual function within the polity. While it is true that fundamental rights are commonly seen to constitute minimum

standards which every political order must meet in order to be legitimate, rights and the mechanisms for their determination are also core
elements of the political process itself. Consequently, far from just
showing an existing common basis of rights on which European integration rests, the debates in the Convention brought to the fore important
conflicts among different understandings of rights and their meaning.
In such a situation of disagreement, the process of listing those rights
which were to be considered 'fundamental' in the EU context was
central. It involved a great number of profoundly political decisions.
Looking both at the process, which was set up to arrive at a definition
of the EU's fundamental rights basis (Chapter 4), and its results (Chapter
5), it becomes clear how the Charter project brought the EU's constitutional questions into the open much more clearly than had previously
been the case. The contribution of the EUCFR to the Union's legitimacy
must therefore be understood as the combined effect of the rights it
contains, of the process which it developed, and of the debates which
it created.

This contribution is part of the wider process of permanently rebalancing the legitimacy of the European Union and it had to have a
positive effect on the perceptions of Europeans. Yet criticisms have been
levelled against the Charter exercise from the start from two different
angles: on the one hand it has been argued that from a legal point
of view the Charter was of little real value as long as it remained
a political declaration, and even after its inclusion in the European
Constitution it carries the danger of raising false expectations and/or
undermining existing systems for rights protection.[6] On the other hand,
some theorists of democracy and constitutional process saw the Charter
project as dangerous because the codification of certain rights and particular values through a process and in a document which itself made
clear references to classical liberal constitutionalism and which has since
become part of the now openly 'constitutional' process of the EU, risks
the closure of the very political debate which is seen as indispensable
in a pluralist setting such as the EU.[7]

Both kinds of criticisms can, in my view, be addressed by focusing on
the interaction of process, contents, and the wider debate about the
EU's future. The fundamental question behind these critical views is
whether the EU is really so diverse in terms of political culture that it
does not make sense to speak of a consensus on certain political values
reached and gradually built through half a century of interaction and
compromise negotiation, and whether the formalisation of the current
contents of this compromise in a document like the Charter really

means that this body of values is set in stone henceforth, and is thus removed from political debate for ever. In substance, this is the perennial problem of how much community is necessary to validate a political organisation and whether this community predates, or is created with, the establishment of political structures.[8] This debate has been intensified at the theoretical level with the drafting of the EU Constitution, but if and when the Constitution enters into force, the debate will also have been superseded to a certain extent by empirical developments – at least for the time being.

The Charter process and its contribution to EU legitimacy

The present volume maintains that the Charter is a positive contribution to the legitimacy of the EU because through its process it generated a debate about what precisely the agreements and disagreements in terms of values and rights were in the EU at the time. Given the institutional history of the EU, it seems safe to assume that such a debate would not have taken place if the Charter project had not provided the focus and forum for it at that particular moment. In this sense, the danger of the Charter 'freezing' the political process was outweighed by the greater publicity and wider reach of the debate which the Charter created. Moreover, both in legal terms and through the role of the Convention as an institutional precedent, I argue that the Charter project was instrumental in generating further openings for political debate. It is thus an important element in the history of the development of EU legitimacy.

The hypotheses guiding the investigation are therefore firstly, that the Charter process has had a significant effect on the legitimacy of the European Union, and secondly, that this is a positive effect because of the political debates it generated and the mechanisms it provided for accommodating differences. The effect of the Charter consisted, and continues to consist in the political choices it embodies, and in the political process from which it emerged, rather than just in its legal contents. From this perspective the legal status of the Charter, which was initially proclaimed at the Nice summit in December 2000 merely as a 'political declaration', was of secondary importance. While the Charter's inclusion into the EU Constitution of course will have significant legal consequences, and in itself constitutes a very important political choice, the Charter in its original status was already a crucial step towards a more legitimate EU because the debate in the Convention and beyond about the fundamental rights on which the EU is built promoted a clearer definition of what the European Union is, whom it is for, who are the actors in it, and by which means it can and should achieve its aims. The later Convention on the future of the EU could build on these debates and on the experiences from the Convention process.

In trying to understand precisely how the Charter, and its drafting process made this development possible, and how this affected and affects the legitimacy of the European Union, the following questions have to be discussed:

- What are the constituent elements which make up the legitimacy of a political order?
- What is the link between the legitimacy of a political order, and a body of fundamental rights which informs the organisation of this order?
- What action has been taken in the past by actors in the European Union to improve the legitimacy of the Union?
- How does the definition of a set of fundamental rights for a particular polity affect the legitimacy of that polity, in this case the EU?
- What effect does the process by which a catalogue of fundamental rights was agreed have on the EU's legitimacy?
- What other elements contribute to the effect of the Charter project on the European Union's legitimacy?

The structure of the volume

Chapter 2: Legitimacy and fundamental rights

Based on these questions, Chapter 2 investigates the notions of 'rights', 'legitimacy', and the link between them. It shows that both rights and legitimacy are complex concepts. Legitimacy conveys authority upon a political decision; rights circumscribe the autonomy of the individual vis-à-vis the collectivity. According to most theoretical approaches to the question of legitimacy, the latter is a multi-layered concept which includes at least three constitutive elements.[9] The first of these is to do with the 'legality' or formal correctness of decisions according to a set of predetermined rules. The second element requires a legitimate decision to be consistent with the identity, or shared ideas or norms of the collectivity which makes up the polity. The third element of a legitimate decision requires some notion of institutionalised consent to, or participation in, such a decision, by those who are affected by it. As far as rights are concerned, the main question is on what basis they rest. Even though most present-day theories of rights recognise that rights are based on some kind of 'contract' between individuals and that rights therefore are not absolute, the concurrent notion of 'innate' human rights with a certain absolute quality to them is still very prominent in the political debate about the protection of rights.[10]

In the case of the European Union, the situation with regard to legitimacy is particularly complicated because the EU is a new and evolving polity which is developing alongside with, and on top of, a number of existing political orders, most notably its member states. This creates a situation in which legitimacy and power are transferred between different levels of governance, a process which in itself requires legitimacy. Analytically, the situation is complicated by the need to distinguish between the legitimacy of the new political order as such ('polity legitimacy'), and the legitimacy of its functioning ('regime legitimacy').[11] Furthermore, the question of rights at the EU level is complicated by the fact that all 15 EU member states which were involved in drafting the Charter in the year 2000, as well as the ten new member states which joined the EU in 2004 and had to sign up to the Charter, do provide protection of a number of fundamental rights in their national constitutions, and all of them are signatories to the European Convention for the Protection of Human Rights and Fundamental Freedoms (ECHR). Europe is a political space in which different systems of rights protection co-exist and interact, and into which the Charter had to be fitted.

The link between legitimacy and fundamental rights is therefore delicate. While at one level, fundamental rights of the individual are the limits to the legitimate power of the collectivity, at another level the organisation of these rights and their internal balance is one central element of the political process. Fundamental rights thus fulfil a dual function in legitimating a given political order. This is captured in the conceptualisation of fundamental rights (understood as inter-subjectively recognised entitlements), and the political process (understood as the recognition of individuals as free and equal holders of rights), as constituting each other.[12] This understanding allows us then to look at the process of drafting a catalogue of fundamental rights not merely as an exercise in legal codification, but as an instance of political decision-making with a profound impact on the legitimacy of the political order within which it occurs.

Chapter 3: What kind of legitimacy for the EU?

The political structure in question here is the European Union. To assess the significance of the Charter process, it needs to be placed in the overall context of the EU's development. In particular, the different ways in which the emerging EU polity has addressed the problem of its own legitimacy in the past are instructive both for their achievements and for their shortcomings. Chapter 3 traces the particular problems of the EU as a constantly changing political order in trying to develop an approach to a legitimacy of its own. The analysis follows the broad categorisation of the main elements of legitimacy, developed in Chapter 2, as input, output, and identity-related. The recognition that any order, to be legitimate, has to be able to generate policy output effectively and efficiently, has produced a number of innovative institutional arrangements at the European level. However, it is not clear whether a stronger EU is improving or exacerbating the legitimacy problem. The construction of input avenues of democratic participation within the EU has followed mainly traditional patterns (i.e. those based on the needs of, and the experience from, the nation-state), which meet with particular problems when applied to a multi-lingual, large, diverse and continuously changing polity. Finally, attempts to invoke or create a European identity through mainly symbolic action have revealed the limits of 'commonness' and emotive bonds between Europeans. Thus none of these attempts to tackle the three elements of legitimacy seems to have been able on their own to sustain 'enough' legitimacy to solve the EU's problem. More recently, the development of a notion of European citizenship, while providing at least the conceptual framework for a more comprehensive approach to the complex problem of legitimacy, has so far not realised its full potential. Yet, if conceived within a broad, political notion of European constitutionalism, the concept of citizenship could become the basis of an independent EU legitimacy. The drafting of the EU Constitution including the Charter and building on the first Convention's experience seems to suggest that the EU will continue to follow this path.

Chapter 4: Drafting the Charter in the Convention

In this situation, the process of drafting a Charter of Fundamental Rights provided an open, institutionalised forum in which to debate EU 'constitutional' questions. The evidence from a close analysis of the debates in the Convention provides an interesting case-study for assessing how the Charter process interacted with the normative foundations of integration. While such fundamentals had until then primarily been discussed and decided by the Members of the European Council in intergovernmental conferences (IGCs), the Charter debates brought together actors from all EU institutions, as well as from national

Parliaments and civil society. The Chapter shows how the debate about fundamental rights in and around the Convention went to the heart of the political process at European level, and required new balances to be found on the four core dimensions of this process, namely: who are its subjects, which spheres should it cover, what is its scope, and which political style should be followed?[13] By demonstrating the need to find answers to these challenges, the Charter project moved the EU legitimacy question on to a new level.

Chapter 5: The impact of the Charter

The Charter and its process have contributed at a number of different levels to a greater legitimacy for the EU. The Charter, even as a political declaration, quickly became a point of reference not only for individual rights litigation before the European Court of Justice (ECJ), but also for the wider EU constitutional debate. Similarly, the process in the Convention itself turned out to be a useful innovation for the particular task of finding and/or constructing compromise in a diverse setting such as the European Union. The Convention's structure with its members from different institutional backgrounds, the particular rules which guided the debates, and the individual as well as the collective standing of the delegates, encouraged in the Convention a deliberative style of debate on many sensitive issues on which agreement in a different arena would have been very difficult. Even though the deliberation in the Convention was not 'perfect', and traditional forms of compromise and bargaining were part of the overall result, the deliberative element was one key innovative part of the process in the EU context. Moreover, the process also contributed important additions to the discourse of the European Union as a community of values. These results of the Charter process have effects on the EU's legitimacy because they set the standards against which the Union has been measured since and will be measured in the future. Together with the certainly significant legal impact of the Charter, especially after its inclusion in the EU Constitution, the overall effect of the document and its process cannot be overestimated.

Chapter 6: Linking rights, process and legitimacy

While some of the Charter's implications will become fully measurable only once the Constitution enters into force, and further research will be needed in this respect, the effect of the 1999–2000 experiment on the EU's legitimacy is already clearly visible. The Charter process focused and expanded the debate about what exactly the Union's legitimacy consists in, which, given the inter-subjective nature of the legitimacy problem, is an essential step towards finding a tenable balance. The drafting process provided a focus and a forum for the first constitutional debate about the European Union outside the diplomatic arena of the European Council meetings. The limits of the deliberation in the Convention of course have to be acknowledged, yet the new style of interaction allowed for agreements to be reached on some very controversial issues. The ensuing steps in the EU's constitutional process did recognise many elements of the Charter process as having provided the basis for the second Convention. A detailed investigation of the former is therefore necessary to take account of the less directly visible contributions of the Charter project to the EU's legitimacy, and to place them in the wider debate about the normative underpinnings of European integration.

The Charter and EU legitimacy

The project of drafting an EU Charter of Fundamental Rights in order to address the EU's legitimacy problem reflects a concern which is becoming increasingly important at the political level. How, by which mechanisms or through which action, can European integration be made *more* legitimate? The single most surprising element of the process of European integration has been its continued dynamics over time, despite an increasing awareness that a growing number of people in the countries of the EU seem to have doubts about it. There are few expressions of outright hostility to the EU, or calls for its demise, so far. As Joseph Weiler notes, '[t]he European construct, democratic deficit notwithstanding, has been approved democratically again and again'.[14] Nevertheless, talk about the Union's legitimacy deficit becomes more and more urgent, not least because subsequent rounds of enlargement of the Union seem to require further steps of integration to be successful, while the downward trend of interest and participation in European politics seems to be unstoppable. The question facing the Union, therefore, is whether at any given moment the legitimacy available to it is 'sufficient' to sustain the next step of political adjustment.

In this debate, the EU faces, in the words of the Commission, a 'real paradox. On the one hand, Europeans want [Europe] to find solutions to the major problems confronting our societies. On the other hand, people increasingly distrust institutions and politics or are simply not interested in them.'[15] Whether the solution to this paradox is a linear and cumulative development towards 'ever closer Union', or even towards a super-state, is subject to inspired but as yet inconclusive debates. In this context it seems of great practical as well as of epistemological interest to pay attention to the mechanics of legitimation at the European level. Given the difficulties highlighted by Philippe Schmitter, i.e. that it is impossible to 'measure' legitimacy, the starting point for such an investigation has to be the political action undertaken in pursuit of legitimacy. By trying to clarify how the creation of a Charter of Fundamental Rights affected the EU's legitimacy and its perception, it might become possible to separate those strategies which are more likely to be successful in improving the legitimacy situation, from those which are less so. This book argues that the Charter initiative did indeed make a contribution to a more legitimate EU, though not necessarily in the way that was expected by those who commissioned it: the EUCFR and its process promoted the EU's legitimacy not (mainly) by answering questions about fundamental rights, but by raising more questions about the constitutional foundations of the EU. The ensuing debate about the core of European integration is a pre-condition for finding a tenable legitimacy balance for the EU in the future.

2
Legitimacy and Fundamental Rights

Introduction: fundamental rights and European integration

As indicated, the mandate setting up the Convention to draft a Charter pre-supposed a strong link between the protection, at the European level, of certain rights and the legitimacy of the European Union.[1] Paul Craig expressed a similar view when he stated that '[t]he most obvious reason' for the EU to develop its own regime of fundamental rights protection 'is that it enhances the Community's legitimacy . . . The greater the powers of the Community, and the more they impinged on matters which were social and political and not merely economic, the greater the need for some quid pro quo in terms of individual rights.'[2] The initiative to draft a catalogue of fundamental rights for the Union, and to do so in the particular process that was devised by the decision of the Cologne Council, in this sense, was a new attempt to redress the delicate balance of EU legitimacy by top-down institutional means (see also Chapter 3). One problem in this exercise, however, was the apparent failure by the authors of the Cologne mandate to recognise how much political dynamite was contained in their proposal. The EU was a complex of overlapping systems of rights, and rights protection, both legally and politically, even before the decision to add another layer to this system in 1999. The idea that fundamental rights in Europe were already so well defined and commonly agreed that the task would be one of *'merely'* making them visible (as transpires from the Cologne mandate), therefore seems somewhat naive, but it reflects a particular understanding of fundamental (human) rights as essentially given and pre-political. Yet, the diversity of traditions, institutions, and understandings of rights within the EU simply *had to* interact with the political nature of the process, to produce fundamental debates about the normative foundations of the EU.

In order to understand the reasoning behind the political decision to draft a Charter, and to assess what effects (whether intended or unintended), this initiative had, it is necessary to clarify the core concepts of rights and legitimacy, and the central link between them. This chapter undertakes such a clarification with the specific problems of both concepts in the EU debate in mind.

Firstly, legitimacy is the quality which confers authority upon collective decisions. The mechanisms by which this is achieved are complex, particularly in a new political entity which is not (yet) based on a clearly defined political space and/or community.

Secondly, rights are understood here in their liberal guise as individual entitlements vis-à-vis the collectivity. This notion of rights has seen a dramatic development since the eighteenth century. Yet, an important problem for any such theory of rights is posed by the question whether rights are inalienable properties of the individual, or whether they exist only in a social context. While the philosophical discussion has provided a number of different accounts of rights and their functioning, most of which recognise that rights are socially constructed, it is important to bear in mind that in the political (and in the public) discourse, the other understanding of rights is still very influential: especially in the concept of 'human rights' the older concept of rights as natural (or divine) endowments of the individual, which are inalienable and absolute, can be traced. This notion exerted an important influence over the debates in the Charter Convention (see Chapter 5).

Thirdly, it will be highlighted that the relationship between the complex concepts of rights and legitimacy turned out to be not as clear and hierarchical as the formula of the Cologne mandate suggested. In fact, rights fulfil a dual function for legitimacy: respect for them is both a precondition for legitimate order (as the Cologne mandate maintained), but at the same time, the realisation of rights is also one of the central aims of the political order. Thus to a certain degree rights justify political order, but they themselves need some kind of justification as guiding principles of political action. This becomes a problem if the traditional notion of inalienable, innate, and unnegotiable human rights is challenged by the contemporary understanding of rights as products of, and subject to, negotiation and compromise between free and equal individuals in a political process.

The drafting of the EU Charter in the wider context of the EU's search for legitimacy brought this conflict to the fore. The Charter process was significant for having provided a constitutional forum, in which the debate about rights, their contents, scope and beneficiaries came to constitute the polity. The debates in the Convention drafting the Charter revealed both substantial differences on some of the issues raised (for example the role of social and economic rights and whether these were to be included as 'fundamental' rights), and a surprising capacity for compromise and ultimate agreement among the members of the Convention, and by extension between the political constituencies they represented. The subsequent analysis of the results of the Charter debates, and of the process which yielded these results, shows how clarification of both agreements and disagreements marked substantial progress on the path to a more legitimate EU polity.

In clarifying the central notions of 'legitimacy' and 'rights', and the link between them, it becomes clear that both concepts cannot stand on their own but need to be linked to, and by, some notion of democracy, in particular in a pluralist setting. The next step therefore identifies the elements of legitimacy, and looks in more detail at the role of fundamental rights in legitimating a political order, in particular the European Union. One plausible way to translate these theoretical notions into political practice is provided by a notion of 'democratic process' in which rights and legitimacy constitute each other. Following arguments advanced by Jürgen Habermas, who sees the 'double answer to the legitimacy question' in 'popular sovereignty and human rights', a process-based account of legitimation will be sketched out which is particularly suited to conceptualise the realisation of fundamental rights in a multicultural setting at the inter- or transnational level.[3] The essence of this process is the act of discursive deliberation which mediates between the two principles and constitutes the polity.[4] The final section returns to the particular case of the European Union and concludes that the Charter process acted as an arena for the deliberation of rights, which in turn helped to consolidate a set of compromises on the constitutional questions of the EU.[5]

Basic concepts

Legitimacy

At its most basic definitional level, the concept of legitimacy is concerned with the mechanism which 'confers upon an order or command an authoritative or binding character, thus transforming power into authority'.[6] It creates a willingness of the ruled to comply with constraints on their individual freedom imposed by the ruler. This conferral of 'binding character' consists of two separate elements: the linking of authority with the order itself, and the acceptance of this link by the ruled. This is what Max Weber tried to capture when he described the state as a 'relation of men dominating men, a relation supported by means of legitimate (i.e. *considered to be* legitimate) violence'.[7] David Beetham, however, is fiercely critical of Max Weber's notion of legitimacy as 'a belief in legitimacy' and calls his influence on the concept of legitimacy 'an almost unqualified disaster' because Weber's emphasis on the belief in legitimacy, in Beetham's view, obscures the objective elements of the notion.[8] For Beetham it is therefore necessary to develop a more complex understanding of legitimacy which, apart from the subjective element, also takes account of the 'legality' of power, and of 'consent' to it.[9] A further problem in understanding legitimacy is added by the fact that, as Andrew Heywood notes, the 'term legitimacy is used differently in political philosophy and political science', where the former is interested in it as 'a rational or moral principle', whereas the latter deals with it as a sociological fact, namely the acceptance of authority by the ruled.[10] One therefore needs to be aware of the multiple aspects of the notion of legitimacy, which determine its interaction with other concepts such as 'power' or 'rights'.

With regard to the latter concept, legitimacy is about the acceptable curtailments of individual freedoms and the need to balance these against a set of individual rights. The notion of rights is itself a complex one and will be explored further below. At this stage it is important to note that there exists a tension between authority, on the one hand, and individual rights, on the other – on both the philosophical and the practical levels. It is the notion of 'legitimacy' that mediates this tension. Legitimacy explains how a system of constraints on the individual can work and become an accepted fact. The rights and freedoms of the individual and the authority of the collectivity need to be organised into some kind of equilibrium, and the mechanisms to maintain and adjust this equilibrium are the means of legitimate rule and legitimation.

Rights

The notion of rights is similarly complex. At its most general, the notion of rights 'implies that some principle or rule gives a person or class of persons an entitlement to the aid or forbearance of others in the pursuit or enjoyment of some good; or the ability to bring about such an obligation on others; or an immunity from being subject to such an obligation by others.'[11] Rights form a central element of human organisation into collectivities. Yet, Peter Jones notes that '[r]ights are so common in our world that we might suppose that they are woven into the very fabric of human existence. But there have been worlds without rights.'[12] This observation is important because it shows that a concept of rights emerged as one particular way of organising the relationships between individual human beings. At the same time, there is a strong conceptual tradition of 'natural law' which assumes that rights are an innate attribute of human beings, and thus endow individuals with equal and inalienable (natural) rights by virtue of being human.[13]

This particular understanding postulates that such rights exist outside of, and prior to, the organisation of individuals into collective groups. Others have argued, however, that the very concept of rights only makes sense within a collectivity of individuals (for example Jürgen Habermas, see below). Whichever position one holds in this theoretical debate about the origin of rights, however, the idea of 'natural' rights is still powerful in political discourse today. It is reflected in the modern notion of 'human rights', in Jeremy Waldron's definition the 'conviction that there are liberties and interests so basic that every society should secure them irrespective of its traditions, history or level of economic development'.[14] According to Peter Jones, these are rights 'which all people are thought to posses whether or not they are embodied in a system of positive law'.[15] In this sense human rights are egalitarian. With regard to the controversies in the Charter Convention as to which rights should be included in the document as 'fundamental rights', it is interesting to note that 'according to the full-blooded version of the doctrine [of human rights], declarations and conventions of human rights do not "create" and "give" rights to human beings; they simply recognise and announce the rights that human beings have'.[16] The precise difference between these two understandings and its implications for the contents of the Charter was a hotly contested issue in the debates in the Charter Convention and ultimately had to be resolved by finding compromises (see Chapter 4 in this volume).[17]

Balancing rights

As far as the link between rights and legitimate power is concerned, the main function of the liberal notion of rights when it developed as a political instrument from the middle of the eighteenth century was 'first and foremost as checks upon political power'.[18] That is to say, rights emerged within the context of the formation of territorially based organisations of human co-existence as a means to balance the standing of the individual against the interests of the collectivity at a moment when it could no longer be automatically assumed that the ruler (who had, until then, claimed to act on behalf of a higher authority), was the best person to rule justly. At the same time, it is clear that not all of these rights are necessarily always compatible or even 'compossible' with each other.[19] In other words, the concept of inalienable rights is challenged by the inevitability of clashes between different rights which must be resolved within a given political system. In order to adjudicate conflicts between rights, the different rights claims have to be weighed against each other. This is usually done with reference to a set of under-lying values, of which the rights in question are seen as expressions. The problem is that values themselves are in conflict in pluralist societies. As Sniderman, Fletcher, Russell and Tetlock argue, '[t]he poli-tics of rights is driven by the irreducible diversity of values in politics and the unavoidability of their . . . coming into conflict with each other.'[20] The challenge for any political system in this understanding is to provide a framework in which conflicting values can be negotiated and rights balanced against each other.

In trying to understand the dynamics of a process of listing a set of fundamental rights in the year 2000, it is important to be aware that both this latter conception, and the natural law based assumption of rights as 'absolute', are still influential in the thinking of political actors, and traces of both became visible in the debates in the Charter Conven-tion which had to balance different, and often opposing claims to rights against each other. This tension was epitomised in the debate whether the Charter was 'just' listing existing, undisputed, 'natural' human rights, or whether it was engaged in a constructive exercise of finding a balance between different rights specific to the circumstances of the European Union at a particular point in time.[21]

This general problem of necessary limitations on fundamental rights is also clearly visible in the European Convention of Human Rights of 1950, which was the main point of reference for the rights of the EU Charter. In 1950, in the real world of a justiciable human rights docu-ment, a compromise had to be found between the common view of human rights as 'inalienable' and based on the 'inherent dignity . . . of all members of the human family'[22] on the one hand, and the need to acknowledge the limitations, and possibly conflicting nature, of some of the rights in question, on the other. The ECHR therefore pro-vides quite specific limitations to certain rights within individual arti-cles. It also allows for a temporary suspension of most of the rights in specific situations such as war or emergency, but within limits (ECHR Art. 15 – but rights which cannot be suspended even under this provision include the right to life (Art. 2), the prohibition of torture (Art. 3) and the prohibition of slavery (Art. 4)). On this basis, it has become 'a principle of interpretation of the Convention that only restrictions that are expressly authorised are allowed' to prevent that the exceptions 'eat out the contents of the substantive rights.'[23]

The same problem informed the debates in the Charter Convention whether limitations to the rights enumerated in the document could be justified. The final document produced by the Convention therefore contained a blanket limitation clause, which envisaged limitations 'if they are necessary and genuinely meet objectives of general interests recognized by the Union' (Art. 52 EUCFR), but there are also specific limitations in some individual articles. Moreover, the qualification of Charter rights by the phrase 'in accordance with Community law and national laws' in numerous articles, and the provision in Art. 52, were introduced as a means to allow for continuing diversity among member states. From a legal point of view, there was some doubt at the time, however, whether the limitations in the Charter were going to be as effective as those in the ECHR, if the Charter was to become legally binding.[24] Yet, for the issue of legitimacy, the question whether ulti- mately diversity or uniformity will be the outcome of the contestations which might arise from these rights, is less important than the need for each new settlement to be the product of compromise and of an appro- priate process. This need to compromise rights is particularly problem- atic where there is no agreement on the moral grounding of the rights in question, or about the political system itself.

Legitimacy and rights in a pluralist world

The focus of this book is the legitimation of a (supposedly) democratic system through reference to a set of fundamental human rights. As Richard Bellamy argues, 'rights and liberties are . . . intimately tied up with the democratic process, which gives them their force, form and content'.[25] This democratic process is thus the arena in which the con- troversies inherent in different notions of rights about their function and justification are mediated and ideally become part of the legitimat- ing force of rights. Since the political system in question, the EU, is a pluralist one, we have to focus the investigation on what Attracta Ingram calls an 'account of individual liberty and rights which is appro- priate to the practice of pluralist liberal democracy'.[26] Such a situation requires a concept of rights that is *not* founded on a single, shared notion of a higher moral authority as the ultimate justification of supposedly absolute rights because there is no agreement on such an authority within the EU. In this context, it needs to be remembered that the issue of legitimacy as a problematic conceptual relationship between rights and authority became a major issue for political thinking when 'modernity' undermined the previously 'universal' belief within most communities that both political authority and rights (where they existed), were derived from God. The debates both in the Convention drafting the EU Charter, and later on in the Constitutional Convention, about a reference in both documents to specific religious or cultural traditions as the foundations of a European political order, showed just how deeply divided the current-day EU is about such pre-political values.[27]

Thus, in a modern world of competing moral notions and different justifications of authority, debate and compromise about the concept and contents of rights are necessary. This debate in turn presupposes the individual's freedom and capacity to conduct such a debate. The necessary pre-condition to enable such a dialogue between individuals as free and equal is captured in the concept of 'autonomy'. In Ingram's words, '[f]or us to come to reasonable agreement on a scheme of rights acceptable to all, the idea of autonomy has to be presupposed.'[28] This autonomy itself is protected by a democratic order because only a democratic order 'simultaneously secures the private autonomy of the individual by certain protective rights, and secures the public autonomy of the individual by a right to participation'.[29]

Ingram also shows how the acceptance of the premises of a pluralist world and liberal forms of democracy and their relations with rights entails three further debates which can be seen as an expansion of what Richard Bellamy calls the fundamental problems of 'contestability' and 'compossibility' of rights.[30] All three are of relevance to the question of how the European Union tries to legitimate itself by reference to rights.

First, there is the underlying incompatibility highlighted above, between 'the orthodox conception of rights – the libertarian view that rights are a species of moral property of one's person', and a concept of justice as a socially constructed compromise on 'what everyone could in principle reach a rational agreement'.[31] This reflects the conflict between the natural-law justification of rights, and the view that rights are meaningful only if understood within a political context. This raises the practical problem of whether rights are subject to trade-offs. In the debate about the EU Charter of Fundamental Rights, as mentioned, this problem became visible in the clashes between those who saw the Charter merely as a means to make 'existing' rights visible, and those

who perceived the drafting of the Charter as an opportunity to introduce new political goals for the European Union. These groups disagreed
not only on the question which rights would fall under the (supposedly
uncontroversial) notion of 'fundamental rights', but also about the
question whether there can be different categories of 'more' and 'less'
fundamental rights. This debate was confused, however, by the fact that
almost all parties claimed that the rights which they were arguing for
had existed as fundamental human rights prior to the attempt to list
them in an EU Charter. A number of different techniques had to be
employed to construct a compromise which could be supported by near
consensus in the Convention, which meant that the result is a complex
package of different conceptions of rights and their conditions.[32]

Second, Ingram points to the ensuing debates about 'citizenship, community and democracy'[33] which also figured prominently in the Charter
negotiations (see Chapter 4). They were focusing on the political context
in which rights can be claimed and protected, and also touched on the
process (legal or political), by which rights are weighed against each
other in cases of conflict. Thus, all three issues have a direct bearing on
the legitimation of the EU's political system and figure prominently in
the debates about Europe's future in general. It is therefore not surprising that they also surfaced in the negotiations about a rights foundation
for Europe and created the need for a more extended debate on who
are the 'subjects' of European integration, and what precisely is the
relevant political context for the protection of their rights.

Third, Ingram indicates the need to 'broaden the appeal of rights'
beyond the traditional division between liberal and republican views of
the role of rights. She argues that:

> we need a doctrine of rights because, as citizens of modern republics,
> we meet as strangers *without* a *common* good except *whatever we can
> forge together* for the advancement of our *diverse* ends; that
> right-holders are *not* the atomistic, radically unsocialized subjects
> bereft of communal allegiances that anti-liberals suppose; and, finally,
> that the form of *liberal community* that a post-libertarian doctrine
> of rights sustains is no less worthy of pursuit than the more
> full-blooded traditional communities of shared ends and intimate
> personal knowledge.[34]

This acceptance of a need for a rights and democracy discourse beyond
the traditional (national) community is of even greater importance
in what Jürgen Habermas calls the 'post-national' constellation.

Traditional frames of community reference (and consequently rights conceptualisation) are challenged by interdependence between states, and by globalisation.[35] This is the challenge of legitimating a political order which can no longer rely on real or presumed ethnic and/or cultural homogeneity and a fixed national frame of reference as the basis for a common good. For the European Union this is of particular importance in response to the argument advanced by some that legitimate order is dependent on a culturally homogenous community as the bearer of sovereign democratic power (see Chapter 5 in this volume).[36]

At the same time, when applying these theoretical considerations to political reality at the beginning of the twenty-first century, it has to be acknowledged that over the past five decades the notion of international 'regimes' of (supposedly universal) human rights in which individuals can rely on external sources of rights against their 'own' states has emerged.[37] The nation-state is becoming increasingly bound to supranational entities which limit or at least reshape its sovereignty. Especially in the context of the European integration process, this internationalisation of rights has provoked speculations about the effect of these developments on the legitimacy of the nation-state and other political structures.[38]

Yet, regardless of which particular structures have gained or lost in legitimacy through the development of international human rights, it is clear that, as Ingram concludes, 'respect for human rights has become an accepted *criterion* of political legitimacy, in domestic *and* international politics'.[39] Thus, every political system in search of legitimacy has to take a stance on the issues of rights and rights protection. As the debates in the Charter Convention have amply demonstrated (see Chapter 4), there is a general, abstract consensus on human rights, but the actual definition of which rights qualify as 'human' or 'fundamental' is contested and requires a legitimate procedure to be mediated. This is all the more important if different understandings of rights are to be brought together, and more important still if these rights are to form the 'founding principles' of a political order. The second half of this chapter is devoted to discussing under which conditions rights can fulfil these functions.

Fundamental rights and legitimacy

The elements of legitimacy

From the forgoing definition of the concepts of 'rights' and 'legitimacy' and the link between them, it has become clear that rights do not in and of themselves provide legitimacy because they themselves are dependent on some kind of justification. This justification derives either from some notion of humans possessing rights 'by nature' or from an understanding of rights as those elements of the social fabric which make human co-existence possible. Both views are present in the current-day human rights discourse, and they appeared also in the debates of the Convention drafting the EU Charter.

Given this ambiguous role of rights, legitimacy cannot be built just on respect for fundamental rights, but needs other elements too. As noted previously, Habermas sees the essence of legitimacy as the tension and mediation between some notion of human rights (whatever their justification might be), on the one hand, and the principle of popular sovereignty, on the other.[40] At the same time, most studies of legitimacy from a political science perspective begin with some kind of threefold typology of legitimacies which mostly echo the seminal distinction of three (ideal) types of 'reasons' for legitimacy proposed by Max Weber at the beginning of the twentieth century. Famously he identified charismatic, traditional and legal-rational authority as his three sources of legitimate authority.[41]

It is of note that Weber refers to legality and not rights in his classification. By pairing legality and rationality, Weber places great emphasis on the structure and process by which legitimacy is conferred by legal-rational authority.[42] What interests us here, however, is that Weber avoids the category of rights, and that legal-rational authority is just one of the three possible bases for legitimacy in his scheme. Similarly, David Beetham and Christopher Lord base their account of the legitimacy of political authority on the three notions of 'legality', 'normative justifiability' and 'legitimation' and expand on these three categories as follows: 'The first of these levels is that of rules; the second that of justification grounded in beliefs; and the third that of acts of consent or recognition.'[43] Interestingly, in this application of the theoretical concept of legitimacy to the concrete case of the European Union, fundamental rights are not mentioned explicitly but seem to be 'contained' as a pre-condition in the concept of legitimate 'rules' on which the polity and its processes are based.

In another important discussion about the specific nature and problem of the legitimacy of the European Union, Markus Höreth also draws on three sources of legitimacy (democratic decision-making, technocratic utility, and indirect legitimacy derived from the member states), and shows how the three resulting types of legitimacy are locked into what he calls the 'legitimacy trilemma' in the EU case.[44] It becomes clear in his discussion that the trilemma is in fact based on the more familiar seminal trilogy of 'input, output and social legitimacy' proposed by Fritz Scharpf.[45] Again, legitimacy on the basis of fundamental rights is not mentioned per se, but to a certain degree the effective protection of fundamental rights can be envisaged as contributing to the 'output' legitimacy of a political system. At the same time, any kind of 'social' legitimacy which reflects shared feelings or expectations of the citizens, also seems difficult to imagine without an underlying notion of fundamental rights in a democratic system where fundamental rights have to ensure the autonomy of the individual. Thus it becomes clear that the notion of fundamental rights cuts across different elements of legitimacy.

More recently, however, and inspired by the discussion about the EU Charter of Rights and the 'finality' of the European integration project, a new body of literature has developed with a clear focus on the role of fundamental rights in legitimating the EU. John Eric Fossum for example, in contrast to the authors cited so far, does explicitly envisage legitimation through 'rights' alongside legitimacy through 'outcomes' and through 'values'.[46] Following Habermas (see below), Fossum stresses the central function of the 'reciprocal recognition of rights' as the basis for a 'sense of community allegiance'. It is this act of recognition which 'constitutes' the democratic polity.[47] Fossum concludes that legitimation through rights is an important element especially in his case study of the European Union, where legitimation through outcomes and values is problematic. However, he also acknowledges that the three 'modes of legitimation' would need to be combined 'to get an overall sense of how entities are legitimated'.[48] In fact, the debates in the Charter Convention showed that the concept of European citizenship is the most likely candidate as the conceptual frame for such a combined approach. The Convention process and the subsequent constitutional developments have both moved the EU further towards a clearer definition of its own political purpose (see Chapter 5 in this volume). In this contexts, rights are important but equally important is the process by which they are defined and realised.

In order to grasp the complex interaction between fundamental rights and the processes by which they are realised in a given political context, a useful conceptual distinction has been proposed by Richard Bellamy and Dario Castiglione: the distinction between the legitimacy of a 'polity', and that of a 'regime'. The 'polity legitimacy' in this scheme concerns the justification of the political structure as a locus 'where collective decisions can be made about particular issues', whereas the 'regime legitimacy' concerns the 'acceptability of the prevailing "regime" or form of governance whereby those decisions get taken'.[49] The significance of this distinction lies in the fact that the mix of the three core elements of legitimacy required to justify a 'polity' or a 'regime' respectively, is likely to differ. The analytical problem is, *how* they differ and what consequences this difference might have for political action to legitimate either a polity or a regime. As far as the drafting of an EU Charter of Fundamental Rights is concerned, while the authors of the mandate of Cologne might have thought they were just embarking on an exercise of regime legitimation (for example through the closure of a gap in the EU's legal system), the debates in the Convention brought out profound questions of polity legitimation as well. The Charter's positive contribution to a more legitimate European Union is precisely its success in opening up the debate about *both* polity and regime.

Legitimacy at European level

All scholars quoted above (with the obvious exception of Weber) developed their understandings of legitimacy with reference to the particular challenges to traditional state-level legitimacy of the late twentieth century from the emergence of new sub- and supra-national political organisations with their own requirements for, and claims to, legitimacy. The European Union as it emerges from the ongoing integration process is of course the most pertinent example, but by no means the only one. The increasing diversification and co-existence of a plurality of political structures changes the patterns of legitimation and requires an adjustment of the relative weights given to individual elements of legitimacy because it is their particular 'mix' which defines the legitimacy of any given polity.

In trying to understand how legitimacy functions, and how a new entity such as the EU can acquire legitimacy in a context of existing legitimacies, we face the problem how to establish empirically on what basis the pre-existing, older legitimacies are founded. A 'traditional legitimacy' in Weberian terms, for example, depends probably at least in part on the 'charismatic authority' of leaders past or present in creating a coherent historical narrative of legitimate action. Therefore, the two can not be separated. Similarly, it is clear that the 'rules', which for Beetham and Lord constitute one distinct level of legitimation, need to be 'believed' to be in the interest of the community, which in turn means that they must 'represent' individual interests or collective beliefs. Finally, Fossum's notion of 'values' is distinct from, but in substantial parts dependent upon, a notion of shared 'identity' to underpin a system of common values. As Fossum recognises himself, both elements need to be combined with legitimation through rights to get the full picture. The key question is then how different legitimating principles relate to one another.

The explanatory force of the concept of legitimacy lies precisely in combining the diverse objective/rational elements, with the equally manifold subjective/emotive elements of collective behaviour. The different elements of legitimacy constantly interact with each other in a dynamic, two-way process. Collective identities and their recognition, for example, shape rules and patterns of participation, but identities are also shaped by them. Thus, even if one does not share Markus Höreth's pessimistic view of 'multi-dimensional legitimacy' as a 'zero-sum game', in which advances in one area of legitimacy necessarily lead to more problems in other areas, his clear acknowledgement of the inter-dependence between the different sources of legitimacy is a useful, even necessary, reminder of the complexity of the problem.[50] It took the EU legitimacy debate a long time to make the transition from isolated, often rather incoherent attempts to tamper with different aspects of the problem, to a more comprehensive approach under the conceptual umbrellas of European citizenship and constitutionalism (see Chapter 3 in this volume).

Rights legitimating the polity

With few exceptions, the issue of fundamental rights does not figure prominently in the theoretical literature on legitimacy in general or of the European Union in particular. The conceptual link between the two is nevertheless close, as Habermas' account underlines: in his view, human rights are one 'half' of the two-pronged answer to the question of legitimacy.[51] Yet, the understanding of this link is made difficult not only by the complexities of the notion of legitimacy outlined above, but also by the ambiguities in the concept of rights already mentioned, and the different functions which rights are consequently supposed to fulfil.

First, there is the question of whether rights, if they are regarded as 'human' or 'fundamental', are self-sustained and self-evident, or whether they are contingent on a system of positive law to 'realise' them.[52] Second, with regard to their role for the democratic system, they have a dual function. On the one hand, respect for fundamental rights is seen as a minimum condition without which no rule is democratically acceptable. In Peter Jones' account, '[t]hose who wielded political power, were obliged to do so in a manner which respected people's natural rights. If they did not, they forfeited their right to rule.'[53] On the other hand, however, rights do not just specify the minimum requirements of a democratic political order, but '[o]f equal and perhaps greater significance is the way in which rights inhabit our ordinary moral and political thinking. Claiming or asserting rights has become the common mode by which people seek to promote an interest or advance a cause.'[54] Rights, and especially human rights, are employed as political tools because they can be portrayed as possessing self-evident moral force in a liberal democratic setting.

If accepted uncritically, this understanding of rights as 'natural' has of course important consequences for the question of the legitimation of political power through rights. The main aim of any legitimate political order in such a view would have to be the absolute protection of the natural rights of its citizens. But this simplified understanding of the link between rights and the legitimacy of political order cannot accommodate those conflicts between different rights claims which are the daily business of any political community. Yet, if we then accept that even what we consider 'fundamental' rights are *not* absolute expressions of some 'superior' moral authority, and thus require balancing, this means that mere reference to these rights does not justify a political order. Rather, as Richard Bellamy argues, it is the democratic constitutional process that justifies rights, and in the same process also the constitution of the polity itself. 'Democracy facilitates this process because . . . it embodies the "right to have rights".'[55] Whether the codification of rights into constitutional documents or charters is, in this context, necessarily detrimental to democracy because it 'freezes' and removes them from the political process, as Bellamy argues, is a separate issue which will be discussed later (see Chapter 5). What matters here is the multiple function of fundamental rights as constituting, animating, and setting the boundaries of, the political process.

By 'merely' pledging respect for fundamental rights, therefore, a political order does not have much to 'gain' in terms of legitimacy. In this sense, it may have been short-sighted when the Cologne mandate seemed to assume that making the 'overriding importance and relevance' of fundamental rights more 'visible to the Union's citizens' would be enough to improve the EU's legitimacy record.[56] Unless, of course, one of the following three conditions applied:

(1) If the lack of legitimacy of the order in question was attributed mainly to a lack of respect for fundamental rights by the powers

within this system, a strengthened commitment to fundamental rights of some description can obviously contribute to solving the problem.

(2) If the order which tries to legitimate itself can convincingly show that it will be able to ensure a 'better' (i.e. a more efficient and/or more effective) protection of the rights in question than other political arrangements competing for legitimacy, it might use the reference to fundamental rights as proof of its (superior) output legitimacy.

(3) Finally, if the reference to the protection of fundamental rights itself can be used to create a shared notion of a 'common good' of the political order in question, it can become part of the 'social legitimacy' underpinning it.

It thus remains to be investigated in the analysis of the EU's Charter process how far these conditions applied and were addressed by the Charter project.

The *process* of legitimation through rights

The common origins of rights and democratic process

From these observations about the function and content of rights themselves, and their link to the notion of legitimacy, it becomes clear that a central element of the legitimating force of rights is the process by which these rights are instituted and by which conflicts between them are resolved. Faced with a secularised understanding of political authority and rights in a pluralistic world, there is a need to found a self-sustaining system of legitimation of power in which individual rights are recognised and fed into the process by which power is exercised. As highlighted, this is particularly important in trying to create a basis for the legitimacy of a new multicultural political entity like the European Union. One attempt at devising such a process-based system of political organisation can be found in the idea of the European Union as a system of and for deliberative democracy, which are based on original considerations by Jürgen Habermas.[57]

For Habermas, the starting point of the debate about legitimacy of political order is indeed his notion of rights, and he notes that modern states are 'essentially built upon subjective rights'.[58] In his view, the mutual recognition of rights between individuals constitutes the foundation of the 'community of rights', which is then expressed in the construction of a 'legal system' and finally in the foundation of some kind of political organisation (i.e. a state) by means of a process of deliberation. Individual rights and freedoms constitute spaces for individual action in which the political process can develop. This process is thus dependent on the delicate balance of 'private and public autonomy of the individual'. This balance in turn is ensured through the institutionalisation of the modern notion that everything is allowed which is not explicitly forbidden. In this respect, a modern system of positive laws is different from traditional systems of moral obligation based on notions of reciprocal duty.

This distinction between the system of 'positive law', and the 'moral universe' is an essential element of a modern political order because notions of universal morality, according to Habermas, are no longer a reliable source of orientation in a pluralist world. Therefore the democratic process has to be based on the acknowledgement of conflicting notions of 'the good', and on the mutual recognition among citizens of each other as equal holders of rights. This recognition allows the democratic process to justify itself and be justifiable, on rational grounds. Habermas makes clear that 'the law obtains its full normative sense not per se through its form, nor through a given a priori moral content, but through a procedure of constituting right, which creates legitimacy'.[59]

At the same time, the rights recognised mutually by individuals constitute constraints on the operation of the system of law emerging from this process. These constraints apply to the mechanisms of enforcement (power) which are necessary to institute the legal community itself: this is the principle of the *Rechtsstaat*, or rule of law. This reasoning underlines once again that 'rights' have the dual function of providing the basis for any social organisation of equals, *and* of setting the limits for that very same organisation. Fundamental rights form the minimum standard for the protection of the individual against the collectivity, but their realisation is also a central element of the political process. In Bellamy's words, '[f]rom this perspective, the protection and realisation of rights and the rule of law fall within rather than outside politics.'[60] In this sense, Habermas envisages rights and political power as '*gleichursprünglich*' (= emerging contemporarily from the same source).[61] Bellamy, however, criticises Habermas' accounts of the European Union and its constitution as a polity in this sense, for being based on a vision of the interplay between 'systemic' and 'social' integration which *does* rely on one pre-dating the other.[62] This debate reflects the fundamental problem of how much common understanding must exist between different individuals *before* they can enter into a meaningful dialogue about their political constitution, and whether there can indeed be 'consensus' on any sort of principle, or whether this is impossible in a pluralist world.

In the actual case of the debate on the EU's Charter, rights were linked to, and used as a means of, legitimation. The question of the interaction between rights and the political system therefore presented itself with a slightly different emphasis. By setting up the Charter Convention, a forum for the exchange of views on these fundamental rights was created which of course operated within the given political context of the EU. Moreover, the debates about fundamental rights occurred in a context where the existence of the ECHR, the judicial practice of the European Court of Justice, and of the Strasbourg Court on Human Rights, as well as the global political debate about human rights, already provided a basis of common understanding of rights, which was often referred to as a 'consensus' on human rights. Therefore, the question here was whether the particular political process that took place in the Convention was adequate to provide a sustainable balance between differing views on the more particular legal and political issues, and whether it broadened the existing basis of common understanding, which would then create legitimacy for the process itself and for the wider political structure which enabled it.

Universal human rights and democratic process

The problem of applying the elaborate conception of the interdependence of rights and political power, in which both constitute each other, to the empirical reality of human rights institutions today, is that it is at odds with the more traditional view that human rights pertain to individuals by virtue of their human nature, and thus pre-exist any form of political organisation. Largely ignoring the question of how these rights are ultimately justified (i.e. whether the individual 'ownership' of rights is linked back to religious beliefs in the value of human beings, or based on other concepts of intrinsic humanity), the idea of human rights existing outside and above human society and thus providing limits for what 'can be done' to individual human beings, is an implicit element of a large part of the modern human rights discourse.

As Michael J. Perry notes, one expression of this belief is the concept of 'human dignity'. Perry quotes several international human rights documents, most importantly the UN Universal Declaration of Human Rights of 1948, the preamble of which speaks of the 'inherent dignity . . . of all members of the human family'.[63] The problem is of course that the concept of 'innate' dignity itself can be contested and therefore is not sufficient as a basis for such rights.[64] Thus, in drafting the EU Charter of Fundamental Rights, conflicting visions of the ultimate justification of rights came to the fore in the debate about whether or not to have a reference to human dignity in Article 1 (see Chapter 4 in this volume). Despite the fact that at the theoretical level no compromise can ultimately be reached between those who see human rights as being rooted in nature or in religious beliefs, and those who see them as human constructs, compromise had to be possible in the political exchange about the content and definition of the rights in question.

Habermas takes account of this incompatibility of the widely diffused notion of human rights as 'self-evident' moral standards, with his notion of their essentially 'social' nature and acknowledges a 'peculiar tension between the universal sense of human rights and the localised conditions of their realisation'.[65] As possible solutions to this tension, he has to envisage either a transformation of all states into democracies based on the rule of law (in which case the problem would become irrelevant) or, alternatively, the institution of a global order beyond the nation-states under which every individual can claim his or her rights as a citizen of the world. But he also admits that there are substantial political problems with the move towards a truly cosmopolitan order: 'In the transition from a nation-state based to a cosmopolitan order, one does not know exactly what is more dangerous: the disappearing world of sovereign subjects of international law which lost their innocence long ago, or the unclear muddle of supranational institutions and conferences which can lend doubtful legitimation, but which are still dependent on the good will of powerful states and alliances.'[66] The problem thus remains, at both the global and the national level, how to mediate conflicting rights claims and how to enforce those rights that have been agreed upon as legitimate. The only solution in Habermas' vision is an open dialogue between free and equal participants to try and reach commonality of understanding between the participants. While at the national level the institutionalisation of rules of procedure already provides a framework for such a dialogue, the international level still has to reach a common understanding of what the dialogue is about. The discourse about human rights seems a useful starting point for this deliberation.

Transnational and intercultural rights discourse

Yet, with this approach the question arises again what degree of common understanding (for example in the area of human rights) has to exist in order to make a meaningful dialogue on these issues possible. In other words, we are faced with a classic chicken-and-egg dilemma of whether a community (on the basis of common descent, common culture, or common rational understanding of certain notions) has to pre-date the political organisation, or whether a common experience within shared organisational structures creates communities. On the practical level, however, at the beginning of the twenty-first century, this is not a real problem: the UN 'Universal Declaration of Human Rights' of 1948, as well as several regional human rights documents such as the European Convention for the Protection of Human Rights and Fundamental Freedoms of 1950, or the African [Banjul] Charter on Human and Peoples' Rights of 1986, demonstrate that many exchanges of views have already taken place at a global level, the results of which have been accepted by the participants to constitute a common body of meaning.[67]

To a degree, these rights catalogues must be seen as the products of some kind of, however imperfect, intercultural dialogue on the issue. These dialogues and their results constitute the context for any new debate on similar issues. The opportunities for such dialogue, and the chances to organise it democratically, are improving in the age of globalisation, according to Habermas' optimistic view. Despite widely differing notions of fundamental rights between different cultures, Habermas stresses that the notion of human rights as it exists today is not so much based on a particular (western) understanding of human nature or civilisation, 'but on the attempt to meet the specific challenges of a social modernity which by now has spread globally'.[68] Thus, both the need, and the possibility, for more intercultural dialogue exist. The challenge then is to institute a level of dialogue and communication beyond the traditional arenas of the state on the subject of human rights which would be both a precondition for, and a substantial part of, the creation of trans- or supra-national fora for legitimate rule.

Yet, the mere agreement on common minimum standards does not solve some of the practical problems with regards to different kinds of rights, and the level at which they should and could be protected. Human rights as a concept and body of law have evolved since the Second World War as a reaction to the blatant violation of rights under fascism and during the war itself.[69] In this sense, it is understandable that the rights which emerged are framed in a way that is supposed to be 'beyond' and 'above' the level of individual states who continue to prove unreliable in protecting rights. Moreover, it is clear that a list of fundamental rights without any enforcement mechanism is of limited value. Unless, of course, the rights in question were regarded and accepted as 'legitimate' by, and thus as producing obligations on, *all* concerned parties. This is not yet the case at the international level and in the absence of a functioning global political system, even compliance with commonly agreed standards cannot always be enforced against supposedly 'sovereign' nation-states.

The European Union and fundamental rights

Constitutional dialogue about rights

There exists of course already one particularly important example of supposedly sovereign nation-states having instituted a cross-national 'community of law' with far-reaching powers of legal control – the European Union. With the EU, the argument about the mutual dependence of rights and political power due to their contemporary emergence from the same source (the constitutional process), comes full circle: the EU as a political entity needs to establish a certain degree of rights protection in order to legitimate itself, but to be able to do so it needs the political power to enforce these rights if necessary against the member states – which raises the problem of legitimacy. Therefore, a Habermasian constitutional process is necessary which would constitute simultaneously the rights and the political power to realise them, one legitimating the other in the process.

The challenge for such a process is how to enable the open dialogue between free and equal participants about which rights all individuals should recognise for each other, and what kind of political framework is legitimated as an 'institutionalisation' of these rights. At the same time, to avoid the 'rigidification' of these rights as might occur when they are written into a constitutional document, the process needs to be kept in constant flux. As Richard Bellamy argues, the 'process of *reconstituting* the polity is a continuous one'.[70] This latter requirement, however, poses practical problems because one essential element of legitimate political order is to create and maintain (legal and institutional) certainty and predictability. This is echoed in Jo Shaw's broad definition of constitutionalism as standing 'for the principle that government ought to be conducted in certain types of ordered and just ways, in the sense of conforming to the well-established and widely regarded principles of the rule of law, checks on powers, and the protection of individual rights'.[71]

Moreover, a 'full-scale' constitutional process debating the fundmental parameters of political order cannot go on for ever. Albert Weale, for example, recognises that a 'constituent assembly would only be a one-off event, and it would not provide a process by which the legitimacy of the constitution could be continuously reassessed and reaffirmed', but he also acknowledges that 'constitutional systems have evolved devices, like amendment procedures and constitutional courts, the role of which is to accommodate the continuing demands for constitutional amendment'.[72] The concept of 'constitutionalism' in the European Union seeks to address these concerns at the trans-national level and the Charter Convention exercise was an important step in the institutionalised constitutional process for the Union which found its culmination so far in the second Convention in 2002/03.[73] For such a process to be legitimate, and to act to legitimate the polity, practical solutions need to be found to the questions of who is representing whom in such a constitutional process; how the 'wider public interest' can be involved in the process; and how the results of the process are presented to, and validated by, the public at large. These are questions of how to 'organise' legitimation by means of a constitutional process which allows adaptation and change of any compromises reached.[74] The first use of the Convention method at EU level provided important insights in this respect which have by now become accepted tenets of the EU's constitutional memory.

In order to turn this constitutional process into a successful tool of legitimation, and to create legitimate outcomes in the Habermasian logic, the process has to be open and inclusive, allowing all voices to bring forward reasoned argument – in other words, it has to be a *discursive deliberative* process.[75] This process involves *justifying* decisions by '*arguing* in relation to inter-subjective standards of truth, rightness, and sincerity'.[76] If successful, this process will lead to what Erik Eriksen and John Fossum call 'normative learning', based on 'arguments of a certain moral or ethical quality', which in turn allow for common understanding of the issues to develop.[77] Such a process would involve debate and deliberation both about the underlying normative assumptions and goals of the polity, and about various aspects of its internal organisation, that is, about the legitimacy of the polity as a whole, and the legitimacy of the regime within that polity.[78]

The dialogue about the fundamental rights that form the basis of, and define the European Union as a new political order, did provide a first focus for such a constitutional debate. This dialogue brought out the normative arguments underlying the integration process and in consequence helped to clarify its organisational structure. Thus, it could also highlight the legitimating force of the rights discourse because, as Fossum reminds us, '[r]ights offer a framework for discourse and are also established through discourse.'[79] At the same time, bearing in mind the interconnectedness of the different elements of legitimacy, it is clear that such a process in the EU could not stop at legitimation by reference to the rights themselves, but had to involve also the other elements of legitimacy usually invoked: shared beliefs and values, a common identity, an implicit or explicit consent of the ruled and notions of effectiveness and efficiency (see also Chapters 3 and 4). In the case of the EU Charter, this proto-constitutional dialogue took place against a backdrop of substantial degrees of integration which facilitate the discursive interaction in everyday EU politics, and which mean that the process could build on the results of previous exchanges on constitutional questions in various European fora. Yet, such a process at EU level also had to contend with ingrained national differences and nationally routinised practices of interaction which did, at times, have a limiting effect.

The EU Charter: legitimation through deliberation on rights

This chapter has attempted to clarify some of the concepts employed both in the academic debate and in political discourse about the grounds for justification of European integration: the concept of legitimacy in its multiple facets, and the concept of rights as a central notion of democratic political theory. We departed from the strong link claimed by the Cologne mandate calling for the drafting of an EU Charter of Fundamental Rights, between the legitimacy of the Union and its respect for fundamental (human) rights. As the analysis has shown, this link does indeed exist in the sense that violation of certain fundamental rights would clearly de-legitimate a political order. In this view, respect for fundamental rights is 'an indispensable prerequisite' (Cologne mandate) for the polity legitimacy of any order, including the European Union.

Yet it has also been shown that the role of fundamental rights is broader than this conditionality, because rights not only set the limits for collective decisions vis-à-vis the individual, but also form a core element of the political process. This second function of rights is implicit in the other part of the Cologne mandate's formula, namely that '[p]rotection of fundamental rights is a founding principle' of the Union. Rights and their protection within the political context form an essential part of 'politics'. Thus the legitimacy of a political order is at least partly dependent on its capacity to provide mechanisms for the realisation of rights. The debate about rights is therefore an important aspect of the legitimacy of a particular regime within a given polity.

The most common understandings of the concept of legitimacy combine different sources of legitimacy (i.e. a political order's capacity to realise its citizens' goals effectively and efficiently, the consistency of collective decisions with established rules, the degree to which such decisions represent and involve its citizens, and the degree to which the political order itself is seen as an expression of their identity and values), and the legitimacy of a specific political order depends on the exact interplay between these different elements. The notion of rights affects all of these sources of legitimacy in different ways under different circumstances. Thus, it becomes clear that the notion of 'legitimation through rights' cannot stand alone but needs to be seen in a wider context of concurrent processes of legitimation.

The concepts of rights, legitimacy and democracy and the relationship between them are not free of tension. There is disagreement about the origin and the justification of rights; about the balance between the private autonomy of the individual described in terms of rights, and the public autonomy which is necessary for the democratic process; about the degrees of stability and flexibility in the rights to be protected, and about the legitimate mechanisms to adjudicate between conflicting rights claims. Moreover, there is disagreement about the different elements of legitimacy and their relative importance; and whether a feeling of community needs to pre-exist the constitution of a polity in order to make the ensuing political order legitimate. In a pluralist and interdependent world, some kind of mediation between these opposing views needs to be found to make co-existence possible, both within and between political systems.

Following Jürgen Habermas' notion of the discursive deliberative process, it has therefore been argued that the debate about fundamental rights, because of its implications for legitimacy and the constitutional issues it raises, is a very valid starting point for a broader democratic and democratising process – even for a new political order such as the European Union. This applies in particular because in the EU there already exists a wide range of institutional arrangements and policies which testify to a substantial degree of common purpose and principles. At the same time, as will be shown in the next chapter, the EU to date has only partially been able to provide the context for a genuinely fundamental debate about the rights and principles underlying the integration project, and the EU's legitimacy continues to be challenged as a consequence.

The debate about the EU Charter marked an important step towards a more comprehensive constitutional debate. The process in the

Convention brought to the fore fundamental disagreements not only about certain aspects of the rights in questions, but also about many core elements of the EU's constitutional structure. Yet on many of these questions, agreement was eventually reached through an open process. Moreover, where such agreement was not reached, temporary solutions were found to enable the Charter to be approved by the Convention. Not least it was possible to reach 'consensus' on the very idea of having a catalogue of fundamental rights for the EU, and drafting it in a body whose composition, working method, and self-description had clear constitutional undertones. The process did highlight the state of affairs, and the areas where further action is needed to find or construct a more permanent entente. Thus the Charter Convention provided an appropriate forum to set in motion a deliberative process to broaden the common basis of the Union, and by this to increase its legitimacy.

3
What Kind of Legitimacy for the EU?

Introduction: the EU's problematic legitimacy

This book looks at the drafting of the EU Charter of Fundamental Rights as a political act to improve the legitimacy of the European Union. In order to assess whether this initiative had positive effects on the EU's legitimacy, and more specifically, what such effects could be, it is necessary to understand why the European Union is commonly seen as suffering from a legitimacy deficit. This chapter discusses the EU's particular problems in being accepted as a legitimate polity by its people over the years, and it looks at the political reaction to these problems by different actors in the integration process. It is argued that, because of certain structural properties of the EU as a polity in the process of formation (i.e. the indeterminacy of its boundaries, its functional scope, its membership, and its internal mechanisms), legitimacy has been an issue in the integration process for at least three decades.

In response, a number of different strategies of legitimation have been employed by EU integration actors in order to ensure that the evolving legitimacy of the EU polity could keep pace with the polity's development itself. Understanding and assessing these strategies involves first an attempt to define what the emerging polity is, and should be, because this determines public expectations as to what kind of legitimacy is needed to sustain the new political system. This poses some particular problems in the case of the European Union which is a polity 'in the making' and as such has not (yet) reached a definite state. For this kind of polity, the need to legitimate the EU in its evolution has prompted different institutional actors in the Union to pursue initiatives to improve the output of the EU system, to create mechanisms for more popular input into the system, and to foster a feeling of common belonging – in other words, attempts to address the three constituent elements of legitimacy. Yet while these attempts to address individual aspects of the legitimacy problems have had some success in the past in their respective areas, the problem remained the need for a more general concept of legitimacy policy to take care of all three different dimensions of legitimacy. The concept of an EU citizenship is presented in the final part of this chapter as the most comprehensive institutional approach to creating the basis of an independent EU legitimacy up to the end of the twentieth century and it is crucial for the further constitutional process which developed after the Charter had been drafted. The citizenship debate itself is in fact a core part of the wider process of constitutionalising the European Union. A broad, political notion of constitutionalism seems thus the best conceptual framework in which to conceive possible progress on the question of EU legitimacy. The Charter process and in particular the debates in the first Convention were crucial in expanding this debate about the need for, and nature of, a constitutional concept for the emerging European polity. The Charter Convention therefore did a lot of important groundwork for the Convention which then drafted the EU Constitutional Treaty in 2002–2003.

As has been stressed so far, the (inter-) subjective, cognitive element of the legitimacy concept means that the question of whether there is a legitimacy problem depends as much on how people perceive the system, as it does on objective qualities or deficiencies of the system. The notion of the EU's 'deficit' of legitimacy suggests that the legitimacy available to the Union is insufficient in the eyes of the public to justify its operation, its further development, or even its existence, at a given point in time. Such judgements are usually based on statistical data of public support for the EU, or on manifestations of 'public opinion' such as referenda or electoral turnout.[1] Yet, the 'amount' of legitimacy necessary to sustain a given political order, or to create a new one, is as difficult to measure as the legitimacy actually available to it.[2] All one can say is that the *expectations* of legitimacy have to be in some kind of balance with the legitimacy *resources* available to the polity at a given point, and a legitimacy deficit arises if this balance is disturbed. Even then it is a matter of degree whether the damage is permanent, or whether the balance can be redressed. The EU might have a problem of legitimacy, and many argue that it has had it for a while now,[3] but as a political order it has been remarkably enduring. In this sense, the EC/EU must by and large have been successful in readjusting/maintaining the balance of its legitimacy.

At the same time, however, one important reason for the EU's perceived problem of legitimacy lies in the fact that it seems less and less clear, what people actually *do* expect from the Union. Since its beginning, the European integration project has tried to shape the expectations of the people by defining itself, and its purposes in the relevant Treaties and through its political actions. Yet these definitions are contested and subject sometimes to rapid changes, and its seems that 'the public' has been confused by developments at the European level, especially since the events of 1989. Both politicians and scientists have become increasingly aware since then that a substantial part of the EU's legitimacy troubles are probably due to what has become known as the 'EU polity problem', i.e. the question what exactly the EU is, and what it should be and do.

The following section of this chapter traces the roots of this problem back to the very origins of European integration: its foundations were laid with the Treaty of Rome and the commitment to 'ever closer union'.[4] This formula suggested an open-ended, but clearly directional process. Both of these fundamental assumptions have been increasingly challenged in recent years. While it is clear by now that a definite answer to the question 'what kind of polity is the EU?' cannot be given because the process of integration is still ongoing and open-ended, the problem of describing which kind of 'beast' we are dealing with, shapes the ensuing debate about legitimacy.[5] Since most accounts of European integration nowadays agree that the Union can no longer be regarded as an international organisation which is completely and exclusively controlled by its member states and thus receives its legitimacy from their consent, the EU is now more than ever in need to define what it is, in order to create its own independent basis for legitimacy.[6]

The analysis then turns to how concerns about the different aspects of the EU's legitimacy have prompted different EC/EU institutions over time to try and redress the legitimacy problems of the emerging political structure. The institutional responses on which the analysis focuses produce a mirror image of real or perceived public concerns about the legitimacy of progressive integration. Thus the chapter examines how supposedly legitimacy-enhancing action has developed alongside the integration process, and in reaction to it. As integration has deepened and widened over the years, the EU and its actors have employed different strategies of legitimation to ensure that the Union's legitimacy keeps up with changing, and possibly increasing, expectations. These were partly strategies aimed at improving what de Búrca calls 'popular legitimacy', when the European institutions tried to enhance the output of the system and the public perception of it, and partly strategies aimed at clarifying the 'underlying questions of normative legitimacy' which are seen to justify the integration project as a whole.[7]

The concept of a European citizenship and its role in legitimating the EU as a way to address the different aspects of legitimacy are presented in the following part. As the account of legitimacy policy shows, Union action in these areas has not always been consistent. Output, input, and identity-related initiatives were not joined by a comprehensive idea of clarifying the EU polity's nature by democratic means. A qualitative shift in this direction did arguably occur, however, with the formalisation of a concept of European citizenship in the Treaty on European Union (1991). Though limited in its immediate legal effect, the introduction of the very notion of citizenship for the Union marked an important statement with regard to what kind of polity the Union is. What particular implications does the application of such an idea to the new European polity have for its legitimacy? In seeking to answer this question, special emphasis is placed on the connection between EU citizenship and the notion of special rights for European citizens, because it was this issue which resurfaced in the exchanges about the EU Charter of Fundamental Rights and its addressees, and which exerted an important influence on the debates in the Convention (see Chapter 4). Moreover it is the notion of the EU as an area of special protection of fundamental rights for its citizens which forms an important part of the discourse of the constitutional process which followed the drafting of the Charter of Fundamental Rights.

It is therefore the concept of a 'constitutional' process in, and of the EU that is examined in the final part of the chapter. Taken not in its narrow legal-institutional, but in a broader political-social sense,[8] constitutionalism presents itself as a tool to understand how parallel processes tie in together in shaping the EU polity and consequently its legitimacy. Important among these processes are the legal development of Community law by the ECJ (European Court of Justice), the ongoing debate about institutional reforms by means of intergovernmental conferences, the incremental growth of new forms of governance, as well as initiatives of political constitutionalisation by means of 'legitimation policy' such as those described above. The broader understanding of the Union's constitutional process is increasingly reflected in a growing interest on the scientific side, and it became increasingly influential at the political level in recent years with the debate about the *finalité* of Europe on the eve of the Union's biggest ever enlargement in 2000.[9] Of course this debate led, together with the Charter Convention experience, to the creation of a second Convention in 2002 to actually draft a document which then quickly acquired the commonly accepted denomination of 'European Constitution', but whether this document actually embodies a broad conception of the unique kind of balance that is needed for a *sui generis* polity like the EU, is still subject to debate.[10]

The chapter concludes that the drafting of an EU Charter of Fundamental Rights with its capacity not only to discuss a set of rights, but also a set of values and principles underlying the creation and functioning of the Union (see Chapter 4), was a highly significant step in the process of 'constitutionalising' the European Union. The Charter process institutionalised a constitutional dialogue at the European level about the nature of the EU polity, beyond the narrow confines of the Council of Ministers, on which the second Convention could and did build. The immediate institutional and political background to this initiative in the context of the impending enlargement of the Union played an important part in bringing about the particular institutional setup of the first Convention with its peculiar structures, which made it an important new tool in the EU's ongoing constitutionalisation. The debates about the Charter of Fundamental Rights not only reaffirmed the Union's claim to an independent polity legitimacy, but they also highlighted the question of *how* such an EU polity should be organised. By stating the indivisibility of social, economic, civil, and liberty rights,[11] the Charter makes an important contribution to defining the 'European model' of political organisation. Together with the procedural innovations introduced and 'tested' in the Charter Convention, the debates on these questions in the Convention improved the legitimacy of the EU.

The EU polity problem

The problem of new polities: naming the 'beast'

At its most basic level, the 'problem' of the EU polity lies in the fact that even after nearly five decades of its existence, the EU is still *new*. Both politically and analytically the voluntary surrender of such important shares of power by supposedly sovereign states to a new set of institutions and actors is without historical precedent in the intensity and speed with which it occurs at the European level. The fact that this is happening raises to a new level a number of questions which have so far been discussed mainly in the national context: why do human beings bind themselves together in collective structures, despite the fact that this means a severe curtailment of their individual freedom? How much of this limitation are they willing to accept and on what conditions? Which level of collectivity is the most suitable to organise legitimate constraints on freedom? How can new levels of organisation be created legitimately, especially if their development and maintenance require a shift of established loyalties on the part of the individuals concerned?

These questions are relevant to any form of human organisation, and have informed the debate about the most prominent and influential collectivities to date, the nation-states, as well as their relations to each other. A number of different concepts have been developed to capture the complex interrelations between the individual and the collectivity, which include the concept of legitimacy itself (see Chapter 2), but also the notions of citizenship,[12] collective/national identity,[13] sovereignty, and democracy.[14] For the European Union as a new kind of structure, this creates a number of difficulties. Much of the analytical debate about how to understand European integration focuses on what kind of 'beast' the EU is, and how it relates to, and compares with, the more familiar structures of nation-states. At the same time, there is a growing awareness of the limitations of this conceptual frame, since the EU is recognised to be neither a nation-state on a larger scale, nor a mere aggregation of its member states. A great number of new labels and approaches have therefore been proposed over the years to capture the uniqueness or *sui generis* nature of the European Union.[15]

One central difficulty in capturing the nature of this new phenomenon, with important implications for the legitimacy of the Union, is the fundamental 'structure–agent' problem of social sciences. This refers to the question whether structures or agents are more important in determining human action, and, like a 'chicken-and-egg' dilemma, a definitive solution is unlikely to be found.[16] Most of the different approaches to conceptualise the EU and its development can therefore be read as proposing new versions of the (inherently subjective) balance between actors and institutions.[17] Yet, despite all ongoing refinement of these approaches, the fundamental structure–agent dichotomy does not go away and has greatly influenced, and continues to influence, the 'original' debate between intergovernmental and neofunctional understandings of European integration.[18]

To summarise this debate in very general terms, the intergovernmental account puts more emphasis on nation-states as actors determining the EU, whereas neofunctionalism and its derivatives pay more attention to the structures which have evolved, and the influence they exercise on the actors. This means that the *mechanisms* by which integration occurs are different: for strict intergovernmentalists, integration happens only if and when sovereign actors decide that it should happen. In the neofunctionalist account, integration also develops its own dynamics (captured in the term 'spillover') which means that once the process is started, individual actors are not always fully in control of it.[19] This is particularly important in the EU context with regard to the role ascribed to supranational institutions (especially, but not only the European Commission) by different theoretical approaches.[20] The disagreement about who or what shapes the outcomes of integration in turn has important consequences for the question of legitimacy, both analytically and in prescriptive terms. It determines crucially, who can be held responsible and accountable and also reflects the debate about the relationship between the individual (and his/her rights) and European agents and/or structures.

What beast do we want? Normative aspects of integration

This insight has led in recent years to a growing acknowledgement that, whatever the EU in its present state can be classified as, decisions within and about its future development must be understood as normative decisions as well as functions of governance. This insight is important for two reasons: firstly, there are those who claim that the *original* attempts at theorising the integration process were 'value-blind', because they did not acknowledge the underlying normative choices implicit in their theories.[21] Thus what was needed, in Dimitris Chryssochoou's terms, was a 'meta-theoretical critique' to highlight where normative choices had biased the traditional theories.[22] The normative angle is also useful because it reminds us of the fact that there is no such thing as a value-free account of human behaviour. This is particularly true with regard to the legitimacy of the Union: as discussed in Chapter 2, one core element of legitimacy refers to a consistency of political decisions with certain normative beliefs.[23] In this sense legitimacy is, among other things, also the expression of the normative validity of political structures. Thus any debate which clarifies the normative foundations underlying the integration project makes an important contribution to the maintenance or development of the EU's legitimacy.

Moreover, in analytical terms the legitimacy debate revolves around what Thomassen and Schmitt identify as the three fundamental questions of the 'demos, or the domain of the political system'; 'the scope of government, or the jurisdiction of the people'; and 'the institutions and processes of government',[24] in other words: who is entitled to decide about what, for whom, and how – bringing us back to both the problem of what kind of polity we are dealing with (analytically), and what kind of polity we want (normatively). Richard Bellamy addresses the same concerns in his four 'dimensions' of the political process, putting a somewhat greater emphasis on the legitimate 'styles' of government, and distinguishing between the 'domain' (in Bellamy's terms the 'sphere') and the 'demos' (Bellamy: 'subjects') of politics.[25] The political process defines, and is defined by, these dimensions.

Yet one fundamental problem of analysis remains: Thomassen and Schmitt quote Robert Dahl's seminal *Democracy and its Critics* with an admission of the inability of democratic theory to define its own 'turf': 'The justification for the unit [within which it is to operate legitimately] lies beyond the reach of the majority principle and, for that matter, mostly beyond the reach of democratic theory itself.'[26] This limitation means that the democratic process cannot decide on its own subjects either. The reason for this is that the democratic process has no means to democratically decide on the inclusion or exclusion of individuals from that same democratic process. This is why many traditional accounts of democratic polities rely on primordial, pre-existing communities to sustain the democratic process. Such an approach, however, creates problems for the European Union where it is not obvious whether a community of some kind pre-existed the foundation of new structures by political (and supposedly democratic) decision – thus we return to the chicken-and-egg problem of the EU polity, and the question, *how much* homogeneity is necessary to enable common political action.[27]

The problem of the EU polity's boundaries

This problem is further complicated by the uncertain nature of the EU's boundaries, in both functional and territorial terms *even after* its 'foundation'.[28] While it is accepted now that the EU in many ways straddles the boundary between domestic and international politics, and that globalisation threatens more traditional notions of boundary anyway, it still seems necessary to define some kind of limitations within which the political process can be organised. But for an EU which is embarked on an ongoing process of (functional) deepening and (territorial) widening, and which had so far only a rather 'thin' definition of membership, it seems very tricky to state clearly in which sphere and for whom it does what it does. As far as the territorial aspect is concerned, Lykke Friis and Anna Murphy note that the recent literature on the EU as a system of governance has not paid sufficient attention to 'the implications of lack of "fit" between membership, territory and function. It is ironic that the application of a concept which assumes a blurring of boundaries between inside and outside . . . has largely ignored or down-played the significance of the "outside" in shaping the "inside".'[29] This is why, at the political level, enlargement has triggered the debate about the future of the Union at this moment.[30]

The functional boundaries of the EU are equally blurred: Weiler, Haltern and Mayer note that '[t]he output of European governance is like that of a state, even a super state' but the 'structure and process of European governance, by contrast, is not at all, in many of its features, like that of a state.'[31] It is these incongruencies between territory, func-tion, structure, and demos, in fact, that lie at the heart of the notion of the EU's democratic deficit. The obvious question arises, whether this 'lack of fit' is only a temporary one because the democratic development of the Union for various reasons lags behind the EU's institutional/func-tional development, or whether it is a structural feature that cannot be remedied at all. Bellamy's concept of the political process as a constant balancing and redefinition of the four dimensions of sphere, scope, subjects, and styles suggests that also in the EU case, the problem is one of balance *at a given moment*. A more legitimate balance might be found if the political process is allowed to fulfil its function, but no permanent 'consensus' on the dimensions could or should be sought.[32]

Permanence in fluidity? The evolving polity

Yet, one of the few things that seems to be certain about European integration is that so far it has developed as a continuous process which, despite temporary setbacks, has been marked by progressive deepening and widening. It has led to an overall accumulation of political power at a level beyond the nation-state. So far no overwhelming and clearly articulated opposition has developed to stop these changes, even after the 'permissive consensus'[33] supposedly ended with the Maastricht rati-fication crises. In fact, Banchoff and Smith argue that, even though the political controversy following the Maastricht crisis was a very serious challenge to the EU structure, this very controversy 'ultimately revealed the reserves of legitimacy that the EU possesses' because the EU found a way out of the crises and continued to develop.[34] This observation in itself does not say much about the predictability of the future trajectory of these processes. It does, however, suggest that by the time the project of a European Union became a reality with the TEU, a sufficient con-sensus on some underlying, admittedly vague, values had emerged to sustain general acquiescence if not support, even in times of crisis.[35]

Moreover, even if there is disaffection with individual policies, de Búrca argues, following Weiler that 'the fact that there may be vigorous debate over the merits of particular Community measures, does not necessarily mean that there is a crisis of legitimacy in the Union'.[36] Empirically it is difficult to establish, beyond the crude measures provided by Eurobarometer, how much the citizens differentiate between discontent with policies affecting them more or less directly, and the overall feeling towards integration. The argument presented here is, however, that in the historical development of integration to date, a broad balance between the two must have been achieved, otherwise the integration process would have come to a halt or would at least have been more seriously challenged. The question then is which role 'institutional tinkering' has played in maintaining this balance in the past, and which role it might play in maintaining and/or restoring it in the future.

In fact, it might be true that the qualitative shift from a 'permissive consensus' to a situation where people became really concerned with the question of what kind of Europe they want, was occurring only at the point where the common currency became a daily reality, and enlargement to include ten new member states in 2004 put the whole EU system under considerable strain. In fact, even though it remains difficult to determine in how far issues of European integration have become a concern of 'the public' (or the publics) of Europe at large, it is clear that the political discussion has intensified since the launch of the debate by Joschka Fischer on 'the future of Europe' which remains a reference point even after the Constitutional Treaty has been signed. The continued urgency of these questions is evident from the dual pressures on the EU, exerted on the one hand from within by signs of public discontent (such as decreasing turnout in European elections and the uncertainty of the ratification of the EU's constitution for example), and on the other hand from outside the Union by the demands for further enlargement.[37]

This attempted explanation points again to the (fundamentally insoluble) circular relationship between causes and effects in complex social phenomena: is the Union in crises, because its legitimacy is perceived as too weak and therefore it has to embark on new political initiatives, or are these political initiatives the root-causes of the legitimacy problems?[38] The Charter of Fundamental Rights and its role for the legitimacy debate is an interesting illustration of this point. As has been shown in Chapter 2, the role of fundamental rights in sustaining a democratic polity is by no means as clear as the public discourse about fundamental rights often suggests. The Cologne mandate itself proclaimed a somewhat dubious causal link between the protection of fundamental rights and the EU's legitimacy (see Chapter 4). This suggested that the protection of fundamental rights was *a means* to legitimate the polity as a whole, and its internal functioning. Yet, this approach is problematic if the polity is as difficult to define as the European Union, and if the rights in question are already protected through other means (under the ECHR and the national constitutions). Thus, the supposed strengthening of the EU's legitimacy basis by reference to a set of fundamental rights raised as many questions about the Union's legitimacy as it provided answers. The Charter exercise in this view could have also led to a further delegitimation of the EU if the disagreements in the Convention had been so profound as to challenge the notion of a common European project. The argument here is, however, that the debates in the privileged environment of the Convention and the ensuing clarification of the limits of agreement on the dimensions of EU politics, were themselves necessary parts of the legitimation process, even though the instigators of the Charter project might not have bargained for this debate at the outset.

Nevertheless, to understand the nature of the debates and their effect, it has to be noted that the Charter was caught from the very beginning in the ambiguity between on the one hand affirming the legitimacy of integration as such (by showing that it does not lead to a decrease in fundamental rights protection), and on the other hand trying to create additional legitimacy for certain aspects of integration (by improving the functioning of the new polity). Claudia Attucci has noted a similar tension 'between the principle of the equal treatment of human beings, and that of respect of diversity between member states' which meant that from the beginning the Charter exercise was 'ambivalently inspired by both normative universalism and particularism'.[39] Before a closer analysis is presented of how this ambiguity affected the debates in the Charter Convention and what consequences it had for the Charter's contribution to the EU's legitimacy, it seems in order to take stock of the other attempts the Union has made at devising and improving its own means of legitimation in the past.

EU modes of legitimation

A polity is a polity . . .

Leaving aside for a moment the fundamental problems that beset, at a theoretical level, the formation of a new polity, one has to recognise that the European Union over the years has developed more and more aspects of a new and independent polity. These developments have in themselves been 'legitimated' in different ways and at uneven paces. Some of the most visible steps towards polityhood of the EU have been the construction of autonomous institutions at a supranational level, the establishment of the principles of supremacy and direct effect of Community law,[40] qualified majority voting in the European Council,[41] the creation of 'classical' representative structures with a directly elected Parliament at their centre,[42] and more recently of course the drafting of a 'Constitutional Treaty' for the EU which defines the EU as based on 'the will of the citizens and States of Europe to build a common future' (Art. I-1). While it is possible to see all these developments as 'instruments' to facilitate, implement, and legitimate European-level policies as the desired outcomes, it is also clear that each step itself depended on legitimation, and expresses certain normative choices about the polity.

At the same time, it remains unclear to date on what kind of 'collective-psychological basis' the structures of the new polity have developed. While a shared identity or at least some sense of commonness seems to be universally accepted as one important element of legitimacy of political organisation (Chapter 2), there is no agreement as to the precise role of such an identity in the European case. Indeed, as William Wallace observes, '[t]he question of expectations, of common identity or consciousness of the emergence of a "sense of community" is the most contested because [it is] the most difficult to measure.'[43] Moreover, there is disagreement whether such an identity has to exist prior to political organisation, or whether it emerges in the process, and if so, whether it emerges automatically as a by-product of political interaction, or whether it can and should be consciously constructed.[44] An important contribution to the understanding of these problems in the EU context has been made by the recent application of constructivist ideas to the integration process which explicitly examine the possibility of 'creating' new identities through political action.[45]

What is of concern here, however, is not so much the theoretical debate about the causal connections between legitimacy and identity, but the empirical attempts by players at EU level to influence the legitimacy problem through political action. Following the three-fold distinction which dominates the debate about the different elements of legitimacy set out in Chapter 2, the EU's attempts at improving its record in the area will be categorised as 'output-related measures', 'input-related measures' and, as an expansion on the notion of 'social legitimacy', the third category will be termed 'identity-related' measures. In each area EU policies have contributed to the legitimacy of the new political order, albeit in a somewhat uncoordinated way. This lack of a coherent vision of the action necessary to provide the EC/EU with a legitimacy of its own is in turn partly responsible for the persistent perception of an EU-legitimacy problem.

Improving the output

In many accounts, the origins of European cooperation lie in an attempt by several nation-states to improve their capabilities by pooling political resources. As Ernst Haas puts it, 'the readiness of citizens and governments to accept the decisions made by the collectivity as authoritative, binding and final has generally been associated with the evolving capability of the collectivity to make decisions which meet the needs and demands of the citizenry.'[46] In this reading, improving efficiency and effectiveness of policy was the supreme aim of integration, and hence the yardstick for its legitimacy. Beetham and Lord distinguish two different strands of this 'performance based' understanding of legitimacy at the EU level, as compared to the national level: on the one hand legitimacy based on the superior knowledge of technocrats, on the other hand the EU's overall superior capabilities to provide solutions to certain cross-border problems.

The latter argument is, according to Beetham and Lord, used both by the intergovernmentalist account of integration (where nation-states only agree to transfer sovereignty on issues where the superior capability of the supranational organisation is clearly beneficial to them), and by the neofunctionalists, who see the superior capability of a larger scale organisation as providing the driving force behind their notion of 'spill-over'.[47] Thus the Union has to improve its performance and to enhance its capabilities in order to be legitimate. At the same time, the acquisition of new competencies by the Union, or the expansion of its legal and/or administrative capacities, is subject to close scrutiny by the member states precisely because of the legitimacy problem. From this point of view, any new competencies for the EU are acceptable only where clear functional gains can be shown.

In this sense, the debate about which kind of output the Union can legitimately hope to produce has intensified as the pace of integration accelerated, and Weiler, Haltern and Mayer speak of a 'practical eruption of the hitherto dormant question of Community "competencies and powers", a question and debate which has found its code in the deliciously vague word, term and concept of "Subsidiarity".'[48] The inclusion of the principle of subsidiarity in the 1991 TEU, which tried to clarify the definition of legitimate EU output as action taken by the union 'only if and in so far as the objectives of the proposed action cannot be sufficiently achieved by the Member States and can therefore, by reason of the scale or effects of the proposed action, be better achieved by the Community' (Article 3b TEU), was seen as a way to settle the issue. Nevertheless, both the ongoing debate about what exactly subsidiarity means, and subsequent calls for a 'catalogue of competencies' to clarify which level does what in the EU, reveal that the question of output is far from resolved.[49]

Thus action taken by the Union can, and will continue to be, contested on grounds of the legitimacy of the Union's competencies.[50] Whether the conflicts which will inevitably arise are best resolved judicially by an independent body (as Weiler proposes with his idea of a Constitutional Council for the EU),[51] whether they can be avoided by the competency categories as introduced in the Constitutional Treaty (part I, title III, Arts I-11-I-14), or whether such conflicts are regarded as the essential contents of a permanent political struggle (as for example Richard Bellamy suggests),[52] are questions that will determine the future of the European Union. Yet, for them to be 'resolved' in a way that is accepted to be legitimate, the other two elements of legitimacy, input legitimacy and social/identity based legitimacy, also have to be addressed.

Improving the input

In Fritz Scharpf's original analysis, the idea of input-based legitimacy is focused on the question 'who governs'.[53] In this sense, it becomes clear that it is the EU's input legitimacy which suffers most from the problem in establishing who/what the polity is. Decisions, in this view, are legitimate if they are based on the participation and the underlying consensus to be bound by them, of all members of the polity. At the same time, Scharpf himself recognises that in a large scale polity direct participation by everybody is impossible. The main question is therefore how to legitimate rule by the majority exercised by their representatives, who are authorised by the electorate (only) at regular intervals. The challenge for the European Union in this view is to organise a degree of participation and representation which ensures at least the right conditions for the other elements of legitimacy (i.e. efficient output/a common identity) to be discussed and developed. The question how this can be achieved is the essence of the debate about the EU's democratic deficit.[54]

The European institutions over the years have tried to improve the Union's input legitimacy mainly through institutional change. The decision by the Paris council of 1974 to hold direct elections to the European Parliament in 1979 marks the first major step in this direction since the foundation of the European Communities with a 'Parliamentary Assembly' consisting of delegated national parliamentarians. Since the establishment of the EP as a directly representative body, most of the initiatives to improve the democratic input from Europe's citizens have been focused on increasing the powers of the Parliament, and making it a genuine co-legislator with the Council.[55] At the same time, there is a debate about the representativeness and intransparency of the Council itself which consists of elected national government ministers, who are, however, only in some cases directly accountable to their national Parliaments for decisions at the European level.[56] Much criticism also focuses on the unelected and unaccountable nature of the European Commission, especially since the Commission combines functions of executive and legislative nature, which in the classical liberal democratic understanding should be separated and subject to more direct external control by the voters. Indeed, one of the main shortcomings of the EU institutional framework in terms of participation is the fact that the voters so far cannot sanction executive power directly by throwing 'the scoundrels out'.[57]

The institutional response to these problems over the years has been a gradual shift towards more parliamentary powers (including an increased involvement of the EP in the constitution and investiture of the Commission). With the introduction first of the cooperation and then the co-decision procedures, the European Parliament has significantly increased its role as a legislator. When it forced the European Commission led by Jacques Santer to resign in 1999, this was seen by some as proof that the European Parliament had reached 'maturity' not only as a legislative body, but also in its function of controlling the other institutions.[58] At the same time, however, it is true that participation in the European political process by means of voting in European elections has been in constant decline since 1979.[59]

In parallel, the European institutions have also explored other avenues to increase popular control of EU-level decisions. The 1991 Treaty on European Union created the office of a European Ombudsman and the right to petition the European Parliament as part of the introduction of a European citizenship (see below). Moreover, forms of 'selective participation' have been experimented with at different levels. The involvement of interest representation groups in the formulation and implementation of policy is in fact one of the most distinctive elements of the European Union today. Some attempts have been made to regulate and formalise these processes,[60] but at the same time they continue to raise 'serious questions about access, privilege, legitimacy, openness, transparency and standards of ethical behaviour in European public life'.[61]

Furthermore, even if the representation of specific interests at the EU level increases the legitimacy of sector specific decisions, this in itself is not enough to legitimate the overall existence of the Union and its capabilities to take decisions that affect all the people living within its boundaries. The 2001 Commission White Paper 'European Governance' examines the possibilities of further broadening alternative forms of participation. These proposals contain useful additions to the EU-level political process, and can help to achieve the original goal of the European Community, as formulated in the white paper, to 'integrate the people of Europe, while fully respecting individual national identities'.[62] Yet, these proposals alone will not solve the legitimacy problem. Walker in fact criticises the White Paper for missing its 'constitutional opportunity' by not addressing more substantially the challenges to the EU on grounds of 'identity' and 'authority'.[63] Even the changes introduced in the Constitutional Treaty, most notably the increase of the European Parliament's influence through the extension of the co-decision procedure, public meetings of the European Council when it acts as a legislator, a new role for national Parliaments in policing subsidiarity, and a new element of direct democracy with the citizens' initiative (Art. I-47.4) do not in themselves solve the problem of EU legitimacy if Europe's citizens do not feel that these channels are there for them to use. As Fritz Scharpf observes, the problem remains that even the most sophisticated models of input-based legitimacy rely on some kind of shared identity for them to work, and 'similar conditions apply even to modern concepts of "deliberative democracy"'.[64] The next section therefore examines the attempts by the European institutions to acquire such an identity as a basis for Europe's legitimacy.

Identity and legitimacy

As indicated in Chapter 2, most accounts of political legitimacy include a reference to some notion of feeling of belonging, commonality or shared identity between the members of a polity. This emotive bond between them is seen as a precondition for the trust which is necessary to sustain stable relationships and make majority rule acceptable in abstract contexts, i.e. in a situation where the polity is so large that the bulk of individuals' relationships cannot be based on actual acquaintance or kinship. At the same time, the discussion so far has shown that the link between identity and legitimacy is unclear, because most democratic theory seems to *pre*-suppose a shared identity to set the boundaries of legitimate government. This of course creates problems for political entities which are visibly pluralistic, like the EU. A possible 'solution' to this is suggested by Habermas' notion that the polity and its institutions (including the laws) constitute each other at the same time (see Chapter 2), but as Scharpf argues, even this concept relies on a minimum level of solidarity and trust, or at least a sense of common purpose, for this 'act of constitution' to take place (see above).

Moreover, empirically the question of identity can only be one of degree, i.e. how much commonness is there between a number of individuals at a given moment, and is this sufficient to support the legitimacy of joint decision-making. At the individual level, the concept of identity is based on a distinction between 'sameness' and 'otherness', which Habermas conceptualises as the 'dialectics of inclusion and exclusion'.[65] The link between identity and legitimacy in this sense lies in the question whether a sufficient degree of 'sameness' is felt between those who decide and those who are decided upon. Thus, despite being a fundamentally subjective phenomenon, identity does have important repercussions for the viability of institutions. Its role is complicated by disagreement on the question whether collective identities 'exist', or whether and how far they are and can be legitimately constructed. It is clear that this question is of particular significance in the creation of a new political entity (such as the EU), on the basis of existing ones (such as the member states) which claim a command over the identity of 'their' individuals.[66]

The available empirical evidence on how integration has affected emotive bonds between individuals and the political entities at various levels is sketchy. Public opinion data (most importantly from Eurobarometer) suggest that some shift of allegiance has occurred (illustrated by the consistently high number of individuals who describe their identity as both member state and European), but this shift is not radical.[67] A very general feeling of community exists, but this gets 'thinner' the more concrete the questions asked become, and there is a declining trend in identification with the Union and its institutions in recent years. At the same time, the data does support the claim by Manuela Glaab, that 'national and European identity-references do not necessarily exclude each other',[68] which points to the possibility of multiple identities co-existing with each other in layers.

With regards to the legitimacy of the EU and its political action it remains to be seen how successful such multilayered identities can be in maintaining the Union in its day-to-day operation and how much differentiation between different parts of the polity/different policy-areas can be reconciled with the legitimacy of the system. At the same time, the EU by now has a considerable history in trying to make use of the identity concept for legitimation purposes. The result is mixed, and the approaches have changed over time. Thus a brief account of some of the most prominent EC/EU attempts to foster its own 'identity' gives interesting insights into how the institutional actors have perceived their role in legitimating the Union. From these historical precedents it becomes possible to place the Charter project in the wider perspective of the ongoing attempt to define, what is distinctly European about the EU and to create an emotive link between the political structure and its people. The 'results' reached in the Charter Convention have formed the basis for, and in several cases were then superseded by, the continuing debate about a European identity in the constitutional process.

While the founding Treaties are silent on the concept of a common identity of the Europeans, the first prominent mentioning of this idea occurs with the 1973 (Copenhagen Summit) 'Declaration on European Identity', which undertook to 'define the European Identity with the dynamic nature of the Community in mind'.[69] Interestingly, the purpose of this exercise was mainly to provide a means 'to achieve a better definition of their [the member states'] relations with other countries'.[70] Thus the identity presented here was directed outward, and no explicit reference was made to the need for a common identity to sustain democratic rule at a supra-national level. Yet, the declaration makes remarkable statements about the perceived origins of Europe's identity. It refers to the overcoming of past hostilities between the member states and the agreement by 'the Nine' 'that unity is a basic European necessity to ensure the survival of the civilization which they have in common'. The EC member states also claim to share 'the same attitudes to life' and a commitment 'to defend the principles of representative democracy, of the rule of law, of social justice – which is the ultimate goal of economic progress – and of respect for human rights'. These principles, with some small alterations, have over the years become core elements of the EC/EU identity discourse, and they also provided the starting point for the debates about the preamble to the EU Charter (see Chapter 4).[71]

With regard to the citizens and their role in the integration project, the 1973 declaration states: 'The Nine believe that this enterprise [i.e. the defence of the above-mentioned principles, but also the preservation of 'the rich variety of their national cultures'], corresponds to the deepest aspirations of their peoples who should participate in its realization, particularly through their elected representatives.'[72] The document thus uses the reference by the integration actors (here the members of the Council) to a community of values which it describes as being 'common' already, to strengthen the EC as an international actor. As far as the subjects of such a community are concerned, the emphasis is on 'their [i.e. the member states'] peoples' as collective entities, represented by the member state governments, rather than as individual political actors.

Subsequently, the idea of a European identity took on a life of its own and became increasingly linked with the growing concern of how to improve the legitimacy of the integration project. The next significant step in this development was the report on the idea of a 'European Union' by former Belgian Prime Minister Leo Tindemans in 1974/75.[73] He argued for a stronger definition of Europe's identity, and launched the idea of a 'European citizenship', which was then developed further in a Commission report in 1975.[74] In this context, Tindemans proposed a series of measures under the heading of a 'citizen's Europe', in order to promote a 'common vision of Europe' and restore the European idea as a mobilising force.[75] The Commission in its own contribution to Tindemans' report recognised that there was a need for the future European Union to react to the 'growing resistance to attempts to centralizing [sic] power', and to find means of power-distribution 'enabling both the efficiency of public administration to be raised and the involvement of the citizens to be intensified'.[76] Significantly, the protection of human rights appears among Tindemans' proposals because the report insists that 'the democratic nature of the European Union, which should be explicitly stated in the Treaty of Union, means that the protection of human rights is a fundamental element in the new political edifice and in the operation of its institutions'.[77]

In the difficult climate for integration which followed the first enlargement of the EC and the oil shock in the early 1970s, little direct action seems to have followed from Tindemans' report. The next significant event, therefore, was the attempted relaunch of the European Union idea with the 1983 'Solemn Declaration on European Union' at the Stuttgart Council meeting. This declaration refers to 'an awareness of a common destiny' and 'of a common cultural heritage as an element in the European identity'[78] among the foundations of the Union. This addition to the previous rhetoric of European identity is significant because the idea of using the cultural heritage to 'advertise' the common identity became the basis for various political initiatives in the area of culture and ultimately led to the introduction of an Article on culture in the Maastricht Treaty.[79] While it seems likely that initiatives in the area of culture have been successful to a certain degree in raising awareness of the European integration project, they have also exposed the fundamental ambiguity of the EC/EU's involvement in promoting both its own common identity, and the distinct identities of its member states: the cultural heritage can become easily divisive, as happened during the debates about the reference to Europe's religious/moral heritage in the Charter preamble and again in the second Convention on the Constitution.

In parallel to the protection of the cultural heritage as a source of Europe's identity, the development of genuinely European symbols of a common identity was also pursued. It was promoted especially by the Adonnino report on 'A People's Europe' in 1985.[80] This document, in the wider context of the relaunch of the integration project under Jacques Delors, addressed a broad range of issues thought to be of concern to citizens. The Fontainebleau summit 1984 commissioned the Adonnino report with the following rationale: 'The European Council considers it essential that the Community should respond to the expectations of the people of Europe by adopting measures to strengthen and promote its identity and its image both for its citizens and for the rest of the world.'[81] This opening statement is significant because it speaks of Europe's 'people' rather than 'peoples', and refers to '*its* [Europe's] citizens' rather then the member states' citizens. This new emphasis on a direct connection between the Community and 'its' people is maintained throughout the document. Moreover, identity here is no longer exclusively aimed at the outside world, but is there 'for its citizens'.[82]

The ensuing report put great emphasis on proposals 'which will be of direct relevance to Community citizens and which will visibly offer them tangible benefits in their everyday lives' because this is seen as being 'of great importance in making the Community more credible in the eyes of its citizens'.[83] The most important addition by the reports' authors to the original agenda set by the Council is the (implicit) recognition of the need to make Community action more legitimate: Adonnino therefore proposes '[a] strengthening [of] the special rights of citizens, in particular voting rights, improvement of citizens' complaints procedures and simplification of Community legislation.'[84] Without mentioning either the idea of a European citizenship, or the problem of legitimacy as such, the report thus anticipates a number of important issues which came to the fore during the negotiations of the citizenship provisions of the Maastricht Treaty, and have remained on the agenda ever since.

Without the framework of a comprehensive citizenship concept, however, the proposals in the Adonnino report appear mainly as haphazard attempts to find policies to 'please' the citizens, and to create an emotive attachment to integration by providing 'added value' and new symbols. With regard to the identity and legitimacy issue, the report states that '[i]t is also through action in the areas of culture and communication, which are essential to European identity and the Community's image in the minds of its people, that support for the advancement of Europe can and must be sought.'[85] Some imaginative proposals are advanced to disseminate or even create a clearer identity for the EC: cooperation on television programmes, a Euro-lottery, a European Academy of Science, Technology and Art, University exchanges, twinning of sports teams and schools, a European Voluntary service, and, most symbolically, the adoption of a flag, an emblem and an anthem 'to be used at national and international events, exhibitions and other occasions where the existence of the Community needs to be brought to public attention'.[86] Yet, the mere strengthening of the 'corporate identity' of the new polity alone did not automatically lead to a stronger identification of the citizens with it.

As far as the symbolic action to endow the European Community with its own distinct identity to underpin political legitimacy is concerned, the Adonnino report marks the first high point of *proto*-state symbolism. During and after the controversies about the Treaty on European Union of 1991, the emphasis of the debate shifted away from the creation of a common identity, but in 2003 a core set of 'symbols of the Union' was introduced in the Constitutional Treaty (Art. I-8).[87] Nevertheless it appears that Union actors have become increasingly aware of the difficulties of proposing a 'uniform' European identity as a solution to the legitimacy problem of the Union. Part of the reason for this reorientation is of course the fact that the 'crisis' following the signing of the Maastricht Treaty did highlight a feeling of threat to national identities from the project of European Union.[88] In the face of such criticism, the Union institutions have tried to stay clear of the problematic idea to define Europe's cultural and political identity in any way which could bring the dividing elements to the surface again. Nevertheless this debate has been re-ignited with new vigour by a possible accession of Turkey to the European Union.

Legitimation policy in need of direction

The persistent tension between the search for a collective identity of the Europeans and the need to respect the diversity of cultures and identities in the EU points to one of the dilemmas of the EU's legitimation policy. While the debate about what the EU is and does gathered pace after the

Maastricht crisis, the actors at EU level seemed for a long time stunned by the open opposition to some aspects of integration which manifested itself during the Maastricht ratification. At the same time, the project of institutional reform of the Union moved on only slowly with the inter-governmental conferences of 1996 and 2000, but then gathered momentum again with the Constitutional Convention of 2002. Nevertheless, the challenges before the Union have developed even faster since the turn of the century: the global changes after 11 September 2001, the enlargement of 1 May 2004, the continued problems of economic performance of the EU 25 and the debate about the future extension of the European Union continue to challenge the existing balance of legitimacy in and of the EU. For the earlier part of the history of integration, the question of legitimacy was either not an issue at all, or it had been debated in a way which did not capture the complexity and interconnectedness of the elements making up the legitimacy of a post-national political system. As has been shown, the response of the EU institutions generally consisted in uncoordinated, sometimes contradictory, political action to tackle particular aspects of the EU's legitimacy here and there, but with no clear overall direction.

This changed to a degree with the Maastricht Treaty. The idea of political union in the post cold-war context brought the EU polity question to the fore, and the concept of a European citizenship laid at least the conceptual foundations for a more comprehensive approach to the legitimacy problem (see below). On this basis, issues of the degree of commonness in Europe, of the legitimate scope and sphere of the EU polity, and of the feasibility of building a common identity, could become prominent during the drafting of the Charter of Fundamental rights in 2000 and then shape the discussions about the Constitutional Treaty in 2002/03. The Charter debates were significant in this context as the first example of an attempt to clarify Europe's nature and identity in an institutionalised public debate. The notion of a European citizenship, which will be examined more closely in the following section, provides a crucial conceptual lens through which older and wider concerns about who is integrating what, for whom and by which means, can be addressed.

European citizenship: defining the EU-demos?

Citizenship beyond the state

As was discussed earlier, one core problem in defining the EU polity is the difficulty of establishing who is entitled to take decisions within it, and which individuals are to be bound by its decisions – in Bellamy's terms the 'subjects' of the political process. This has important consequences for the democratic nature of the polity and the process by which it is legitimated. Defining the 'demos' is therefore a necessary condition for the legitimacy of any political order.[89] A concept of citizenship is thus, amongst other things, a set of criteria to define membership of the polity. This is of particular importance in the case of a new polity being created, such as the EU. Since it has widely been accepted that the EU is more than just a cooperative arrangement between sovereign nation-states, but itself takes sovereign decisions in important areas, the issue has arisen for what purposes and on which conditions individuals are members of Europe. The concept of European citizenship is an attempt to respond to these questions. While European citizenship is still an incomplete concept, especially because it is still dependent on member states' own rules of membership, it will be argued that the debate about citizenship provides a useful framework for the wider questions of the definition and legitimacy of the EU polity.[90]

The problem of defining individual membership of the EU is exacerbated by the fact that historically citizenship as a concept has been tied up closely with the modern state. The tight link between state and citizenship, further complicated by the intricate connection between concepts of 'state' and 'nation', has shaped our understanding of citizenship.[91] This creates ambiguities once citizenship is applied to the EU which is neither a state nor a nation. Nevertheless, in what Siofra O'Leary calls a 'constitutional choice',[92] the EU did adopt the term 'citizenship' in its own attempts to clarify the question of what kind of polity it is. Interestingly, despite the widely differing views on what exactly this constitutional choice entails in legal and political terms, the very choice itself seems to be uncontested: there are few who argued or argue now for a removal of the actual term 'citizenship' from the Treaties or the European debate altogether.[93]

A closer look at the origins of the institutional debate about European citizenship as a means to legitimate the EU polity shows that the development of a notion of European citizenship as part of the wider concept of a 'European Union' first emerged, and then received special attention, in moments of particular crisis of the integration project. In this reading, the citizenship notion can be seen as part of a growing set of 'tools' used by European institutions to legitimate the Community/Union, as the deepening and intensifying process of integration revealed that the indirect legitimacy derived from the member states might not be sufficient to sustain the new polity. The debate about the general meaning of citizenship in a post- and supra-national context, and about its repercussions at the European level, touches upon all dimensions of the legitimacy problem because it concerns the emotive tie between rulers and ruled, as well as the institutional structures, and the ability of the political order to fulfil citizens' expectations of effective and efficient governance. With the drafting of the Charter, this discussion was moved one step further towards a general constitutional debate and set a number of important markers for the exchanges which followed in the second Convention.

European citizenship: rights and practices

The concept of citizenship is, in this sense, clearly more than just the citizenship provisions originally introduced under Article 8 of the TEU (Arts 17–22 since the Treaty of Amsterdam, now taken up in Art. I-10 of the Constitutional Treaty). Antje Wiener, for example, argues that over the years, long before the Maastricht formalisation of EU citizenship, there had been a continuous growth of both formal and informal 'resources' in the EU context of citizenship which she calls 'European citizenship practice'.[94] By taking this broader view, she can include in her analysis aspects of citizenship which go beyond the mere letter of legal documents and which are directly relevant to the issues of legitimacy. She concludes that citizenship has increasingly influenced the European debate 'as [a] concept which is, on the one hand, intrinsically and crucially linked with the political project of state building . . . and which has been highly contested in theory and practice, on the other'.[95]

   This is due to the fact that the EU's citizenship provisions as they stand today are both reason for, and expression of, the EU's fundamental ambiguity between supranational quasi-state and international cooperative arrangement. As Bellamy and Warleigh observe, in the formalised concept of European citizenship of the TEU, the member governments still act as 'gatekeepers of EU citizenship'. At the same time, 'the provisions [of European citizenship] also reflect, and to a limited extent promote, a direct relationship between citizens and the Union'.[96] The ambiguity of this relationship, which was discussed in the Charter Convention, has subsequently been explicitly recognised (rather than resolved) in the text of the Constitutional Treaty which 'establishes the European Union' based on 'the will of the citizens and States of Europe' (Art. I-1). In this respect, Union citizenship represents one layer of the multiple citizenships and *demoi* to which people increasingly belong.

The question is how this multiplicity of *demoi* and citizenships can co-exist and legitimate different levels of political power.[97]

The role of citizenship in legitimating the EU polity

What is the role and potential of this additional layer of citizenship in legitimating a new level of political organisation? Citizenship in this context fulfils a number of different functions. Paul Close, for example, extracts two main elements from his (non-exhaustive) list of different, partly overlapping concepts of what citizenship is and does: the 'relational' and the 'individual' aspect of citizenship. The 'relational aspect' here refers to the connection which citizenship establishes between the individual human being and the collectivity (through rights and duties, or a status of membership), while the 'individual aspect' refers to the part which citizenship plays in constituting the identity of the individual.[98] A similar duality features in most citizenship theories, and it is echoed in the notion that citizenship is composed of the two central aspects of 'rights and identity' used by Bellamy and Warleigh.[99]

Both of these elements are relevant to the legitimation of a political order, but the role of both rights and identity is also problematic: the discussion in Chapter 2 has shown that the origin and ultimate justification of some of the rights in question (i.e. universal human rights) makes them unsuitable to define a traditional kind of citizenship as an (exclusive) community. Moreover, it is unclear whether rights are best understood as a precondition of membership of a polity, or whether they form the contents of the actual political process. With regards to the 'relational' aspect of citizenship, problems of identity have been highlighted in the European context, especially if belonging is understood in a 'thick', culturally based way.[100] On the other hand, there are those who maintain that a different kind of citizenship, 'thinner' and based on a 'civic' rather than 'ethnic/cultural' understanding of belonging, could emerge once citizenship is freed from its historical entanglement with nationality and the nation-state.[101]

Bearing these difficulties in mind, the main interest here is the institutional use of the terms 'citizen' and 'citizenship' by EC/EU actors in their attempts to provide legitimacy for integration and the functioning of the new polity. In this context, it is necessary to remember that, as O' Leary points out in her history of the development of EU citizenship, many of the elements of EC/EU policy which are now regarded as citizenship-based 'could have developed anyway on the basis of free movement provisions and Article 6. Indeed, many of them were in place before an article on citizenship was introduced into the Treaty.'[102] One has to note, however, that this observation reflects a widely shared understanding of citizenship as being largely based on rights. Indeed, the Treaty on European Union, which formalised the concept of European citizenship, did so to 'strengthen the protection of the rights and interests of the nationals of its [the EU's] Member States'.[103] Yet, one important problem with this understanding in the European context is that, even if the rights in question might be regarded as citizenship-related by the EU actors, very often EU citizens do not share this view. They take such rights for granted or as necessary corollaries of economic integration. This makes such rights unsuitable for providing the 'added value' of European vis-á-vis national citizenship.

Moreover, the reduction of citizenship to consisting almost exclusively of 'extra' rights, raises important questions about the teleology of the EU in developing the citizenship notion:[104] the question whether citizenship is ultimately seen as a legitimating goal *in itself*, or whether it is a *means* to make other aspects of integration acceptable. A look at the Treaties themselves confirms the ambiguity of the Union on this point. The goals of integration as originally spelled out in the Preamble to the EC Treaty (most famously to 'lay the foundations of an ever closer union among the peoples of Europe', but also the 'preservation and strengthening of peace and liberty'), do not seem to require further justification. It is interesting to note that citizenship is not mentioned among them. Citizenship is thus clearly not a goal in itself for the European *Community*.[105]

The *Union* Treaty of 1991, on the other hand, does list the establishment of a 'citizenship common to nationals of the countries' both in its preamble *and* among the objectives which the Union set itself under Article B. Especially this latter reference is important because it clearly indicates the instrumental character of union citizenship: the objective of the Union is 'to strengthen the protection of the rights and interests of the nationals of its Member States *through* the introduction of a citizenship of the Union' (emphasis added). In a narrow reading, this formula would suggest that it is not the rights that derive from citizenship, but that on the contrary the rights already exist, and citizenship is 'just' a means to 'strengthen and protect' them. This view is in line with the traditional approach to fundamental rights as existing 'naturally', outside the political process, which was discussed in Chapter 2. This view also informed the (contested) understanding of the Charter Convention as a body to merely list 'existing' rights (see Chapter 4). At the same time, such a narrow view of the relationship between rights and citizenship seems to be at odds with the understanding which emerges from the Charter as it was proclaimed at Nice, because there the preamble makes the rights themselves *means* to the end of preserving and developing a set of 'common values'. Finally, in the 'new' definition of the 'Union's objectives' (Art. I-3) developed by the Constitutional Convention, neither citizenship nor specific rights are mentioned, but they are referred to in separate articles (I-10 and I-9 respectively) – which seems to follow a more coherent logic from the general principles to the more specific provisions in part one of the Constitutional Treaty.

European citizenship history

Thus the role of a concept of European citizenship needs to be seen in the context of the notion's historical development. Interestingly, the main 'events' in this trajectory closely follow the chronology set out above for the notion of a 'European identity': from its beginnings in the early 1970s, via major reports of 1975 and 1985, to the Maastricht Treaty and beyond. Despite the fact that 'identity' and 'citizenship' have rarely been directly linked in the official documents, they have developed in parallel. Thus both Antje Wiener and Siofra O' Leary start their accounts of citizenship development with the Paris summit of 1974 (that is, after the 1973 declaration on European identity), when a working group was set up to 'study the conditions and timing under which the citizens of the nine Member States could be given special rights as Members of the Community'.[106] This must be seen also against the backdrop of the earlier judgements by the European Court of Justice in *Van Gend en Loos*,[107] which had established that the European Treaties could confer rights directly on individuals, and *Stauder*, which had stated that fundamental rights were fundamental principles of Community law.[108]

Following Antje Wiener's 'socio-historical institutionalist approach', the new concern with 'special rights' which developed in the early 1970s on this basis, appears as a reaction to the internal and external changes of the Community and its environment which had occurred in the previous two years.[109] Despite the EC's 1972 commitment to reach 'political union' within the decade, by 1974 circumstances had changed: the joint effect of the first enlargement of the EC, the collapse of the Bretton-Woods system of financial stability, and tensions between the nine members in reaction to the first oil crises in 1973, had increased pressure on the community to act more decisively. Despite, or maybe because of, their inability to agree on substantive political decisions, the heads of state and government tried to make some headway at least on some less tangible issues of political integration such as 'identity' and 'rights'. The 1973 Declaration on European identity and the commissioning of the Tindemans report in 1974, as well as several statements during the Paris summit, suggest, according to Wiener, a new awareness of the 'missing link between citizens and the Community as [being] one reason for the crises at this time'.[110] Moreover, despite the fact that according to Desmond Dinan 'nobody (including Tindemans) expected the report on European Union to produce tangible results',[111] in the event the report did anticipate many issues of the later debates on European citizenship. In parallel, the Commission drafted its own report 'Towards European Citizenship' in 1975, envisaging citizenship based on two elements: 1) a 'passport union' (with the abolition of internal frontier controls, a common regime for third country nationals, and the issuing of a uniform Community passport), and 2) the granting of 'special rights' for people living in a member state other than their own.[112] It was thus clear that the European dimension was supposed to provide 'added value' in terms of rights protection – even though it was not clear which rights this could include.

The Tindemans report, which was published shortly after the Commission report on citizenship, offered a little bit more clarity on this question because it clearly made the protection of 'rights and fundamental freedoms, including economic and social rights'[113] an issue for the European institutions. Thus it brought the political-institutional debate in line with the ECJ jurisdiction, which had been developing its own concept of fundamental human rights since 1969.[114] The Commission, in its contribution to the Tindemans report, recognised that 'the democratic nature of the European Union, . . . means that the protection of human rights is a fundamental element in the new edifice'.[115] This protection of rights was, however, not to be an end in itself. The main aim at this point was to create a European identity, and the measures proposed (including rights protection), were seen as means to that end.

At the same time, important steps were taken to give substance to the commitment to democratic procedures and thus democratic 'rights'. The 1974 Paris summit had decided to hold direct elections to the European Parliament from 1978 onwards. In Wiener's words therefore the new 'citizenship practice' which emerged in the early 1970s was based on three pillars: '[p]assport policies, special rights for citizens of Member States, and voting rights to the European Parliament'.[116] In addition, underlining the new concern with (fundamental) rights as a way of binding the people to the new institutions, the European Parliament took up the call for the inclusion of 'special rights' in its 1977

'Scelba report',[117] and in the same year all three EC institutions (Parliament, Council and Commission) signed an inter-institutional agreement on the 'respect for fundamental rights'.[118]

At the same time, however, the European Commission had to acknowledge as early as 1975 in its report on citizenship that 'the Community Treaties contain no provision giving an immediate power to act with regard to political rights, even under Article 235 of the EEC Treaty'.[119] There was thus no legal basis for major institutional progress on these issues. Even though this did not seem to pose a major problem in the 1970s, the political situation changed with the revitalisation of integration in the early 1980s. Because the Single Market programme brought the promise of free movement to the top of the agenda, it became clear that certain 'flanking measures' were necessary in order to make the internal market work, and to encourage Europeans to avail themselves of the new freedoms. Moreover, with the renewed effort to achieve a genuinely integrated market came the formalisation of qualified majority voting (qmv) in the Council of Ministers under the Single European Act, which moved the community beyond the veto of individual member states, and thus changed the nature of the EU's 'constitutionalism'.[120] This development in turn reignited the debate about who constitutes the EU and exacerbated the problems of legitimacy because if individual member states could be outvoted at EU level, it was clear that the legitimacy derived from the member states was no longer sufficient to sustain integration.[121]

In response to this changed situation, the EP proposed its own Draft Treaty on European Union in 1984, and in 1989 its declaration on the Union's 'Fundamental rights and Freedoms'[122] to underline the need for a more 'political' approach to integration. Meanwhile, as described, Adonnino and his committee had prepared their report on 'a People's Europe' (NB not a 'citizens' Europe'!). Apart from the suggestions examined before concerning a European identity, Adonnino stressed the need for 'special rights of citizens, in particular voting rights, improvements of citizens' complaints procedures and simplification of Community legislation' to achieve a Europe closer to its people.[123] The report devoted a separate chapter to 'special rights' and included among them: a uniform election procedure for European elections; a right to vote in these elections for citizens resident in another member state; a right to petition the European Parliament; the idea of a European Ombudsman; local voting rights in the member state of residence; a 'guarantee that citizens of another member state enjoy the same rights of freedom of speech and assembly as nationals of the member state of residence';

rights of consultation for other member states' citizens on issues directly concerning them (for example language matters); initiatives to simplify Community law; a Community driving licence; and diplomatic protection in third countries.[124] Even though in some cases it took a very long time to implement these proposals, most of them did subsequently become European 'practice' and paved the way for the eventual formalisation of citizenship.

That final step occurred under very different political circumstances which again changed the main policy paradigms. The events of 1989 and what Jacques Delors called 'the acceleration of history'[125] led, similarly to the crises of 1972–73, to a new impetus for political integration. In this context, both the European Parliament in its Martin report,[126] and the Belgian government in March 1990, argued for a closer link between citizens and the Community.[127] Only a month later, Helmut Kohl and François Mitterrand called for a second IGC, on Political Union, in parallel with the IGC on Economic and Monetary Union.[128] Kohl and Mitterrand wanted the following four issue areas to be discussed in the political IGC: 'stronger democratic legitimacy; more efficient institutions; unity and coherence of economic, monetary and political action; and a common foreign and security policy'.[129] Thus the issue of legitimacy had made it to the top of the European agenda.

The initiative to include a citizenship provision in the new Treaty as one way of addressing the growing legitimacy problems thus gathered momentum during the IGC in 1991.[130] The idea to include a charter of fundamental rights in the treaty based on the EP's 1989 declaration of rights also circulated, but it fell victim to the political conflicts between the EP and some more pro-citizenship member states on the one hand, and those member states who favoured a minimalist approach on the other. This resulted probably from a growing sensitivity of some national actors to the threat of 'competition' for legitimacy from the EU level. In the end the Treaty on European Union contained only the commitment, in article F (now article 6) to 'respect fundamental rights, as guaranteed by the European Convention for the Protection of Human Rights and Fundamental Freedoms . . . and as they result from the constitutional traditions common to the Member States', the formula which in 1999 was to become the basis for the Cologne mandate for the Convention to draft the Charter.

Despite this failure to include a catalogue of rights in the Treaty on European Union, the formalisation of European citizenship in the TEU does represent, in Wiener's words 'a shift of the normative ideal underlying EU governance towards legitimacy and democracy as challenged principles in a multi-level polity', and also triggered a significant mobilisation around citizenship issues in the run-up to the 1996 IGC.[131] This mobilisation was partly due not just to the treaty itself, but came also in response to the Maastricht ratification crises. The strong reaction against the TEU in some member states (notably Denmark, but also France) had taken many political actors by surprise, and clearly demonstrated that the concerns about democratic legitimacy and public acceptance of integration had not been successfully addressed by adopting the Maastricht-kind of citizenship. In response, the hearings of NGOs organised by the European Parliament prior to the 1996 IGC expressed, and in themselves raised, high expectations for further change. They also established for the first time a kind of institutional channel for claims of a constitutional kind directly at the highest European level and thereby set the precedent for a similar approach adopted during the negotiations of the EU Charter and the Constitutional Treaty.[132]

The outcome of the Amsterdam Treaty, however, disappointed many of these expectations. As far as citizenship was concerned, Amsterdam did little but reaffirm the fundamental limitations of the European citizenship concept: its dependence on the nationality of a member state, and the narrow scope of the rights that individuals derive from it. Nevertheless, Wiener notes '[w]hile the formal institutional aspects of the citizenship *acquis* thus largely remained the same, the Amsterdam stage of citizenship practice produced more changes with regard to the routinization of informal resources as the Brussels based institutions began to work with national representations, national parliaments, and NGOs to address the citizens' demands in order to fight the rising discontent'.[133] This in turn has had a significant impact on the role that citizenship, understood in modern participation-focused terms, can play in legitimating European-level politics.

At the same time, integration continued with some incremental progress on the inclusion of visa and immigration policy in the first pillar, and the EU summit meeting in Tampere in October 1999 formalised the EU's commitment to create an area of freedom, security and justice to strengthen policies regarded as relevant to the citizens. Moreover, the Council at Tampere agreed on the modalities for drafting a Charter of Fundamental Rights of the European Union with important implications for the citizenship debate (Chapter 4).[134] The Treaty of Nice, however, which was supposed to make the EU fit for enlargement, did not really address the problem of a worsening legitimacy crisis in an EU of more than 20 members. No sustainable results were reached on issues crucial to the procedural legitimacy of the EU, such as the weighting of votes in the European Council and the number of seats in the European Parliament, and the negotiations failed to address wider issues of membership and participation. Similarly, the mere 'proclamation' of the Charter of Fundamental Rights as a non-binding document disappointed many who had placed high hopes in its capacity to expand the notion of European citizenship.[135] Nice did, however, specify this issue, together with the 'delimitation of competencies', the 'simplification of the Treaties', and the 'role of national parliaments in the European architecture', as the contents for a future IGC.[136] Subsequently these and other questions were taken up in the Laeken Declaration which formed the basis of the Constitutional Convention.[137] It is early yet to decide whether the questions mentioned have been 'resolved' by the Constitutional Treaty, and only time and a developing European 'constitutional practice' will tell. Yet it is clear that with the consolidation of the EU Treaties into a 'constitutional' document, with the inclusion of the Charter of Fundamental Rights as part II, and with important changes to the voting mechanisms and other elements of the EU's institutional framework, the history of EU citizenship has entered a new phase in which a new balance between individual membership and collectivity will have to be found.

European citizenship: the balance

The assessment of the development of EU citizenship so far is therefore a mixed one. Citizenship is a useful conceptual approach to the legitimacy problem, because ideally it addresses all three of its elements: it can potentially ensure legitimate output by enforcing subsidiarity and citizens control over EU action; improve the democratic input by defining the demos and enhancing participation; and foster social legitimacy by creating a civic European feeling of belonging. Over the past three decades, there has been a continuous growth of concern with the role of citizens in the integration project. The understanding of citizenship has expanded to include concepts of multiple belonging, overlapping identities and new and varied forms of participation. The EU's institutional response to the challenges of changing patterns of membership has, however, often been based on a narrow notion of citizenship with a strong emphasis on (special) rights for European citizens and a traditional (nation-state) kind of symbolism. As far as the capacity to provide legitimacy for the new political entity is concerned, this approach has been only partially successful. On the one hand, growing pressure for new forms of inclusion of public opinion have allowed for new institutional arrangements to emerge, and some of the European symbols have acquired a stable position in the collective consciousness. On the other hand, uneasy feelings about a 'legitimacy deficit' are likely to persist, regardless of how measurable they are.

It is partly for these reasons that the *process* by which the Charter of Fundamental Rights was drafted, became so important. If one adopts a process-centred approach to political legitimation, and follows Haber- mas' notion that the rights and the polity contemporarily constitute each other, the process of deliberating on fundamental rights is one way of shaping the political organisation while empowering the citizens in the process. Legitimation in this understanding springs from the recog- nition of those involved in the constitutional process as being free and equal in their deliberations.[138] In the case of the EU, this approach is a particularly fruitful one to explore because even more than national polities, the Union is characterised by an ongoing process of negotiation and renegotiation, not only of the policies of the day, but of its very structure. Continuing enlargement, a series of intergovernmental con- ferences of treaty changes, and last but not least the activities of the European Court of Justice mean that the constitutional framework of integration is under constant reconstruction.

The academic literature has taken note of this situation in recent years with a growing emphasis on the link between the legal and the political aspects of this constitutional process, where the political aspects also include a concern with legitimacy. This approach is summarised in the following as EU 'constitutionalism'. In this context, constitutionalism is to be understood not as a distinct form of legitimation (such as iden- tity building or the improvement of input or output), but rather as an analytical prism which tries to bring the different elements together. It then becomes possible to see the drafting of the Charter not as the starting point, nor as an isolated instance of a European constitutional debate, but rather as one step in the process, albeit one that is significant for its institutional innovations, for the comparatively prominent posi- tion it achieved, and for its importance in preparing the next step, i.e. the drafting of an EU Constitutional Treaty – a development which cannot be understood without the preparatory work which the Charter Convention provided.

EU constitutionalism: defining the EU polity?

What constitutionalism for the EU?

It is usually the ECJ which is credited with, or blamed for, the develop- ment of a quasi-constitutional order of the EU which it derived from the original EC Treaties, but which was not mentioned therein explicitly.[139] With its doctrines of 'direct effect' (developed in *Van Gend en Loos*), the ECJ established that the Treaties confer 'individual rights which national courts must protect'.[140] Thus it made Europeans themselves, not just their states, subjects of Community law, which profoundly altered the legal nature of the Community. Moreover, the ECJ then also developed the doctrine of 'supremacy' of EC law over national law in *Costa* v. *ENEL*,[141] even though this notion is contested with regards to constitutional provisions on fundamental rights (see below). According to Weiler, these two principles constitute the foundations of the constitutional development of the EC/EU. They are essential because in '[w]estern, liberal democracies, . . . public authority requires legitimation through one principal source: the citizens constituting the political subjects of the polity.'[142] But, as Weiler goes on to argue, paradoxically the ECJ's judgements made European union citizens subject to EC law only with regard to the *effect* of those laws, not with regard to the *making* of the laws, because EC law was for a long time created through the member states in the Council of Ministers with only very limited input from the citizens.[143] Thus, even though the ECJ later on, in the judgement in *Les Verts*,[144] referred to the European Treaties as a 'constitutional order', there continue to be serious challenges to the legal notion of EU constitutionalism which have not been resolved, according to some, with the Constitutional Treaty.[145]

Consequently the following is based on an understanding of 'constitutionalism' which goes beyond the legal notion of the term. As Jo Shaw clearly states in her account of European Union constitutionalism, the latter 'is not . . . just about institutions and structures, but also about ideas and values'.[146] The problem, in Shaw's analysis, is that despite the fact that the ECJ did develop a legal idea of constitutionalism based on sometimes generous interpretations of the language of the Treaties, the sources of EC law are wider than that. They include 'institutional practices including legislation and measures akin to constitutional conventions which govern the conduct of the Member States and the Union institutions themselves' as well as the letter of the founding treaties.[147]

Yet, legally the functioning of the 'constitutional construct' of the European Union depends on the goodwill of the major actors, especially that of the national courts which have, in many cases, the task and power to safeguard national constitutions against illegitimate encroachments from the supranational level. The most obvious, and for the EU most dangerous, expression of this dilemma so far has been the challenge against the constitutionality of the Maastricht Treaty brought before the German Constitutional Court (*Bundesverfassungsgericht*, BVG). Joseph Weiler uses the metaphor of the cold-war doctrine of 'mutually assured destruction' (MAD) to describe the situation of (potential) stalemate between national constitutional courts and the ECJ which arose from this judgement.[148] Most importantly as far as the Union's legitimacy is concerned, in Weiler's interpretation the BVG in its judgement in 1993 'rejected the ECJ's claim to exclusive judicial *Kompetenz-Kompetenz*'.[149] This means that in complete defiance of one of the central pillars of European constitutionalism, EC law would not be supreme over national law anymore because it could be struck down by national courts as anti-constitutional at any time. Weiler calls this the 'paradox of constitutionalism'. He concludes that the solution to this legal impasse can only be a political one.

Constitutional dialogue in the EU

Similarly, Shaw also argues for a European 'constitutionalism as a discursive process . . . to accommodate diversity' in a much broader political sense.[150] This echoes calls for a broad and inclusive process of constitutional debate put forward by political theorists. Moreover, Shaw argues that the 'self-evident federalization of law . . . has been buttressed by the Court's discovery and construction of a doctrine of fundamental rights within the EU legal order (as opposed to the imposition of external systems of fundamental rights . . .)',[151] and takes this as evidence of a set of 'key constitutional principles', which in turn are based upon recognizable "constitutional" value systems'[152] as expressed in Article 6(1) of the TEU. The problem is that these principles are nowhere as clear-cut as constitutional rules usually are in national contexts. Furthermore, with the pillar structure of the EU up to now, a growing number of informal principles and actors, and the increasing importance of flexible integration, the EU constitutional framework in a formal sense is far from coherent. For Shaw this state of affairs represents an 'opening' for future change rather than a permanent deficiency, because it allows for a 'dialogic constitutionalism' in a 'post-national' context based on the essential 'contestation' of the European project to develop.[153] The argument, whether the Constitutional Convention and its result are just a more prominent version of such a dialogue, or potentially might mark an end-point and freezing of this necessary conversation, is still ongoing.[154] In fact, even though legally the Constitutional Treaty does not seem to challenge this balance, because it still is an international treaty entered into by sovereign states, it remains to be seen if its political impact over time might not trigger further changes or challenges to the national systems of constitutional law.

The argument about permanent constitutional dialogue does, however, run the risk of ending up in an infinite regress on the question of how to determine by means of a constitutional process who is entitled to participate in the constitutional process. This problem has already been encountered in three different guises: in the legal theoretical version of how the polity and the rights can constitute each other at the same time (Chapter 2), in its political theoretical version as the question how the boundaries of the polity can be defined if we do not have a predefined ethnic or cultural community to constitute the polity (Chapter 3 above), and finally in the democracy-theoretical recognition that the democratic process is simply unable to define by democratic means who is part of it (Chapter 2). Antje Wiener and Vincent Della Sala noted in 1997 that because of this problem, the contemporary debate on EU constitutionalism had 'taken place almost completely isolated from another raging debate, that of citizenship'.[155] This, they argued, led to the paradoxical situation that there was very widespread consensus on the principles and objectives of what they call 'old con-stitutionalism' (such as the need to constrain the power of government to ensure individual freedom, or mechanisms like separation of powers, transparency and accountability to achieve this),[156] while at the same time there was no common 'understanding how individuals come together and create a sense of belonging, demand and recognize recip-rocal rights and duties'.[157]

Since the two strategies open to classical liberal constitutionalism, i.e. assuming a pre-existing community, or embarking on a project of élite-led creation of a community, are not available at European level or seem not acceptable from a democratic point of view respectively, European constitutionalism must either be abandoned or find an alternative solu-tion. While Wiener and Della Sala acknowledge that theories of 'new constitutionalism' do represent some progress, because they take account of an enlarged, politically aware demos, and of the influence of institu-tions on the sense of belonging of the citizens, they argue that only a notion of 'citizenship practice' can bridge this 'democracy gap'.[158] With this affirmation, the argument about who constitutes the polity has come full circle: how much common understanding, shared values, or will to cooperate must exist between free individuals (or sovereign states, as the case may be) before the construction of common rules and institutions becomes acceptable to each and every one of them? The increasingly popular application of deliberative democracy approaches to the process of EU constitutionalism does not purport to solve this basically unsolvable problem, but it does offer an new analytical way to understand the dynamics of the process once it has started.[159]

Conclusion: problems and solutions of EU legitimacy

Polity, citizenship, and constitutionalism

The debate about the EU's legitimacy is intensifying both at the academic and at the political level. As the Union's activities become ever more invasive of peoples' lives with the progress of integration, and as new enlargements challenge the very concept of 'Europe', the legitimacy of the entire process depends more and more upon the Union's ability to legitimate itself independently of the member states. A coherent approach to this problem is, however, made difficult by the many uncertainties about the nature of the polity emerging at the European level, and the ensuing lack of adequate analytical and normative concepts.

At the same time, as the overview has shown, different European-level actors have long been concerned with the need to legitimate integration in the eyes of the citizens. The actions which were prompted by these concerns may often appear rather disparate, but certain continuities are clearly visible. Over the years, the Union has managed to expand its output and is trying to improve its efficiency and transparency. The democratic input has been constantly increased since the first direct elections of the European Parliament. There have been attempts at fostering a European identity, both through progress in the other two areas, and through symbolic action in culture, education and the 'public relations' of the Union. In this context it also has to be mentioned that a growing number of rights of individual citizens has come to be protected at the European level, courtesy of the European Court of Justice which over the years has continuously expanded its rights protection on the basis of the ECHR and the constitutional traditions of the member states.[160] Moreover, as was argued, the notion of a European citizenship is an increasingly important conceptual frame to address all elements of the legitimacy question. It is not possible to measure empirically the success or failure of these initiatives with precision, because of the complex psychological and subjective nature of questions of belonging, identity, and legitimacy, but what can be stated is that there was sufficient legitimacy so far to prevent the disintegration of the Union, but evidently not enough to make the legitimacy problem go away.

This is not surprising, given the gradual and ongoing nature of the constitutionalisation of the EU. In the process of establishing and re-establishing the balance of how much political integration is 'acceptable', and which kind of legitimacy it requires, the empirical yardstick to measure the existing levels of commonality can only be the preceding stages of integration which have been accepted. In this sense, the fact that the commitment to the 'ever closer Union' has never seriously been challenged; that only one member state has left the EC/EU so far;[161] that all twelve heads of state or government accepted the project for a Treaty on European Union in 1991; that fifteen of them endorsed the drafting of an EU Charter of Fundamental Rights in 1999; and that 25 member state heads of state and government signed the EU's Constitutional Treaty in October 2004, are all expressions of the 'constitutional consensus' that exists. At every juncture in the process, this consensus is re-evaluated – at least by those members of the 'national élites attentive to integration issues'.[162] In addition, progress has been achieved in opening up the debates about these issues to organised interests at different levels, and in certain cases to a wider public. Moreover, analysts agree that even in the 'constitutional moments' of the Union, the emphasis has shifted recently towards new modes of legitimation based on a deliberative understanding of constitutional dialogue.[163]

With the Charter towards the Constitution

The EU Charter of Fundamental Rights and its drafting was a further step in this development. It marked both a symbolic and a substantive move towards a constitutional process which allowed the debate to address the wider issues of the legitimacy of the integration project as such (i.e. the polity legitimacy), and of the more concrete questions of how to organise the project legitimately (regime legitimacy).[164] In drafting the Charter, this necessary distinction between the two aspects of creating legitimacy was not always clearly drawn, which meant that the process on several occasions was at risk of being overloaded with questions of fundamentally different attitudes to European integration (see Chapter 4). Yet, the Charter drafting process was successful in bringing out the common foundations shared by most, while at the same time providing a mechanism (deliberative exchange and 'consensus' in the Convention), by which agreement could be found on some of the more divergent notions.

Thus, while at the theoretical level the polity-question remains insoluble, a combination of institution-led/élite-engineered action to legitimate the Union and evolving citizenship practice have created an *acquis* of legitimacy resources on which the current EU edifice rests. The drafting of the EU Charter represented a new institutionalised forum in which these resources could and were, at least partly, operationalised. As with many of the individual steps taken in the past by the institutions to legitimate themselves and the European Union, the Charter changed the EU's constitutional trajectory by its very existence and by how it came into being. As an anonymous editorial commentator put it in 2001, 'it is now there, nourishing debate as to its significance for the entire process of European unification and integration' – a prediction born out by the subsequent debates in the second Convention.[165] Moreover, the process by which the Charter was conceived provided a number of elements which themselves became 'routinised' and have been included in the Constitutional Treaty (Art. IV-443), and thus will shape future debates on the legitimacy question. In order to assess the potentials of this development, the next chapter offers an account of the drafting process and its results from the perspective of how it shaped the four dimensions of the political process at European level.

4
Drafting the Charter in the Convention

Introduction: the dimensions of the EU polity

The legitimacy of the EU and its functioning have been a concern for major actors at the European level for a considerable period. How does the initiative to draft a special document of fundamental rights for the European Union fit into this ongoing 'quest for legitimacy'? The argument here is that the EU Charter of Fundamental Rights, despite the fact that it was initially only proclaimed as a political declaration, was a significant development for the legitimation of the European Union because the Charter process went beyond a debate about the specific rights-protection aspect of the EU regime, and brought into the open a whole host of questions concerning the legitimacy of the EU polity which had previously been debated mainly under very specific circumstances (during the IGCs) by a very small group of nationally legitimated EU policy makers (mostly national ministers and/or heads of state or government). The Charter Convention not only broadened and publicised this debate, but it also found a number of new solutions to old problems, and most importantly established the Convention method as a new tool for debating issues of 'constitutional' significance for the EU. The following account of the working of the Charter Convention highlights its important contribution to the EU's legitimacy by exploring the following questions:

- How did the definition of a set of fundamental rights for the EU affect the particular legitimacy balance of that polity at a given point in time (i.e. in 1999/2000) and the further trajectory of the development of the Union?

- What role did the process by which a catalogue of fundamental rights was agreed upon play for the EU's legitimacy?
- What other elements contributed to the effect of the Charter project on the European Union's legitimacy?

In order to address these questions, the analysis focuses on four particular aspects of the debates which can be seen as corresponding to Bellamy's four dimensions of the political process:[1]

- the discussions on the Charter's *purpose*, as set out in the Cologne mandate, because they spilled over into wider debates about the more general reasons for European integration (Bellamy's *sphere*);
- the notion of a *common European identity* as expressed through a European citizenship and its role in sustaining the legitimacy of a (new) polity by defining its membership (Bellamy's *subjects*);
- the discourse of *EU-level common values*, and the way this discourse was developed in the drafting of the Charter as a measure for the purpose and legitimate extension of integration (Bellamy's *scope*);
- finally the *quality of the Convention process* and how it differed from the traditional settings of intergovernmental and parliamentary debate. The process was particularly important because it encouraged a deliberative style of debate which in itself became a significant contribution to the legitimation tool-set of the EU (Bellamy's *style*).

Thus the theoretical dimensions of *sphere*, *subjects*, *styles*, and *scope* of politics are 'translated as' the variables of purpose, identity, values, and process because the debate about the *purpose* of the Charter (and, by extension, of integration) expressed clearly a concern with the legitimate *sphere* of political organisation at European level and how far it should go; the need to define the *identity* of both the authors and beneficiaries of the Charter's rights (embodied in the debate about European citizenship) aimed at clarifying the *subjects* of European political action; and the novel *process* in the Convention clearly indicated a fundamental change in the *styles* of EU-level constitutional politics. Finally a relation can be conceived, although a less clear one, between the issue of the European value discourse and Bellamy's dimension of *scope* which he explains as follows: 'the scope of politics has to do with its aims and the claims it makes upon people within its designated spheres'.[2] The scope establishes how much, and which kind of political action is acceptable within an agreed sphere. In the context of the EU Charter, the dimension of scope was partly embodied in the debates about the purpose of the Charter, i.e. the question if, and how, the EU could take action to actively protect certain rights. At the same time, the value discourse in the Charter debates also touched on the dimension of scope because if the Union is portrayed and accepted as a community of values (i.e. the EU is more than a free-market organisation), the claims to legitimacy it can make on the basis of its role as a rights-protecting agent are greatly enhanced. The Charter project made use of this connection because it cast the EU in the role of 'contributing to the *development*' of certain values (see below).[3]

Furthermore, it became clear in the course of the debates that the main disagreement about the EU value discourse in the Convention was about the unclear division of competencies between the Union and the member states with regard to legitimate Union action in promoting values (see for example the issue of the religious heritage below). This controversy once more brought out the close connection and frequent overlap between issues of scope and sphere of legitimate EU action. Yet, it is important to note that this question was addressed in the Convention several times couched as the legally-technical need to clearly define the *scope of the Charter*, in order to avoid Charter rights from becoming extensions of EU competencies by stealth. It thus seems feasible to look at the Charter's contribution to the EU value discourse from the perspective of the legitimate *scope* of integration politics. This debate was of course carried over into the Constitutional Convention two years later, where both the issues of the values defining the EU, and of the legitimate scope of EU fundamental rights protection and of European integration writ large, were still hotly contested. This development further illustrates that the Charter Convention did not, and in fact could not resolve these issues, but the Charter Convention found some new balances between divergent views and interests on important aspects, many of which have been included unchallenged in the Constitutional Treaty.

It thus emerges that the Charter process touched upon all four dimensions of politics. Since, in Bellamy and Castiglione's scheme, it is the legitimacy of the polity which 'concerns the *subjects* and *sphere* of politics', whereas the legitimacy of a regime 'concerns the *styles* and *scope* of politics', the debates about the Charter clearly were significant at both levels of legitimacy.[4] It was the particular structure of the method by which the Charter was drafted which interacted with the particular nature of its subject (i.e. fundamental rights) in a climate of uncertainty about Europe's future to allow a wider discussion of aspects of both polity and regime legitimacy to develop. In this process, each of the four dimensions produced its own kind of interaction, which were intimately linked.

This chapter therefore addresses the different dimensions in turn: despite the fact that the purpose of the Charter as set out by the European Council appeared initially to be very limited, the Convention succeeded in exploiting the ambiguities contained in the Cologne and Tampere mandates to broaden its own remit. The debate on what the Charter was for at several junctures led to more general exchanges about the reasons behind integration. The Charter project, therefore, produced a new view on what the legitimate *sphere* of integration should be. The next section reveals that this definition was seen to be encouraged by, and in turn strengthened, the notion of a common identity for Europeans. The contribution of the Charter process to the development of this concept is based on two parallel effects of the project. On the one hand, the perceptions and the understanding of a European identity by the Convention members converged as a result of the process on which they were embarked. On the other hand, the Charter forced new solutions to the question 'who is European' in terms of the beneficiaries of the rights defined. The compromise solutions which had to be found in balancing universal rights and more restrictive rights for EU residents or citizens have the potential to broaden European citizenship and thus opened the debate towards a more comprehensive account of the *subjects* of Europe's integration.

The fourth part of the chapter looks at how the Charter process consolidated and advanced the discourse of EU-Europe as a community of values. More particularly, the debate about the Charter's preamble highlighted both the potentials, and the limits of the value discourse at that juncture, and thus provided the basis for the following debates on the issue in the second Convention and beyond. It showed that a broad consensus exists about the legitimacy of the EU as a polity, as well as on a number of basic values (and related principles) within the European Union, which form the yardstick against which to measure the legitimate *scope* of EU politics. At the same time, the clashes over the reference to Europe's religious heritage also indicated where the limit of this value consensus lay at that moment in time.

The fifth section of the chapter investigates how these outcomes were helped by the particular nature of the process which the Convention operated. The way the Tampere provisions were interpreted by the Convention and the novel composition of the body allowed a process to emerge which contained important elements of deliberation and encouraged the formation of argued compromises. A debate about fundamental rights, with its particular capacity to solicit exchanges on underlying convictions rather than technical detail, turned out to be a particularly adequate subject matter for a more deliberative interaction. Even though the deliberation in the Convention was far from perfect, a large majority of Convention members recognised the benefits of this new kind of process, which for the first time gave full involvement to both national and European parliamentarians at the EU constitutional level. The Charter process tried, tested, and showed the need for improvements in this kind of process, which thus constituted an important precedent for this new *style* of politics at EU constitutional level.

It is concluded that the *Charter and its process* provided new benchmarks for all four dimensions of politics in the European Union. Some of these have been developed further, but not necessarily superseded, by the Constitutional Convention. The analysis thus vindicates the claim that the Charter project was an important extension of the EU's legitimation basis because it opened a debate about the purposes underlying the integration project, strengthened a notion of a European identity, consolidated the discourse of the EU as a community of values, and did so by means of a novel process which itself commanded a comparatively high degree of legitimacy due to its transparency and deliberativeness. By instigating this debate, the Charter process created one of the necessary preconditions for a more legitimate process of EU-constitutionalisation.

Creating, defining or just summarising rights?

The purpose of the Charter: the Cologne mandate

In trying to evaluate the Charter's role as an institutional attempt to improve the EU's legitimacy, it is necessary to examine first the task set for the initiative by its creators. Success or failure of the Charter both for the actors involved, and in the perception of the wider public, depends on the aims which it is measured against. The starting point for any such analysis must be the mandate given to the specially created 'body' by the European Council meeting in Cologne in mid-1999, and specified by the European Council in Tampere in October of the same year, to draft a Charter. These expressions of political will by the heads of state or government of the EU proved to be the main guideline for the Convention throughout its work, despite, or maybe because of the fact that the interpretation of these 'mandates' was contested on several occasions.

The conclusions of the *Köln* summit read:

European Council Decision on the drawing up of a Charter of Fundamental Rights of the European Union

Protection of fundamental rights is a founding principle of the Union and an indispensable prerequisite for her legitimacy. The obligation of the Union to respect fundamental rights has been confirmed and defined by the jurisprudence of the European Court of Justice. There appears to be a need, at the present stage of the Union's development, to establish a Charter of fundamental rights in order to make their overriding importance and relevance more visible to the Union's citizens.

The European Council believes that this Charter should contain the fundamental rights and freedoms as well as basic procedural rights guaranteed by the European Convention for the Protection of Human Rights and Fundamental Freedoms and derived from the constitutional traditions common to the Member States, as general principles of Community law. The Charter should also include the fundamental rights that pertain only to the Union's citizens. In drawing up such a Charter, account should furthermore be taken of economic and social rights as contained in the European Social Charter and the Community Charter of the Fundamental Social Rights of Workers (Article 136 TEC), insofar as they do not merely establish objectives for action by the Union.

In the view of the European Council, a draft of such a Charter of Fundamental Rights of the European Union should be elaborated by a body composed of representatives of the Heads of State and Government and of the President of the Commission as well as of members of the European Parliament and national parliaments. Representatives of the European Court of Justice should participate as observers. Representatives of the Economic and Social Committee, the Committee of the Regions and social groups as well as experts should be invited to give their views. Secretariat services should be provided by the General Secretariat of the Council.

This body should present a draft document in advance of the European Council in December 2000. The European Council will propose to the European Parliament and the Commission that, together with the Council, they should solemnly proclaim on the basis of the draft document a European Charter of Fundamental Rights. It will then have to be considered whether and, if so, how the Charter should be integrated into the treaties. The European Council mandates the General Affairs Council to take the necessary steps prior to the Tampere European Council.[5]

The text of the Cologne mandate is a central piece of evidence in trying to understand how the process developed and why, because it became the main point of reference for all members of the Convention in their debates about what precisely they were supposed and entitled to do. It is interesting to note that, despite disagreement about the interpretation of the wording of the mandate (see below), there were no real challenges from Convention members to the text itself and they apparently accepted it as given.[6]

On the crucial question *why* a Charter of Fundamental rights should be added to the EU's existing Treaty documents, the Cologne mandate postulates a direct link between the protection of fundamental rights and the EU's legitimacy because the former is described as 'a founding principle of the Union and an indispensable prerequisite' for the latter. Based on this statement, the mandate then claims that 'there appears to be a need, at the present stage of the Union's development, to establish a Charter of fundamental rights'. This statement of purpose reiterates the very ambiguity regarding the role of rights as both *limiting* and *constituting* the legitimate polity (see Chapter 2). Also, it is curious that the protection of rights is quoted as a 'founding principle' of the EU, but the necessity to list these rights in a Charter seems to have arisen only 'at the present stage of the Union's development'.

Moreover, the reason given for drafting a Charter is not about *improving the protection* of the rights in question, but the aim is to '*make their overriding importance and relevance* more visible' (my emphasis), and this is based on the assessment by the members of the European Council, that there 'appears' to be a need for this kind of clarification now. Thus it is the *perception* of the citizens which is the main target of the project of drafting the Charter according to the Cologne mandate, not the *substance* of the rights concerned. The rights themselves are therefore used instrumentally to ensure the EU's legitimacy. The 'visibility' formula was subsequently used on many occasions by those who argued that the mandate of the Convention only allowed it to list 'existing rights' (a term that does not appear in the mandate itself), rather than drafting new rights or adjusting the rights found in the sources of fundamental rights which are referred to in the second paragraph of the mandate. The description of the Convention's task by Lord Goldsmith (representative of the British government) as '[t]o make existing rights visible'[7] was the synthesis of this approach, as opposed to 'inventing' or modernising rights.

The purpose of an EU Charter according to this argument of visibility was based on the belief that, even though the protection of fundamental rights is highly developed in the European Union member states under national constitutions and the ECHR, the variety of different legal mechanisms for their protection curtails their effectiveness in the eyes of citizens. In order to know which rights an individual actually has, and how they can be protected, one needs to consult several different legal sources, including those listed in the Cologne mandate, but also the different European Treaties, the ECJ's case law, as well as a substantial body of secondary legislation. In this situation, it is difficult for members of the general public to be aware of their rights and the appropriate legal remedies when dealing with a presumed violation of fundamental rights in the European context. This, the argument ran, is detrimental to legal certainty and thus undermines the legitimacy of the system which claims to protect citizens. In this view, the purpose of a new catalogue of fundamental rights was indeed 'just' to show that the EU institutions are already bound by the fundamental rights as they have emerged from the development of the EU Treaties, as well as from the jurisdictions of the European Court of Human Rights and of the European Court of Justice. The aim in this view was to stress the legitimacy of the EU polity as a structure which protects the rights of its individual members 'at least as much' as their national orders do.

A clear limitation for the Convention's remit was, however, difficult to construe on the basis of the formula in the Cologne mandate. A large part of the contestation especially in the early stages of the debates was therefore focused on what precisely the Cologne mandate instructed the Convention to do. Twenty-three Convention members who were asked about their understanding of the mandate held widely differing views on the task given to them, ranging from 'concretising the European order of values',[8] to the minimalist position of 'making existing rights visible' quoted above. Given the disagreement on these issues, the Convention had to make 'political' choices on whether it wanted to restrict itself to accepting the status quo of the rights in the documents specified in the mandate, or whether it wanted to adapt the rights to the EU and find context specific definitions of the 'four dimensions' of sphere, scope, subjects, and styles. The work of the Convention in the end produced a compromise between the more narrowly defined purpose of visibility as it transpires from the Cologne mandate, and the more ambitious plans for a creative and innovative Charter harboured by a large number of Convention members.

A centrally important issue in this debate was the question of the Charter's legal status once it had been drafted. By stating '[I]t will then [i.e. after the proclamation of the Charter by the three institutions] have to be considered whether and, if so, how the Charter should be integrated into the Treaties', the Cologne mandate left open by whom this question would have to be considered and ultimately decided. There were some debates in the early stages as to whether the Convention could and/or should attach a recommendation on the possible inclusion of its draft in the Treaties, but it soon became clear that disagreement on this question could block any progress on the contents of the document. Many members did, however, express concern throughout the Convention's existence that it was impossible to draft a text without knowing exactly what legal status it would have. The implication of this argument was that, if the Charter was to remain a political declaration only, it would be drafted in more accessible (i.e. less legal-technical) language and could contain much more ambitious promises. A majority of thirteen out of twenty-three Convention members interviewed supported a legally binding Charter, with six others referring to the mandate to state that it was not for them to take this decision or that it was a decision for the future. Only four respondents clearly said that they would prefer the Charter to remain a mere political declaration.[9]

Roman Herzog's pragmatic decision to curtail debate about this thorny issue, and to draft the Charter text 'as if' it was to become legally binding, proved vital for the success of the Convention in reaching agreement within the specified time limit.[10] By removing the imminent necessity to decide on the legal status of the new document, the Cologne mandate gave greater flexibility to the Convention to deliberate freely. As Olivier De Schutter notes, this openness of mandate was important for the success of the Convention because it 'broadened the range of subjects of discussion: if no consensus was reached on the basic issues, it could at least be found on the procedures, thus avoiding the risk of deadlock.'[11] It is to Herzog's credit that he succeeded in steering clear of the controversial question of the Charter's legal status most of the time, thus allowing the Convention to continue debate despite fundamental differences on this point. Many Convention members might indeed have shared the feelings of those who expressed relief that somebody else would have to take this politically sensitive matter in hand.[12] The question of the legal status of the Charter was then included in the Laeken declaration as one core issue to be decided by the next 'round' of EU-level constitutional decision-making and was debated extensively in the second Convention. Here Antonio Vitorino, who had already been a member of the first Convention, chaired a special working group on the question of inclusion of the Charter in the draft Constitution. This working group by an overwhelming majority supported the Charter becoming a legally binding part of the Constitutional project and the

Constitutional Convention followed this recommendation, even though some changes were made to the horizontal articles of the Charter (see Chapter 6 below).[13] Yet, the Charter Convention could develop its debates because the question of the document's legal status was 'trimmed' off the agenda in the early stages.[14]

With regard to the purpose of the Charter as it was intended by the heads of state and government at the Cologne summit, it is also instructive to look at the list of legal sources which they considered as the relevant references for fundamental rights in Europe. By providing a list of documents to guide the Convention in its work, the Council tried to limit the scope of what the Convention could propose. Many Convention members, however, pointed to a much wider range of instruments that have developed in the past decades in the area of international human rights, as the relevant basis for a comprehensive list of fundamental rights.[15] The limited list of Cologne is a recognition of the fact that the notion of 'fundamental right' itself was contested, but that it was, at least in the Cologne mandate's understanding, *not* the task of the Charter to define conclusively what these rights are.[16]

The first element on the list provided by the mandate is the European Convention of Human Rights and Fundamental Freedoms (ECHR). Both its contents, and the unique enforcement mechanism which has developed for it with a permanent Court of Human Rights since 1998, make the ECHR the most advanced international human rights protection system to date and consequently also the most important reference for an EU initiative in this area. Virtually all actors involved in drafting the EU Charter seem to have accepted the ECHR as the natural starting point for the new project, and as marking the minimum standard of what constitutes fundamental rights in Europe. The European Convention also provided the common basis for the discourse of common values in the EU (see Chapter 5 below).

The next item in the inventory of sources of European fundamental rights provided by the drafters of Cologne (the rights 'derived from the constitutional traditions common to the member states, as general principles of Community law'), is particularly interesting as a statement of the assumed degree of 'commonness' which supposedly already existed among EU member states. Following the relevant jurisdiction of the ECJ,[17] this formula reiterated the fact that certain fundamental rights have already been part of the sphere of European integration since the judgements by the ECJ in the late 1960s. These rights, the Cologne text suggests, are common and universally accepted because they are *shared* by the member states and have been recognised by the ECJ as general principles which not only underlie national legislation but also inform EC law.

The item that followed in the list (those 'fundamental rights that pertain only to the Union's citizens') was probably meant to be uncontroversial because it referred to a clearly circumscribed body of legal provisions (i.e. the rights contained in Arts. 17–22 of the TEU after Amsterdam). It did highlight, however, the dilemma of the dual purpose of drafting the Charter. If the idea of the Cologne text was indeed just to make existing fundamental rights visible, it seems strange that among these reference is made to rights which pertain *only* to a special category of people. This element of the Cologne mandate was therefore understood by many Convention members and observers as indicating a second purpose for the Charter, namely to increase the EU's legitimacy by giving more substance to the concept of a Union citizenship as an expression of, or at least condition for, a European identity. In the event, the contradiction between these two different understandings of the purpose of the exercise led to a Charter which does contain some substantial new rights for citizens (most importantly the right to good administration, Art. 41; and the right to access to documents, Art. 42), and also includes an interesting new approach to the question of 'inclusion and exclusion' by opening up several previously exclusive rights to non-citizens. It was, however, not accepted by all that this was a legitimate purpose of the undertaking. Nevertheless, a clear majority of the interview respondents did think that the Charter should and would have a strengthening influence on European citizenship, whether that had been part of its original purpose or not.

The most controversial part of the Cologne mandate as far as the precise task of the Convention and the scope of its competencies was concerned, however, turned out to be the last category on the list of sources, because of its ambiguous wording and the unclear legal status of the documents cited: 'In drawing up such a Charter, account should furthermore be taken of economic and social rights as contained in the European Social Charter and the Community Charter of Fundamental Social Rights of Workers (Art. 136 TEC), insofar as they do not merely establish objectives for action by the Union.' This clause was controversial firstly for the instruction it gave ('account should be taken'), which for some members of the Convention just meant to acknowledge the existence of the legal documents mentioned, whereas for others it clearly meant that the rights contained in the said documents should be included among the rights of the Charter. Secondly it was not clear from the mandate whether the 'European Social Charter' referred to here was supposed to be the original

European Social Charter of 1961, ratified by all EU member states, or whether the Cologne mandate also validated references to the 'Revised European Social Charter' of 1996, which had at the time (1999) only been ratified by three EU member states and which covers a much wider range of issues.[18] The social rights that were eventually included in the Charter are in most cases based on the original Social Charter, but in some cases the revised version is referred to in the explanations by the presidium.[19]

The limitation 'insofar as they do not merely establish objectives for action by the Union' took on particular significance in the exchanges about the purpose of the Convention. The main concern of many Convention members and observers was that introducing political aspirations into the document would amount to an extension of the Union's competencies, especially if the document was subsequently to become legally binding. But while it was generally accepted that the Convention did not have the mandate to extend the EU's competencies (see Art. 51.2 EUCFR), it was by no means clear what was to be understood by provisions which *merely* establish political objectives. A clear distinction between rights and objectives, especially at constitutional level, could not be reached because as a legal concept the notion of objectives has developed separately in different constitutional traditions.[20] The 'solutions' to this problem which were found by the Convention differ now from article to article.

The Charter's preamble for example does recognise a role for common principles which do not confer individual rights, but which inform the actions of the Union (see Chapter 5 below). In some of the articles on social rights, in contrast, a narrow reading was adopted to prevent an expansion of social rights beyond the actual competencies of the Union. The proposal of a 'right to work' which was originally discussed in the sense of 'a right to employment', for example, was later reformulated as a mere 'freedom to choose an occupation and . . . to engage in work' (Art. 15). At the same time, however, the example of Articles 37 and 38 on environmental and consumer protection, which clearly set political objectives for the Union, shows that a debate about the fundamental rights underlying European integration in order to increase its legitimacy could not avoid the question of the Union's objectives. The Charter therefore also stirred a debate about the purpose of the integration project as a whole.

The purpose of integration: the preamble

This became most evident in the debates about the Charter's preamble. In these debates attention was drawn both to the purpose of the Charter and fundamental rights in sustaining the legitimacy of the integration process, and to the purpose of the EU itself. The presidium's first draft for the preamble,[21] which was to be subject to numerous alterations, lists the founding principles of the Union (dignity of the human being, freedom, equality, solidarity, democracy, and the rule of law), and establishes an important role for the Union by stating: 'the Union *contributes to the development* of these common values' (emphasis added). This wording reflects the 'activist' terminology in the Cologne mandate which had referred not to the *respect for*, but to the *protection of* human and fundamental rights. While it is not legally tangible what exactly constitutes a 'contribution' to the development of 'values', it is clear that such a wording seems to assign a certain role to the Union to intervene in order to 'promote' the development of these values and principles. It clearly goes beyond the formula 'recognises and respects' which was later used in those areas of the Charter where, it was argued, the Union had (as yet) no competencies to 'guarantee' the rights in question. This was most controversial in Art. 34 on 'access to social security', and in Art. 36 on 'access to services of general economic interest'.

Paragraph six of the presidium's first draft preamble is significant with regard to the purpose of the Charter because it contains an unusual 'statement of mission' for a document mainly concerned with supposedly pre-existing universal rights: '[the Charter] *adapts* the content and the scope of these rights to the development of society, to social progress and to scientific and technological development' (emphasis added). Such an open recognition of the relativity of the rights in question to time and circumstances seems to be at odds with the 'traditional' rhetoric of timelessness and universality associated with the natural law tradition of fundamental human rights (see Chapter 2), and with the originally rather conservative thrust of the Cologne mandate. The Charter, rather than listing rights enshrined elsewhere, is thus given the purpose of changing these rights to make them fit current EU-circumstances. The phrase was, however, subsequently changed to sound less activist (see below).

The wording of this first draft preamble was changed considerably in the process of three redrafts by the presidium, and in response to a number of alternative proposals from individual members. The presidium's first draft prompted serious criticism from several Convention members and generated a lively debate in the Convention plenary.[22] One important contribution to this debate with regard to the purpose of the integration project at large, came from Piero Melograni, Forza

Italia (opposition) representative of the Italian Chamber of Deputies and professor of history, and Peter Mombaur, German Christian Democrat MEP. Their joint proposal for a preamble put strong emphasis on the historical context of the Charter as a constitutional document, and took issue with the idea of a 'shared destiny' of the peoples of Europe introduced by the presidium. In the debate Mombaur noted that the first sentence in the presidium's draft put the sequence of events (in a temporal and a causal sense) in the wrong order: they [the peoples of Europe] do not have the same destiny *because* they created a Union, but the other way around.[23] In his own proposal with Melograni, the first sentence consequently read 'The European peoples share common challenges. For this reason they have created an ever closer Union between them.' For the general understanding of the purpose of European integration, it does of course make a considerable difference whether the Union is projected as a given fact that has emerged from the will of its peoples in the distant past and thus is the *reason* why these peoples share a common destiny, as transpires from the presidium's draft, or whether the Union is projected as an *instrument* created to respond to common external challenges, as in the Melograni/Mombaur proposal.[24]

In response to the ensuing debate, the presidium presented a second draft preamble as part of the first complete draft Charter at the end of July 2000.[25] The preamble had undergone substantial change at this stage. The first indent still suggested that the establishment of the 'ever closer union' was a 'fait accompli' because it still read 'The peoples of Europe *have* established', (my emphasis), but the 'shared destiny henceforth' had been deleted. Instead the peoples of Europe were described as being '*resolved* to share a peaceful future based on common values' (my emphasis). This is an interesting alteration on the previous version, because the notion of the 'peaceful common future' brought back the primary aim of the Schuman declaration of 1950, while at the same time sounding suitably progressive. Frederik Korthals Altes, representative of the Dutch government had actually suggested a direct reference to Monnet and Schuman, recalling Europe's main goal of creating and maintaining peace.

On the overall rationale of having an EU Charter in addition to the existing systems of fundamental rights protection, the statement that 'the protection of . . . rights and their visibility to all *requires*' their listing in a Charter (Convent 43) was replaced by the somewhat clearer '[I]n adopting this Charter the Union intends to *enhance* the protection of fundamental rights . . . by making those rights more visible'(Convent

45, my emphasis) which goes beyond the original limited Cologne intention. With Convent 47 (the third draft), this phrase became linked more directly to the overall aim stated in the previous paragraph, namely the Union's contribution to the development of common values: 'To this end, it is necessary to strengthen the protection of fundamental rights in the light of changes in society, social progress and scientific and technological developments by making those rights more visible in a Charter.' Once more this formula stresses the instrumental role of fundamental rights as *means* to further the *end* of 'preserving and developing' the values mentioned in the preceding paragraph. In this context one should also note that the very last sentence of the preamble in the final draft reads now: 'The Union therefore recognises the rights, freedoms and principles set out hereafter.' This formula is a deliberate step back from the earlier drafts which spoke of a much more ambitious 'guarantee' of the rights.

Thus the preamble drafts reveal a gradual development of a common understanding of what the real purpose of the Charter was, and how it was to relate to the overall goals and purposes of integration in the course of the Convention process. Partly this was a consequence of the ambiguous definition in the Cologne mandate of the purpose of drafting a Charter. At the same time, this clarification was also due to the fact that the debates about the foundations of European integration in fundamental rights raised wider questions about the aims of integration in general. This had repercussions for the question of the Charter's role in the legitimacy question. The clear link between the protection of rights and the legitimacy of the EU which had been postulated in the Cologne mandate does not figure in the Charter preamble. The reasons for this significant omission was probably the fear by the drafters that tying the Charter in with the legitimacy of the Union too closely would appear as an overt admission that there was indeed a legitimacy problem. At the same time, the emphasis of the successive preamble drafts shifted considerably towards the common value discourse as an expression of one, if not *the*, purpose of integration. Especially the casting of the EU as 'contributing' to the 'development' of common European values (as expressed in the extremely controversial second paragraph of the preamble, see pp. 98–107 in this volume), goes well beyond the more limited readings of the Cologne mandate and seems more reflective of the majority of Convention members who saw the Charter as a tool to actively use the protection of fundamental rights as a means of legitimation.

The Cologne mandate and the ambiguities behind it were therefore important elements of the Charter process itself. While not contesting openly the parameters set by the heads of state and governments, the Convention as a body developed its own understanding (albeit not always a clear-cut one) of what the purpose of the initiative was. On the one hand, this testifies to the malleability of the Cologne text, despite the fact that several Convention members claimed it to be 'clear' and unambiguous.[26] On the other hand, it shows the independent dynamic of the Convention with its multiplicity of actors, and its peculiar style of debate which allowed for a broadening of visions despite different views at the outset. The Charter's preamble as it developed in the Convention was the most prominent statement of the overall aims of integration since the preambles to the founding Treaties were written in the 1950s, and testifies to an expansion on the original resolve to 'preserve and strengthen peace and liberty' by 'laying the foundations of an ever closer union among the peoples of Europe'[27] towards a 'peaceful future based on common values.'[28] The Constitutional Convention two years later opted for a similar emphasis and thus confirmed (and built upon) the compromises found in the Charter Convention, even though it is interesting that the reference to the less-than-peaceful past of Europe ('reunited after bitter experiences') now included in the Constitution's preamble was only added by the Intergovernmental Conference. Nevertheless it remains a peculiar compromise that the Constitutional Treaty as it stands now has one preamble at the beginning (drafted by the second Convention) and a second preamble at the beginning of its part II, the original Charter preamble.

European identity and the EU Charter: who and what is Europe?

Special rights for whom? The Cologne mandate

The notion of a European identity has played an important part in the debate about the legitimacy of political organisation at European level, and in the institutional attempts to clarify what kind of structure is being built. This notion developed in response to the perceived need to define who and what is European, and how European those subjects are at a variety of different levels. As discussed in Chapter 3, one important institutional expression of this complex of questions is the concept of European citizenship. The Charter process played an important role in developing the idea of European citizenship further, and thus in consolidating previous institutional attempts at fostering a European identity. In the context of a rights-based understanding of citizenship, the Charter represents the most explicit expression of what is regarded as

the achievements of the EU polity in defining the 'subjects' of integration. By establishing the European Union as a Union 'reflecting the will
of the citizens and States of Europe' (Art. I-1) and elevating the Charter
rights to constitutional level, the Constitutional Treaty consolidates this
definition of what it means to belong to the EU.

It is therefore interesting to trace how the Charter Convention handled
the question of who are Europeans in terms of who was to benefit from
the rights in the Charter, and which particular balance was found
between inclusion and exclusion. These questions are of special poig-
nancy, given that the decision to draft a Charter was taken on the eve
of the biggest ever enlargement of the EU with a view to consolidating
the basis for a much wider and more diverse Union. Furthermore, the
discussion on the question whom these rights were going to be for also
highlighted the tension inherent in the idea of bolstering an identity
for a distinct political entity by reference to supposedly universal rights
(see Chapter 2).

The Cologne mandate's call for the Charter to include also those
'fundamental rights that pertain only to the Union's citizens' was an
important illustration of the fact that the instigators of the Charter
process wanted a document which strengthens an EU-specific vision of
fundamental rights. There is no other possible explanation for such a
phrase in a list of rights otherwise focused on internationally acknowledged *universal* human rights. At the same time, the wording of this part
of the mandate is interesting because it does not mention 'citizens'
rights' as a separate category stemming from the citizenship provisions
of the Treaties, but suggests a 'special kind' of fundamental rights for
Union citizens only. This seems to reflect the old idea of giving substance to European citizenship by granting 'special rights' to European
citizens in order to show the 'added value' of membership in the European polity (see Chapter 3). While most members of the Convention
seem to have subscribed to the notion of fundamental rights as universal (despite the contestability of this understanding on theoretical
grounds, see Chapter 2), many respondents from the Convention also
accepted the Cologne mandate's proposal of a role for rights reserved
for European citizens in fleshing out European citizenship. Yet, the
debate about the 'categories of rights holders' in the Charter brought
out some interesting differences of view on this issue, and led to some
innovative, albeit sometimes ambiguous, solutions.

Citizens' rights in the Convention

Given the link between the legitimacy of the Union and citizens rights
which the Cologne text had introduced, a number of Convention

members were asked how they thought the Charter would affect EU citizenship and consequently the potential to improve the EU's legitimacy through a concept of citizenship. Against this background, only three out of twenty-three respondents expressed clearly that in their view the Charter would have no impact on citizenship at all – either because they dismissed the concept of citizenship itself as 'artificial' and therefore meaningless,[29] or because they maintained that the Charter would and should be mainly concerned with *universal* rights.[30] Of the other respondents, most thought that the mere inclusion of the citizenship rights already contained in the EU Treaties would increase peoples' awareness of their citizenship status, and thus strengthen it. Many were, however, aware of the problem which this provision would create in terms of discriminating against non-EU citizens. Guy Braibant, French government representative, was most critical of the provision of the Cologne text on citizens' rights, when he said 'I think it was a mistake to make them [citizens' rights] a separate category.'[31]

In the Charter debates this became an important issue when the problem arose in connection with several individual articles, whether the right in question would be granted to 'every person', to 'every person legally resident on the territory of the EU', or to 'every European citizen'. This was particularly problematic with regard to some of the social rights, such as access to social security (Art. 34) or the freedom of establishment (Art. 15.2). In both cases, the Charter now contains interesting variations on the traditional clear-cut distinction between insiders and outsiders in terms of citizens' rights: Article 34 (Social security and social assistance) is now a right dependent on living legally on the Union's territory, but not on citizenship. Article 15 (freedom to choose an occupation and right to engage in work) contains three different categories of rights holders: Art. 15.1 (right to engage in work) is a right of 'everyone', Art. 15.2 (freedom of establishment and freedom of movement in pursuit of employment) is a right of every EU citizen, and Art. 15.3 contains a right for equal working conditions for 'nationals of third countries who are authorised to work in the territories of the Member States'. Similarly, Art. 45 (Freedom of movement) is limited to Union citizens (45.1), but it contains a specific clause which allows for its extension to legally resident third-country nationals (Art. 45.2).

Strengthening rights-based citizenship?

With regard to the building of a European identity by means of strengthening EU citizenship, it is to be noted that in the context of the Charter a classic liberal notion of rights-based citizenship seems to have prevailed in the Convention. This is not surprising given the emphasis on rights as the purpose set by the Cologne mandate, under which the debates (and consequently the interviews), were conducted. Only three of the respondents referred, more or less clearly, to concepts of citizenship which included other elements in addition to rights: Frederik Korthals-Altes, Dutch government representative, mentioning representation as an element of citizenship, and Johannes Voggenhuber (MEP – Verts/ALE), speaking about the problem of demos formation, while Peter Mombaur (MEP – EPP) stated critically: 'Citizenship is maybe shorthand for the feeling of belonging of the Europeans. I doubt whether such texts [as the Charter] have a major contribution to make on this. The belonging of the Europeans will be promoted more likely through facts, such as a common currency for example.'

Thus the role of citizenship in improving the EU's legitimacy seems to have been conceived by many in the Convention in a rather narrow way. Several respondents explicitly emphasised the exclusionary aspect of citizenship as the best way to tie the citizens to the integration project: 'The Charter will strengthen European citizenship if it recognises that some rights . . . are, probably legitimately, applied only to European citizens and not to everybody . . . if European citizenship is to mean anything at all, then there are bound to be some political rights that are going to be reserved for European citizenship.'[32] Georges Berthu, who had earlier in the interview dismissed European citizenship as meaningless, was even more outspoken on this point. He recalled that he had tabled an amendment to the article 'everybody is equal before the law', which proposed to add: 'specific rights and duties can be attached to the status of [national] citizenship' because in his view, 'if foreigners have the same rights as citizens, then there is no Europe, there are no nations, there is nothing anymore'.[33] It was in this context that the notion of the 'added value' of European citizenship was clearly formulated by another respondent: 'there are . . . rights that are restricted to Union citizens in the area of professional liberties, and that is right, because the Union citizens must have an advantage from belonging to the Union after all.'[34]

Inclusive or exclusive rights?

At the same time, there were also several voices which advocated a more inclusive approach and therefore favoured a very restrictive reading of those rights reserved for EU citizens. Stefano Rodotà (Italian government representative), formulated it most comprehensively: 'the Charter will be beneficial if citizens see that it raises the level of rights protection. But the Charter should be applicable to all residents of the Union territory. Thus we would have a much richer concept of citizenship which would make Europe a legal space in which everybody's rights will be protected.'[35] In fact, this broader view of a rights protection based on residence rather than (ultimately nationally defined) citizenship, seems to have gained in importance during the debates in the Convention. Jöran Magnusson (Swedish Parliament representative) observed: 'As I understand it, in the beginning in the Convention it was far more obvious that the aim was to create a European citizenship; . . . [this] has diminished during the discussion, and most of the articles are now about persons legally residing in the EU Member States.' Magnusson's perception of a growing awareness of the need to be less exclusive is supported by the example of successive proposals for the article on the right to good administration. This important new right was originally drafted as 'Every person residing in a Member State of the Union has the right', and in its third paragraph stated: 'every citizen may address' the Union in his/her language'.[36] By July 2000, towards the end of the Convention's work and after several redrafts, however, the territorial condition ('residing in a Member State') had been removed entirely from the first paragraph, and the third paragraph had duly become a right of 'every person' to write to the EU institutions in one of the official languages of the Treaties.[37]

At the same time, often problems which arose from the question of inclusion and exclusion were 'avoided' rather than 'solved', by adopting an impersonalised wording. This is particularly interesting in the example of the reference to political parties at the European level.[38] While originally proposed as a right of 'every citizen' to 'form and to join political parties' (Convent 17 of 20 March 2000), a lively debate followed on the question whether this right could and should be restricted to Union citizens, and if there was a place for political parties in a Charter of fundamental rights at all. Many Convention members were opposed to the second sentence of the proposal: 'Political parties at European level contribute to forming a European awareness and to expressing the political will of the citizens of the Union', which they rejected as an objective rather than a right, and as an attempt to push a federalist agenda into the Charter. The presidium reacted to this debate by deleting this second sentence in its draft in Convent 28 of 5 May 2000, and by rephrasing the first sentence as: 'Every citizen has the right to found a political party at the level of the Union and everyone has the right to join such a party', thus creating a curious inclusion-exclusion fault line *within* the same right. After further debate, and several individual amendment proposals, however, the problem was avoided by deleting the separate article on political parties from the Charter's chapter on citizens' rights, and instead inserting the old formula 'Political Parties at European level contribute to expressing the political will of the citizens of the Union',[39] as paragraph two in the 'everyone right' to freedom of assembly (Art. 12).

These examples show that the Convention members had to be aware of the problems of inclusion and exclusion in the context of European citizenship, and that 'pragmatic' solutions had to be found to conflicts which arose. In some cases, these somewhat ambiguous formulas hold the potential for a gradual opening of individual provisions in the future. In this context, it is noteworthy that a substantial new right like the 'right to good administration', while proposed as part of the 'citizens rights' chapter, had been phrased from its very first draft as 'Every person residing in a Member State has the right',[40] and was subsequently made even more inclusive, as indicated above. Thus the deliberation in the Convention encouraged the development of a more inclusive approach to rights.

Whose rights?

At the same time, however, virtually all interviewees accepted that the Charter would contain at least three different categories of rights (i.e. rights of every person, rights of every legal resident, and rights of every citizen). In the event, the Charter also contains a fourth category, namely rights of 'every citizen and any natural or legal person residing or having its registered office in a Member State' (Article 42 on access to documents, Article 43 on petitioning the European ombudsman, and Article 44 on petitioning the European Parliament).[41] This categorisation of rights beneficiaries represents a marked difference of the Charter from other (international) human rights documents. On these grounds, there were, for example, lengthy debates about the right to asylum in the Convention, which many wanted to phrase as an 'everyone' right. This was rejected by those who were afraid of the political consequences of member state nationals claiming asylum in another member state, and therefore wanted this right restricted to non-EU citizens.[42] The problem was 'solved' in this case (as in the case on the political parties above) by not granting an individual right to asylum, but just referring to the relevant international legal documents in Article 18. This article in particular has been criticised as a step back compared with the most advanced international rights documents, but it is in line with the legal practice of most member states.[43]

At the same time, the significance of the Charter process for the identity-legitimacy complex goes beyond the legal-technical question

of who would be able to claim particular rights. The Convention provided a novel institutional setting to debate the question whom European integration is all about, and who are its authors. Fundamental
rights provided a useful focus and starting point for this debate because
they necessitated a context-specific response to the question how the
EU polity constructs its own membership. On this point, several Convention members expressed uneasiness about the chosen formula 'the
peoples of Europe' in the opening statement of the preamble. Jo Leinen
(MEP) proposed an opening statement making the 'people' of Europe
(German: *Menschen* rather than *Völker*, emphasising the individuals'
rights and their direct link with the European polity, as opposed to a
concept of indirect membership through belonging to pre-established
communities of nations, states, or ethnic 'peoples'), the subjects of the
Charter's first sentence.[44] Gabriel Cisneros (representative of the Spanish
Congress), in contrast, suggested that the preamble should explicitly
mention the role of the nation-state as the constitutive element of the
Union.[45] Andrew Duff (MEP, ELDR) argued that one of the distinguishing features of the Union was the fact that power (and legitimacy)
flowed from *both* the states and the people, and that this should be
acknowledged in the preamble.[46]

Despite these alternative suggestions, all following drafts (Convent 45
mentioned above, Convent 47 of 14 September, and the final draft,
Convent 50 of 28 September) left the reference to the 'peoples of
Europe' unchanged. In the absence of voting in the Convention, it is
unclear whether those who wanted to change this formula constituted
a majority of Convention members. The presidium's decision not to
propose a different wording despite the obvious lack of agreement on
the 'peoples of Europe' does show that the presidium exercised far-
reaching discretion in deciding when further debate was necessary, and
when note would be taken of divergent opinions voiced in the Convention. This handling of the debates provoked criticism from some
members of the Convention who challenged the legitimacy of the
presidium's decisions in some instances (see pp. 116–17 in this volume).
The subsequent Constitutional Convention adopted a completely
depersonalised wording for its preamble, but does establish, as mentioned, the Union as based on the will of the 'citizens and States' (Art.
I-1) of Europe, suggesting that the debate has continued since the
Charter Convention.

In the event, the Charter contained a mixed balance of inclusion and
exclusion. While the underlying understanding of the EU's membership
seemed to have been still a rather traditional one of a Union made
up of nation-states and individuals mainly as rights-holders, some

important rights were opened up, or at least hold the potential for future development in that direction. How open and inclusive a document the Charter will in effect be, depends to a large extent on its legal status and that of the Constitutional Treaty, and on the use which the ECJ is going to make of it, whether the Constitution is formally ratified or not. Yet, the (sometimes ambiguous) 'solutions' found by the Convention certainly had and have a guiding effect on the conduct of the inclusion-exclusion debate at EU level. In the ongoing legitimation process, these 'interim' solutions provide the basis for the next steps of debate, and for discursive development of new solutions to the problems. The exchanges in the Convention gave important indications how these might look. The next section investigates how the development of the discourse of the EU as a community of values affects the discussion on fundamental rights and their contribution to the overall legitimacy of the EU polity.

Deliberating the common value foundation of Europe

Common values as a basis for legitimacy

The notion of the European Community/Union as an embodiment of such values as peace, liberty, democracy and respect for human rights has been a feature of the integration discourse for a long time. Attempts to strengthen and to publicise these elements of integration have often been undertaken at times of economic and/or political crisis, when the material benefits of closer cooperation between Europe's nation-states were perceived to be less tangible for the citizens. In the 1990s, with the prospect of enlargement towards a large number of 'young' demo-cracies of central Europe, and with integration in general moving into more sovereignty-sensitive areas such as foreign and defence policy and home affairs, the invocation of common values has become even more urgent in the European discourse in the attempt to define the legitimate *scope* of EU action.[47] Merlingen, Mudde and Sedelmeier in their analysis of the sanctions against Austria in 2000 (see also Chaper 5 below), note that this discourse has a growing influence on the Union's policy options because 'the increasing salience of EU-level norms related to the promo-tion and defence of fundamental rights and democratic principles endowed EU policy-makers with identities that, in the case at hand, prescribed a particular course of action'.[48]

The link between such a value discourse and the overarching problem of legitimacy is a strong one: if certain values (and related expectations as to the actions and shape of political organisation), are common to all members of the European Union, then the portrayal of the common institutions as embodiments of these values is a central part of their legitimacy. This reasoning does, however, tend to conceal the two separate problems included in the idea of common values as a basis for legitimacy, i.e. the question whether certain values are shared among the 'members' of a given community (which regard the question of the legitimacy of the polity as such), and secondly the question which particular institutions or practices are the best possible way to realise and protect those values that have been identified as common (which touches upon the legitimacy of a particular regime).

The sources of Europe's common values

In the case of the Charter, the two elements did appear in conjunction, of course, and need to be treated as a complex. The starting point is once more the text of the Cologne mandate, which listed as one source of the rights to be included in the Charter the 'constitutional traditions common to the Member States, as general principles of Community law'. As mentioned, this formula draws on the ECJ jurisdiction in the fundamental rights area where the Court had developed the notion of 'fundamental human rights enshrined in the general principles of Community law' in the 1969 case *Stauder*, and quoted as its own source for such rights the 'constitutional traditions common to the Member States' in the 1970 case *Internationale Handelsgesellschaft*.[49] It has to be noted here, that this latter judgement was primarily aimed at preventing violations of *national* constitutional provisions by EC law, which means that the Court would have to strike down any measure that was seen to be in conflict with the constitutional tradition of the member states.[50] Since, as Weatherill and Beaumont argued in 1993, '[o]ne issue that remains uncertain is the number of constitutions . . . that must contain a particular fundamental right before the European Court will regard it as a general principle of law', the Charter has an important role to play in this context.[51] All rights that have been included in the Charter are now likely to be regarded as 'general principles of law' by virtue of their acknowledgement in the EUCFR, and thus as expressions of values common to all member states.

Yet, the debates in the Convention showed clearly that the 'constitutional traditions of the Member States' were seen in many cases as expressions of particular, often nationally defined, values. These national traditions contain different value-based balance-judgements on the relative importance of different rights or categories of rights. At the same time, Tania Bossi notes that 'in the [basic] constitutional structures of the fifteen Member States, a relatively high degree of homogeneity can be found' with regard to a core set of fundamental rights.[52] These common elements have been significantly extended over the past decades by the European Convention on Human Rights and its influence on national jurisdictions, as well as by common membership in the EU, and by the impact of the ECJ's jurisdiction. Bossi also notes, however, that there are still important differences in the emphasis which is placed on, and the protection which is afforded to, certain rights, especially social rights in the different systems.[53] It was thus in the area of these rights that the debates were most controversial in the Convention.

Yet, the wording of the Cologne mandate also evoked Article 6 of the TEU, which prior to the elaboration of the Charter provided the most comprehensive and legally the most relevant statement of the underlying values of the European Union. It lists the 'principles of liberty, democracy, respect for human rights and fundamental freedoms, and the rule of law' as the foundations of the Union and as 'common to the Member States'. The Cologne mandate reiterated these principles, but also brought the ECJ jurisdiction indirectly into play by referring to the 'general principles of Community law'. It was not specified, however, which concrete principles, values, or rights were supposed to be 'deriving' from these common traditions, and whether this was to mean just those rights which are common to *all* member states' constitutional traditions. Again, this ambiguity opened up certain opportunities for the Convention to go beyond the Cologne mandate, but only after significant contestation.

The 'value' of solidarity

The most extended debates took place on those social rights which are not part of all national constitutional traditions. The debates highlighted the general problem whether the value of solidarity for example, as expressed in such social rights, was indeed a common value of all EU member states, and, if so, *how* it was to be included in the Charter. It has to be noted that this was problematic despite the fact that 'solidarity (albeit between the *peoples* of Europe, not as a principle governing individual relations) had already been included among the considerations which precede the Treaty on European Union in 1991.[54] Thus, it became clear that the reference to a widely shared tradition alone was insufficient to justify certain rights. It was rather the debates themselves which created the 'common' basis of understanding for rights which had not been 'shared' before. As Bossi observes, a 'right to work', for example, is recognised in most EU member state constitutions, but not in Austria and Germany, nor in the British constitutional tradition.[55] Despite the large majority of national traditions which do contain the right to work, the debates on this right were highly controversial, and much resistance came even from some countries which already recognise the right to work in their constitutions. The formula reached in the end (a right to 'engage in work and to pursue a freely chosen or accepted occupation', Art. 15) represents a hard-fought compromise which might, in due course, become the basis for a more genuinely 'common' approach to a right to work at European level as an expression of the value of solidarity.

In trying to assess the role of such common values, the analytical difficulty lies in the fact that hardly any member of the Convention would openly object to such positively connoted terms as 'solidarity' on fundamental grounds, but many claimed that their 'operationalisation' through social rights was problematic. Lord Goldsmith, for instance, representative of a British government weary of any extension of social regulation that could be induced by strong social rights in the Charter, had been very critical of the 'abstract principle' of solidarity as an element of a legal document.[56] Nevertheless, the proposal by Jürgen Meyer (German Parliament representative), to anchor the principle of solidarity in the preamble, and as one of the chapter-headings of the Charter, was in the end successful. Interestingly, in the debate about Meyer's proposal on 28 April 2000, several Convention members referred to the notion of a distinctly European social model which should be consolidated by the Charter's social rights. This prompted once more debate about the precise nature of the Cologne mandate, and how far the Convention was allowed to be creative. Guy Braibant (French Government representative) probably spoke for many Convention members, however, when he stressed that an increase in the protection of social rights marked the main added value of the EU Charter vis-à-vis the European Convention of Human Rights of 1950.[57] Thus, a consolidation of Europe's common values seemed to have been a relevant goal of the Convention in the eyes of many of its members. Once more it is significant that the Constitutional Convention in 2002–2003 repeated some of the discussions of the Charter Convention, and eventually found an even more comprehensive list of values which are enunciated as 'common to the Member States', including solidarity (Art. I-2).

Common values in the Charter's preamble

The debates about the Charter's preamble turned out to be a particularly clear focus for the question of Europe as a community of values.[58] A first debate over whether a preamble was to precede the Charter took place

on 12 May 2000 on the basis of a draft for a prologue by Andrea Manzella (Italian Senate representative), Elena Paciotti (MEP) and Stefano
Rodotà (Italian government representative). In this discussion a majority of interventions argued in favour of a preamble in order to explain
the reason 'why a Charter was drafted', even though Peter Altmaier
(deputy representative of the German Bundestag) warned against an
'inflation' of preambles if the Charter were to become part of the EU
Treaties. A first controversy erupted in this debate between those who
were in favour of a strong invocation of the historical traditions of the
notion of fundamental rights in Europe (notably the Christian and
humanistic heritage),[59] and those arguing against such references on the
grounds that they would compromise the universality and timelessness
of the rights in the Charter.[60] This controversy clearly brought out the
different understandings of fundamental rights as 'culture specific' on
the one hand, and as 'universal' on the other.

These different visions of fundamental rights, as well as their influence on the contents of the preamble became the focus of increasingly
heated debates with the successive drafts for a preamble proposed by
the presidium. The presidium's first draft preamble was debated on 19
July. It stated the 'indivisible, universal principles' on which the Union
is founded. Interestingly, this list not only featured the principles of
Article 6 TEU (freedom, democracy, respect for human rights and fundamental freedoms, and the rule of law), but also included 'dignity of
the human being', 'the equality of all persons, both men and women,
and . . . solidarity'. The draft went on to ascribe to the Union a role in
the 'development' of these principles, which clearly went beyond the
aim of the Cologne mandate to merely make the rights 'visible' and
'underline their importance'.

With regard to this list of principles it is interesting that in one case,
namely regarding the principle of democracy, the presidium had proposed earlier to devote a separate article to it. The first draft on the
'rights of the citizens'[61] in its article A, entitled 'Principle of Democracy',
stated that 'all public authority stems from the people', then repeated
the wording of the current Article 6 TEU, and included the provisions
on the elections to the European Parliament currently contained in
Article 190 TEC. Such an article could have clarified and given substance
to the otherwise rather abstract 'principle of democracy' at the EU level.
Yet, the first paragraph of the proposal particularly provoked strong
criticism. It was argued by some government representatives that this
passage created the false impression that the EU's power emanated
directly from the people, which was not the case due to the indirect

legitimacy of the EU as a Union founded by states.[62] Lord Goldsmith even pointed out that not all EU authority could stem from the people because there were several monarchies in the Union.[63] But even the reference to EP elections proved controversial, because the question arose whether a right to 'free and equal' elections to the EP would mean the imposition of a uniform electoral system. The whole article was therefore subsequently dropped, despite the fact that several interventions in the debate supported it.[64] This example demonstrates once more that the principle (of democracy) was accepted by all, but that the concrete wording of its legal consequences was beyond agreement.

Europe's 'religious heritage': an uncommon value

The question of what Europe's value basis precisely meant provided the clearest example of the limits of the Convention process. In an attempt to give substance to the common values invoked in the first paragraph of the preamble, the third draft preamble (Convent 47) stated: 'Taking inspiration from its cultural, humanist and religious heritage, the Union is founded on . . .'. This paragraph also included references to Union citizenship, and to the programmatic aim of an 'area of freedom, security and justice', and claimed that the Union 'places the individual at the heart of its activities'. This latter affirmation is in itself a rather strong statement in terms of value-choice for a collectivity like the EU, but it was mainly the 'cultural, humanist and religious heritage' which ignited the debates.

To understand the exchanges that followed, it is important to note that the presidium had decided to hold the last round of meetings before the final plenary debate (25/26 September) in the 'delegations' (of national government representatives, national Parliament representatives and European Parliamentarians, respectively) rather than in the plenary of the Convention. This is significant because the clash about the role of 'religion' as a founding element of Europe's value order thus occurred within the institutionally pre-defined groups of European Parliamentarians, national Parliamentarians, and government representatives, and was then channelled through, and 'mediated' by, the five-member presidium. In the delegations, traditional ideological and national cleavages played a greater role in influencing the style of the debate, and made persuasion through deliberation more difficult, than in the Convention plenary which was characterised by its public nature and multidimensional cleavage structure.

Consequently, tensions rose very high on the preamble issue, especially in the European Parliament delegation and among some national governments, because the question of the religious heritage became a matter of principle expressed in terms of party ideology or national tradition.[65] The French government representative Braibant on this occasion apparently intimated to the presidium (of which he was by then a member as the representative of the French presidency of the EU), his intent to block any draft Charter which included the word 'religion' in the preamble, because that would be incompatible with the *laicist* (secular) founding principle of French democracy. Thus what had been intended as an asset in strengthening the common value foundation for Europe's legitimacy turned into a highly divisive issue.

In the EP Delegation, with the mediating effects of the multipolar Convention plenary removed, the debate on the reference to Europe's 'religious' heritage became an ideological battle between (mainly German) Christian Democrats and (mainly French and Italian) laicist Social Democrats. There were heated exchanges in the delegation meeting on 12 September 2000. The disagreements were, admittedly, not only about the preamble. There were also rows over the need to limit the right to property in Article 16 (vindicated by the left), and the resistance to a right to strike in Article 26 (strongly expressed by the right), but it was the religious reference which epitomised the differences. The constructive atmosphere of the Convention seemed to have evaporated. The tensions were exacerbated by the fact that the only avenue open for change at this stage was an intervention of the delegation president, Iñigo Méndez de Vigo, in the presidium's drafting committee.

Interestingly, the disagreement in this situation was not about the values and principles in the preamble themselves, but just about their 'rootedness' or otherwise in the religious tradition. The argument was clearly one of inclusion and exclusion. Early on, some members had argued for an explicit reference to the Union's Christian heritage, but had been reminded that such a reference would at least have to acknowledge Europe's 'Judeo-Christian' heritage. It was then made clear by the opponents of any religious reference, that the heritage of Islam had also shaped Europe, and that an infinite number of other religious and non-religious traditions would also have to be mentioned to avoid unfair discrimination.[66] Opponents of the religious reference also cited past religious wars and contemporary sectarian violence as proof of the divisive role of religion in European history. The same arguments were used later in the Constitutional Convention and during the intergovernmental conference of 2003/04, in the same debate – an illustration of the fact that the Charter Convention had only found a very temporary 'solution' to this problem which goes to the heart of the European identity question.

In fact, the Charter Convention 'resolved' the issue by a package deal which involved a trade-off between the left and the right within the EP delegation, where the main battle had been fought. This 'package' included the preservation of the formula 'cultural, humanistic and religious heritage' in the preamble, and no further limitations to Articles 15–17 on the freedom to chose an occupation and to own property. In return for these propositions which were meeting demands from the right, the left obtained the inclusion of a right to strike in what was to become Art. 28, and stronger provisions for consumer and environmental protection (finally Article 37 & 38).

EP delegation president Méndez de Vigo, in extension of the practice of the presidium for the Convention as a whole, had taken the 'decision' not to allow voting in the delegation. He therefore offered the whole package as a 'take-it-or-leave-it' option to the sixteen delegation members. Two titular members said they would not support it. Before the EP delegation decided on its final position, however, the Convention presidium tabled a new compromise (Convent 48) which avoided the issue by replacing the word '*religieuse*' in the French draft with the less controversial '*spirituelle*'. Several members of the European Parliament delegation from both sides of the debate were still unhappy with this part of the preamble. Some challenged the concept of 'common heritage' itself now, on the grounds that the heritage was backward looking and not so common after all (Paciotti, Lallumiere).[67] Others insisted that 'spiritual' was too weak an alternative to the original 'Christian', which had already been weakened to 'religious'. Nevertheless, the new formula had taken the sting out of this particular debate. In a general climate of relief at the resolution of this problem, the contemporary change of 'cultural' heritage to 'moral' heritage went largely unnoticed.

In an interesting aside, three Christian-democratic members of the EP delegation, two German and one Dutch (Friedrich, Mombaur, and van Dam), argued that the appropriate translations of the French '*spirituelle*' in some other languages would have to include a reference to religion in order to be clear. The German members were successful in this, and the German text now speaks of the '*geistig-religiösen und sittlichen*' heritage. Friedrich and Mombaur managed to obtain a written confirmation of this special translation from Roman Herzog (a member of the German Christian Social Union, CSU), who was in hospital at the time. The Dutch version, however, does follow the other languages and just mentions the *'gesteelijke en morele erfgoed'*. It is thus only the German text which differs on this issue from the European mainstream. The problem was thus 'papered over' by an act of linguistic 'segregation'[68] which was carried over into the Constitutional Treaty, of which now also the Polish language version includes a reference to the 'religious heritage'.[69]

Common values consolidated: the final draft

The final draft for the preamble proposed by the presidium also contained some other changes. Significantly for the question of the EU value debate, the wording on the 'indivisible, universal values of human dignity, freedom, equality and solidarity' was changed again: while they had been referred to as 'principles' in the old draft (in line with Art. 6 of the TEU), they had now become 'values' in themselves, whereas the term 'principles' was reserved for 'democracy and the rule of law'. Daniel Tarschys observed on this formula, that the notion of *indivisible* values might sound good, but did not make much sense logically.[70] These changes were most likely an attempt to raise the level of rhetoric in the preamble, and the idea was to draw a distinction between the founding values underlying (and legitimating) the EU's creation, and the 'principles' which inform its operation.

What emerges from this account of the debates about Europe's value foundations, is the realisation that there were, by the time the Charter Convention set to work, a number of substantial values which were recognised by all actors as being important and common to all. There was also agreement that the European Union has a role in 'developing' these values, and that the protection of fundamental rights plays a central part in this. Moreover, the Convention debates moved the understanding of these common elements forward, with the recognition of 'solidarity' and 'human dignity' as substantial elements of the European value set even beyond the principles of Art. 6. The more concrete contents of these common values, however, was much more problematic. The controversy about the 'religious heritage' revealed how 'nationally' defined cultures clashed on the relative importance of different elements of the 'common heritage' and indeed its 'commonness' itself.

Nevertheless the Charter provided the first institutionalised public occasion to exchange views on these questions, and a number of novel elements were integrated into the EU body of high-spirited value language. In contrast to the preambles of the various Treaties constituting EU primary law, in the Charter case the 'peoples of Europe' themselves appear as the authors of the preamble, not the 'high contracting parties' (i.e. heads of state). While it is clear that this form could only be chosen because the Charter was not, at the time, conceived as in international treaty, it is a significant statement by the Convention and testifies to the 'constitutional ambitions' which the first Convention developed. Moreover, the reference in the preamble to a 'peaceful future based on common values' was the most prominent recognition of the value dimension of integration at the time and is echoed now in Art. I-3 of the Constitutional Treaty which lists the promotion of 'peace, its values and the well-being of its peoples' as the foremost aims of the Union. The values listed in the Charter preamble (human dignity, freedom, equality, and solidarity) are then reflected in its chapter headings and thus linked to concrete rights in the Charter's body, and the individual (rather than the 'peoples', the member states, or abstract goods such as 'ever closer union') is placed firmly 'at the heart' of the collective European endeavour. Finally it is stated clearly that it is 'to this end' (i.e. the development of the values mentioned) that the protection of fundamental rights needs to be strengthened. The Charter's preamble is therefore a particularly important step in the development of the EU's value discourse because the debates about it touched upon key questions of EU legitimacy and resulted in an advanced version of the Union's value narrative.

The Charter process: a deliberative experiment in new styles

The origins of the Convention method

The decision by the heads of state and government to set up a new kind of body to draft the Charter is one of the most significant innovations of the entire Charter project. The origins of the idea to set up the body in the particular way that it was, lie in the mid-1990s and seem to have originated in the German debates preceding the Treaty of Amsterdam. Jürgen Meyer, member of the German Bundestag, referred to a new method for the preparation of a fundamental rights document by a body consisting mainly of national and European Parliamentarians, as early as 1995.[71] On the more precise formula for the Convention, an official from the German Ministry of Justice who was closely involved in drafting the Cologne mandate, said that it was 'one of those ideas which emerged spontaneously between me and my colleague [from the Foreign Ministry], where you later on do not know exactly where it came from'.[72] His colleague from the Foreign Ministry argued that the structure of the Convention was born out of the necessity to find a system that would be a 'substantial improvement' vis-à-vis the IGC system, which could be 'realised in the short term, especially without prior treaty amendments'.[73] In fact, the German EU presidency of 1999, politically committed by its new social-democrat/green coalition government to the idea of a catalogue of rights for the EU, brought together a conference of high-level experts and politicians from all member states under the leadership of the then Minister of Justice, Hertha Däubler-Gmelin, in March to discuss the structure of such a body as well as the potential remit of its mandate.[74] The proposal for a new kind of body met with widespread support.

Intensive lobbying from the German and the European Parliaments, who had also been able to convince MPs in other member states (notably in Great Britain and France) to push with their governments for a new method to prepare a catalogue of fundamental rights, and the support of the German government meant that the proposals were passed, both by the group preparing the Cologne summit within the Committee of Permanent Representatives (COREPER), and later by the EU leaders themselves, apparently without changes. In the account of one close associate with the process, there were three reasons for this somewhat surprising agreement among the members of the European Council: first the fact that the Charter project, including the Convention method had been well prepared at the scientific and at the political level.

Second, the fact that the Cologne summit was strongly under the impression of the Kosovo conflict. On 24 March 1999, NATO had started air-strikes against Yugoslavia in response to violations of human rights in Kosovo. In the words of one German official present at the meeting, the Cologne summit therefore was all about 'Kosovo, Kosovo, Kosovo, and then it was all about unity, unity, unity'.[75] Consequently there was a certain willingness among otherwise reluctant members of the European Council to grant the new German government a success on their Charter project, in order to present to the outside a united Europe which could take decisive action on human rights. As Merlingen, Mudde and Sedelmeier note, 'by the end of the 1990s, the idea of protecting democracy and human rights in Europe became a central component of a common identity shared by key national and supranational decision-makers in the EU'.[76] The notion that the EU derives part of its legitimacy from its role as a guarantor of human rights therefore shaped the options available to EU leaders. Following a 'logic of appropriateness', they had to make a statement that showed the EU's firm commitment to fundamental rights.[77] At the same time, the impending election to the European Parliament in 1999 could also have been a factor in their desire to do 'something' to address the Union's problems of legitimacy. A third element was the unquestioned recognition of the professional and political authority of Roman Herzog who had already been selected as the German government figurehead for the project.[78] In any case, the meeting adopted the German Chancellor's proposal for the mandate of the new body apparently without debate and without changes.[79]

The Cologne conclusions thus set up the 'body' containing four categories of representatives (national and European parliaments, national governments and European Commission) as nominally equal partners, as well as observers from the European Court of Justice, the Economic and Social Committee, and the Committee of the Regions. Moreover, it stated that 'social groups as well as experts' should be heard by the body, and that the Council Secretariat should provide organisational support. The precise structure of the Convention and its process was then decided by the Tampere Council meeting based on proposals made by an 'ad hoc working group' within the framework of COREPER II with strong cooperation between the outgoing German and the incoming Finnish presidency.[80] On this basis, the Tampere Council:

- stipulated the number of representatives from each institution: one from every head of state or government, two from every national Parliament, one from the Commission, and sixteen from the European Parliament in a deliberate attempt to show that the EP is not composed of member state representatives.[81]
- decided that the 'body' should elect its own president for the whole duration of its work. The original proposals from the working group had envisaged the presidency of the 'body' to rotate with the Council presidency, but the summit meeting in Tampere chose to give the Convention a higher profile by providing its president with greater continuity.[82]
- added a representative of the European Court of Human Rights to the list of official observers (who intervened frequently in the Convention debates, especially on the relationship between the Charter and the ECHR texts).
- specified that the Ombudsman and the applicant countries would be invited to give their views before the body.
- probably most importantly, emphasised the importance of transparency of the proceedings by stating: 'In principle, hearings held by the Body and documents submitted at such hearings should be public.'

This last provision, in the event, turned out to be one of the most innovative elements of the Charter process because the Convention secretariat followed it up by creating a website on which both documents produced by, and contributions submitted to, the Convention were made public.[83] Moreover, not only the hearings organised by the Convention, but all its formal and informal meetings were held in public.[84] This is of particular significance in comparison with, and in contrast to, the parallel process of the 2000 intergovernmental conference (IGC) which was characterised by the secrecy of traditional international diplomacy. With these new elements, the Charter Convention became the reference point for the subsequent initiatives to improve the EU's legitimacy through a second Convention.

The Convention method at work: debate and decision-making

One important structural feature of the Convention method was that the Tampere mandate gave a particularly influential role to the body's president, not only because he was to be elected by the body for the whole duration of its work, but also because, on the question how the Convention was to reach decisions, Tampere stated:

> When the chairperson, in close concertation with the Vice-Chairpersons, deems that the text of the draft Charter elaborated by the body can eventually be subscribed to by all the parties, it shall be forwarded to the European Council through the normal preparatory procedure.

This provision was important for two reasons: firstly it formed the basis for the interpretation by the Convention's presidium (consisting of the president, the elected heads of the national Parliament and the European Parliament delegations, the Commission representative and a representative of the acting Council presidency), that the draft Charter had to be approved by 'consensus' (see below). Secondly, it made the Convention president or his deputy the ultimate arbiter of this consensus. This situation gave great (and some argued, excessive) discretion to the presidium in guiding the Convention's work.[85] The problem was that it was not clear what exactly 'consensus' meant. Some assumed it to mean 'unanimity' of all Convention members which would have given each individual Convention member a de facto veto. Yet, the Convention presidium interpreted the notion of 'consensus' pragmatically by stressing the need to achieve unanimity between the four constituent delegations of the Convention, rather than between all 62 Convention members.[86] In fact, the final draft of the Charter was approved by acclamation without vote, by all but two titular members.[87] It is interesting that the 'consensus formula' which Roman Herzog had extracted from the vague Cologne mandate, was made explicit by the Laeken mandate but it remained undefined – a fact which many saw as a key factor of the functioning of decision-making in the Convention(s).[88]

It was also the opinion of the Convention's president, contested at times by individual members (see below), but in the end prevailing, that the Tampere formula meant that votes within the Convention should be avoided. In fact, while President Herzog himself did on several occasions invoke the possibility of having indicative votes, only on one occasion a vote was called in Herzog's absence.[89] This attempt to put a presidium proposal to a vote by Mendez de Vigo in order to end an inconclusive debate, nearly led to a breakdown of the session because several members of the Convention insisted that majority decisions were explicitly excluded by the Cologne/Tampere mandate and threatened to walk out.[90] While this interpretation does not seem to be supported by the texts of the mandates, all members of the presidium standing in for Roman Herzog later (Iñigo Méndez de Vigo, Gunnar Jansson, Guy Braibant), followed Herzog's interpretation of 'no voting' after this incident.[91] This decision greatly influenced the style and the content of the debates.

It was partly these particular institutional arrangements which turned the Charter Convention into an arena for an open debate in which different points of view could engage with each other without the immediate pressure of voting and majority decision-making (see also Chapter 5 below). The realisation of the benefits of such a process, however, depended to a large extent on the members of the Convention and their attitude towards making the process work. Despite differing views on what precisely they were there to do, in the course of the Convention process the sense of common purpose grew. The Charter drafting was a test-run for a new kind of style of politics, under particularly strict experimental conditions and close scrutiny.[92]

The Convention members' view on the process

Thus, when asked about their own perception of how adequate the process was to the task set by the Cologne mandate, and whether they thought it a suitable model for future initiatives, virtually all respondents stressed the forward-looking and experimental nature of the Convention-method. The conclusions they drew as to the possible use of the method in the future were, however, quite different. A majority of respondents (fourteen out of twenty-three) did see the Convention as a positive experience which could and should, albeit in some cases with alterations to the procedure, be used in the future. Among the six national government representatives interviewed, three were clearly in favour of using the Convention method again, while others thought a Convention-type assembly was useful as an advisory body, but not as an instrument of decision-making.[93]

Especially with the approaching conclusion of the Intergovernmental Conference towards the end of 2000, and with its problems becoming more and more apparent, it is not surprising that the parallel between the work of the Convention and the IGC was drawn by a growing number of Convention members as time went on. It is noteworthy, though, that the reason why the Convention might be more successful than the IGC was not only seen in particular institutional arrangements, but also in the prevailing atmosphere. As one respondent put it: 'there was a much more cooperative spirit [in the Convention]'.[94] Iñigo Méndez de Vigo put it more bluntly: 'The IGCs are dead, they don't produce results – the Convention has produced results, so that is the way we should go.' Here an argument based on superior procedural efficiency of the Convention method is suggested, partly in response to what is perceived to be a common criticism of EU democratic procedures as slow and inefficient. In any case, the conclusion of the IGC at Nice with a minimal result seems to prove that agreement (admittedly on very different matters) was apparently even more difficult to reach among fifteen members of the European Council, than it was to find quasi unanimity among more than sixty members of the Convention.

In support of the argument that the difference between the Convention process and the IGC process lay as much in the different 'style of debate' as in the actual institutional structures, many respondents put a lot of emphasis on the need for, and the possibility of, dialogue within the Convention between 'national and European elements, and between lawyers and politicians'[95] (Braibant), or between '[a]ll those who will have to ratify the text' (Mombaur).[96] Stefano Rodotà saw the Convention as an 'indicator for a general tendency: that the European and the national institutions have to create formal arenas for dialogue'.[97] Commissioner Vitorino observed: 'it is interesting to see that we are not biased [in the Convention] on the intra-community institutional debate, which sometimes is a very closed debate'.[98] Convention members thus felt and reciprocated the open atmosphere with a strong interest in constructive dialogue in the Convention.

Significantly, even a strongly Charter-critical Georges Berthu, while rejecting the Charter-project as a whole and challenging the Convention's constitutional connotations, admitted: 'The "body" (because the "thing" called itself "Convention", but in reality it is a working group of the Council . . .) is formed in an original way' and recognised that it provided a 'useful forum for discussion'.[99] At the same time, Berthu also stressed that the Convention should not think of itself as a body of decision-making, a limitation echoed by Lord Goldsmith who said: 'I don't think it is a very good body as it has been operating, to create new legislation . . . but it is a very transparent process, which is good, it is a very accountable process, which is good, and it is a very legitimate process, which is good.'[100] The Dutch parliament's representative Pateijn was the most critical on this aspect of the process: 'No, it is not the right body, because if you want to negotiate a legal text you have to have a body, or representatives with full powers to negotiate something. And you have to have rules of procedure on how you agree on something.'[101]

The role of Convention members in the process

At the same time, it was not always clear which exact powers the Convention members *did* have. As mentioned, several Convention members believed that each of them did 'technically' have a veto or at least the possibility to 'block' consensus. The evidence from individual members trying to pull their weight on particular articles does suggest, however, that the situation was not the same for all. The Government representatives used the threat of a veto, though more implicitly than explicitly, on several occasions (for example Lord Goldsmith calling the 'solidarity' chapter 'unacceptable', and Guy Braibant/the French presidency making it clear behind the scenes that a reference to the 'religious heritage' in the preamble would not be accepted by France). Some national government representatives thus brought the weight of their governments, who would ultimately decide about the Charter in the Council, to bear on their own position in the Convention. There is no evidence of members from either the national or the European Parliament having tried to influence the presidium in its drafting in a similar way. Here there was much more emphasis on building alliances and mustering support across political, national, and institutional divisions (see below).

This throws an interesting light on the structural imbalance between different categories of Convention members, who were not, after all, fully equal. The excess of power of the national executives was strongly criticised by Johannes Voggenhuber, both inside the Convention and afterwards. In his view, the national governments had had to accept a majority of Parliamentarians in the Convention for 'reasons of legitimation', but by denying them 'the application of parliamentary methods [i.e. majority voting]', the national executives had made sure that nothing passed which would alter the balance in the EU's power structure in favour of 'true parliamentary control'.[102] Moreover, the question of whether anybody did have a veto and whether it was used, unlike other questions of procedure, was never openly debated in the Convention, and in those instances where it seems to have been used, this was done behind the scenes. This points to important gaps in the Convention's structure which decreased the legitimacy of the process as a whole because they cast doubts on the equality of the participants in the deliberation (see pp. 147–8 in this volume).

There was thus no agreement among the interviewees (and neither, it appears, among Convention members at large), about the 'consensus' method and whether votes should have been taken at any stage during the process. A majority of respondents argued that a document like this Charter could clearly not be adopted by a narrow majority, but several acknowledged that 'absolute consensus' (= unanimity) was unrealistic to expect, and agreed that some kind of compromise had to be found. It is important to recall here that all interviews but two, were taken before the final meeting of the Convention on 2 October 2000. In their perspective from 'within' the process, many Convention members expressed fears that if voting was to be used, it would lead to a deepening of divisions within the Convention and would make compromise more difficult. Only two respondents explicitly criticised the lack of transparency of the presidium's role in deciding when consensus had been reached.[103] With the benefit of hindsight, however, the advantages of the consensus method which Iñigo Méndez de Vigo described as a 'compromise' between the 'intergovernmental logic and the parliamentary logic in the Convention',[104] do seem to have outweighed its disadvantages because it encouraged open, non-partisan debate and fostered the deliberative style of most of the Convention debates.

Cleavages in the Convention

The deliberative element in the Convention in contrast both with intergovernmental, and with parliamentary fora, is borne out by the universal acceptance by the interviewees that cleavages in the body were not clearly defined along either national, or party, or institutional lines. Rather, the divisions observed by the participants appear to have been fluid, and to have changed according to issue over time. Despite the fact that many respondents introduced their observations on the cleavages in the Convention by stressing one or the other of the divisions proposed in the question (national, institutional, ideological), they usually added other layers to their accounts, so that a multiple-cleavage structure emerged. This perception of the Convention members is compounded in most cases by the accounts of their own most important contacts with other members of the Convention: many participants were closely involved in consultations with other representatives of their nationality, as well as with colleagues from their party groups and/or from their Convention delegation.

Moreover, if one looks at the Charter debates as a means of consolidating a set of common values in order to build a European identity as a basis for Europe's legitimacy, another fact with regard to the divisions in the Convention is interesting to note: even though cleavages based on national, ideological, or institutional fault-lines were suggested in the question, several respondents supplemented or supplanted them by other cleavage categories based on their own observations. Lord Bowness, for example, observed: 'there always tends to be a northern European and a southern European point of view',[105] and Guy Braibant expanded on the same theme: 'there is a north–south divide. The north and the south in Europe do not have the same legal, or even political culture.'[106] At the same time, these cultural divisions do not seem to have created permanent argumentative alliances and, since they were not consolidated by voting patterns, remained visible and open to change.

Consequently, individual perceptions of which cleavages were to what extent important, vary considerably between respondents. This is further confirmation that divisions changed over time and were clearly less rigid than in a classical parliamentary or intergovernmental setting. Sylvia Kaufmann (MEP), for example, placed the main dividing line 'if anywhere between parties, that is to say, according to fundamental political convictions, value ideas, and of course a clear division line between Parliamentarians and government representatives'.[107] Heinrich Neisser (Austrian government representative), in contrast, said 'I have noticed least of all divisions along party lines. There are [also] some coalitions based on regional proximity.'[108] Other respondents just affirmed that all three divisions were relevant in parallel.[109]

An interesting exception to this varied picture is, however, the European Parliament delegation. Six out of seven interviewees from the EP delegation clearly indicated that the delegation as a whole was their main point of reference on a personal level.[110] Moreover, the special role played by the European Parliament delegation because of its relative coherence and ability to formulate common proposals, is one of the few points on which several respondents converged in the context of the cleavage question. This view was expressed both by members of the EP delegation itself, regardless of whether they shared what they saw as the EP's common position (Berthu, Duff, Mombaur), and by members of other groups (Griffiths, Magnusson, Neisser).

The will to reach consensus

There was, at the same time, a strong emphasis among respondents on the importance to overcome cleavages of any kind in the attempt to reach consensus. Several of them stressed the non-adversarial style of the Convention debate as a means to facilitate agreement. Commissioner Vitorino said: 'We are supposed to work to get a consensus. So the whole exercise requires smoothing the lines of division, not emphasising them.' Frederik Korthals Altes, in reply to whether he saw coalitions emerge within the Convention, said 'I don't think it is useful in finding a solution to make "coalitions". You have to discuss with all the people to find a common solution, and coalitions are obstacles to common solutions.' Michiel Pateijn, on other aspects a strong critic of the Convention, summed up this aspect of the process in a statement which clearly shows elements of a deliberative understanding of the debates: 'No, there are no [coalitions] – if there is a general consensus growing, it is because by having debated certain issues two or three times, the matters become clearer for the participants.'

Evaluating the performance of the Convention method

There was, as has been shown, a widespread understanding that the Convention provided a useful forum for an open and relatively free debate on issues of central importance to the constitutional future of the European Union. Nevertheless, even for those who wanted the Convention method to be used in the future, there were some serious flaws in the way it had operated during the Charter debates. Jürgen Meyer, for example, stressed the need to endow any future Convention with a clearer mandate and rules of procedure, because the role of the presidium and the absence of a clear mechanism to decide the 'results' of the debates had been singled out for criticism.[111] In fact, Johannes Voggenhuber came closest to questioning the legitimacy of the entire Charter process when he claimed: '[I]n those areas where the Charter has failed, and these are not just a few areas, . . . this was the consequence of a massive, direct challenge to the independence of the Convention by the governments . . . To put it bluntly, the Convention has turned out in some points as a means for the governments to write the Charter for themselves.' Nevertheless, while Voggenhuber did declare the result of the internal procedures of the EP delegation as 'unacceptable' on one occasion,[112] he did not reject the draft Charter on 2 October, and thus did not challenge the legitimacy of the result of the drafting process in the end.

The process which developed on the basis of the Cologne and Tampere mandates thus seems to have been overall a successful one. A constructive atmosphere prevailed in the Convention which was conducive to reaching agreement, or at least understanding, among a very heterogeneous group of actors on a set of controversial issues. Two Convention members explicitly articulated a change of perception that they had undergone in the course of debating the Charter. Caspar Einem stated: 'At the beginning of my membership in the Convention, I rather had doubts whether it was the right kind of body, but after several months of cooperation I am very convinced now that the combination [of different kinds of delegates] is a very fortuitous one.'[113] Frederik Korthals Altes simply remarked: 'when we started I did not think we would get this far'.

The investigation of the process also shows that some gaps in the Convention's mandate (especially the lack of a voting procedure), played an important part in shaping the debates and their outcome. While the obligation to reach a consensus was certainly fruitful as an overall principle, a provision to allow indicative votes would probably have improved the legitimacy of the results produced by the Convention. The shortcomings of the process were most visible in the heated exchanges, and ultimate weak compromise, about the reference to Europe's religious heritage in the preamble. It is important to bear in mind, however, that these debates were conducted in the constituent delegations of the Conventions where, especially in the European Parliament delegation, the isolation from the broader concerns of the Convention plenary exacerbated the party-political divisions. The example of the religious heritage is therefore another argument in favour of the more open, more deliberative style of the Convention as a whole.

Moreover, the lack of transparency in the workings of the presidium was also noted as problematic and could easily have led to a more widespread perception that it arbitrarily favoured certain positions in its decisions and was hostage to certain pressures from outside. Such a view, if it had been shared by a majority of Convention members or outside observers, could have undermined the legitimacy of the entire project. A crucial factor mitigating against this perception, and enhancing the legitimacy of the presidium's conduct, was the personal standing of Roman Herzog. As the former president of the Federal Republic of Germany, and of the German constitutional court, Herzog enjoyed high respect both as a politician and as a legal expert. His contribution to the success of the Charter project was afterwards widely acknowledged within the Convention and beyond. At the same time, however, the successful use of the veto by some national governments did constitute a violation of the 'equality of standing' of the Convention members and showed the limits of the independence of the Convention and its presidium. Moreover, it also raised the wider question of how, and on which legitimacy basis, representatives should be selected for an exercise of this kind (see Chapter 5 below).

Nevertheless, the Charter process, and in particular the Convention method, have yielded significant results on two separate accounts: on the one hand, the Convention delivered a draft Charter in the remarkably short time of ten months. On the other hand, the Convention showed the potential for, and the limitations of, the open process aimed at achieving consensus through deliberation. Significantly, several of the shortcomings of the process, in particular the problems related to the equal standing of Convention members, the unclear role of the president and the presidium with regard to the concept of 'consensus', and the question of political pressure on the body from outside, have all been repeated in the evaluation of the second Convention experience.[114] Yet, also the achievements (a comparatively high degree of 'efficiency' in reaching agreement on divisive issues, a markedly more transparent and consequently more legitimate process as compared to the IGC process) have been noted for Convention II. It thus seems that the Convention method has survived its 'trial' period and will continue to be a reference point in the EU decision-making system.

Conclusion: the Convention – what kind of legitimacy through deliberation?

Purpose, identity, value discourse and process

The Charter project's role for the legitimacy of the EU has to be measured by its contribution to the debate about the scope, sphere, subjects, and styles of politics. Only if it can be argued that the debates in the Charter Convention provided meaningful additions to the ongoing balancing and rebalancing of these dimensions can the project be considered to be legitimate itself, and as a contribution to the overall legitimacy of the European Union. In this chapter, four core variables were used to analyse the drafting of the Charter in the Convention, and to clarify its impact on the four dimensions: what was the *purpose* of the undertaking, what impact did it have on the notion of a *European identity*, what was the role of the European *value discourse*, and what were the effects of the peculiar *process* that was chosen? The analysis has shown that in the context of the ongoing European integration process, the Charter exercise provided the first prominent institutional attempt at an open debate on the four questions, and it marked evolutionary progress on all of them which then formed the basis in many respects for the debates in the second Convention.

The purpose of drafting a Charter, though supposedly stated clearly by the Cologne mandate, was subject to substantial debate, not least because of the alternative existing systems of protection for fundamental rights under the European Convention of Human Rights. The answer which emerged from the Convention's deliberations stated that an EU-specific document of Fundamental Rights only made sense if it went beyond the rights already recognised in the ECHR. The Charter consequently includes a wide range of economic and social rights, as well as the traditional fundamental, political, and civic rights. Moreover, in trying to define the purpose of the Charter, the debate spilled over into the question of the purpose of integration itself. Following the track indicated by the Cologne mandate, the protection of fundamental rights in this context was mainly cast as a tool to legitimate the existence of the European Union. This in turn re-enforced the trend to project the EU more clearly as a community of values, the protection and promotion of which is becoming an increasingly important *raison d'être* of the Union. At the same time, many members of the Convention also saw the Charter as an instrument to bind the Union's institutions, and to limit the expansion of its policies. These parallel perceptions once more reflect the dual purpose of rights in the legitimation of a political system, and the Charter's concern with the legitimacy of the EU polity as well as with its regime.

Given the limited legal scope of the Charter (even now that it has been included in the Constitutional Treaty, its rights are aimed only at the 'institutions and bodies of the Union . . . and [at] the Member States only when they are implementing Union law' (Art. 51 EUCFR)), the effect of the Charter must also be seen in its contribution to the political process. As discussed, the Charter, according to its preamble, now provides one of the mechanisms to ensure that political organisation at European level can 'contribute to the development' of the values which characterise the Union. These values in turn were debated and expanded in the Convention to include a clear statement of human dignity, solidarity, and equality as fundamental values of the Union along with the principles of freedom, democracy, the rule of law and respect for human rights. The role of the EU as a means to 'promote' these values has been raised to further prominence by the Constitutional Convention.

This commitment to values in turn is supposed to strengthen the notion of a European identity. If the EU is increasingly defined as an entity which is committed to the values cited above, it needed to give itself the means to protect and develop them. Moreover, the Charter debates brought to the fore the problem of how to distinguish between insiders and outsiders in the context of fundamental, and supposedly universal, rights. The Charter debates resulted in a number of new, temporary balances between inclusion and exclusion. These debates also triggered a clear commitment to the place of the individual 'at the heart of integration', and made the *peoples of Europe* the actors of the process. Thus, while it is clear that the Charter debates did not 'resolve' the problem of identity, they did provide a useful opportunity to reconsider traditional concepts of inclusion and exclusion, and the Charter holds some important potential for broadening the concept of a European citizenship.

Finally, the process by which the Charter was drafted was, as has been shown, a substantial innovation in the framework of EU policy-making. By encouraging a mostly constructive, deliberative debate on highly complex matters, while allowing for a high degree of transparency, it showed one possibility for broadening the political process at EU level. It is clearly not the solution in itself to all procedural problems of the Union's democratic legitimacy, and some of its weaknesses have been repeated by the Constitutional Convention. When decisions had to be made, traditional forms of political decision-making (like bargaining, coercion or compromise) were also used at times, but deliberation played a large part in bringing about the agreement on the draft Charter. The process was thus successful, and by EU standards has managed to combine a high degree of democratic legitimacy with effectiveness and efficiency.

Sphere, scope, subjects and style of European integration

Linking these results to Bellamy's four dimensions of the political process, the Charter project marked significant progress. It provided a new understanding of the *sphere* of European politics by making explicit that the European Union sees a role for itself in protecting fundamental rights in order to aid the development of the values it has defined for itself. Even though it is clear that this concern with fundamental rights is by no means new (see Chapter 3), and even though Joseph Weiler remarks that the Charter falls far short of, or might even be a threat to, a more comprehensive human rights policy by the EU,[115] the Charter does mean a consolidation at a high level, of the EU's commitment to the rights and values in question. This will have effects on the future routinisation of policy in this area, and the gradual construction of a Community *acquis* on fundamental rights.

With regard to the *scope*, in several articles the Charter proclaims to set limits to what the EU will legitimately be allowed to do in the agreed spheres of politics. It lies in the nature of an evolving polity that its scope is constantly renegotiated. Many of the debates in the Convention focused on this question. The 'recognition' by the EU of certain social rights for instance was promoted as protection against pressure from the Union to harmonise these rights for integration-related reasons, which could threaten social standards in some member states. This fear was expressed, for example, by some Scandinavian countries with regard to the provisions on social security. The development of the principle of subsidiarity (see also Chapter 3), which is referred to in Art. 51 and in the preamble, is of crucial importance in defining the scope of possible EU action. One noteworthy contribution of the Charter to the balancing act of defining the legitimate scope of action at different levels of governance, is the empowerment of individual citizens in Articles 41 (on good administration) and 42 (access to EU documents), to police themselves that EU activities do not exceed the agreed scope of policy. With the solutions found in the Constitutional Treaty (notably the strengthening of the control of subsidiarity and the new categories of competencies), the agreements in the Charter have not, however, been superseded: in particular the inclusion of the Charter's rights for individuals will be crucial if the constitutional arrangements are to work effectively to ensure a legitimate *scope* of EU action.

As far as the *subjects* of integration are concerned, it has been highlighted that the Charter contains some innovative solutions to the question of inclusion and exclusion in the European polity. The members of the Convention were acutely aware of this problem, and the link they perceived between the notion of a European citizenship, the Charter, and the legitimacy of the EU underlines that the citizenship debate is the most comprehensive framework so far to address the complex of legitimacy problems. The particular, and in some cases peculiar, balances struck in the Charter rights must be regarded as temporary ones, and in several articles the solutions are unsatisfactory: the unclear fate of third-country nationals with regard to freedom of movement in Art. 45, and the problems of the right to asylum (Art. 18), have been mentioned earlier. At the same time, a surprising number of articles are formulated as 'everybody has the right', including the right to good administration and most of the other citizens' rights. This augurs well for the development of a more inclusive notion of the subjects of the European political process.

Finally, the Charter debates have innovated the *style* of integration politics. The Convention for the first time institutionalised an inclusive deliberation at an EU constitutional level. Even though the Convention process raised numerous questions about the representativeness of its members, the transparency of their appointment, the role and account-ability of the presidium, and the quality and quantity of civil society and applicant country involvement (see Chapter 5), it did show the advantages of including a deliberative element in EU 'history-making' decisions. The direct comparison with the not very successful IGC leading to the Nice Treaty works clearly in favour of the Convention method. It quickly became a point of reference for the following steps in the constitutional development of the European polity.

5
The Impact of the Charter

Introduction: is the glass half full or half empty?

Initial reactions to the completion of the Charter Convention's works in October 2000 were mixed with one observer describing the likely effect of the Charter as that of 'water on marble' (i.e. none),[1] while others hailed it as giving a 'heart to the technocratic EU',[2] or even as a 'milestone for European integration'.[3] These assessments came in response to the symbolically-charged adoption ceremony of the Charter draft by the Convention, during which all but two Convention members rose to their feet and listened to Beethoven's *Ode to Joy* as they applauded the successful completion of their task.[4] However, what role does the Charter and its process play in the wider debate about the legitimation of the European Union?

This chapter argues that there are three distinct levels at which the Charter's impact on the EU's legitimation needs to be examined. These are the Charter's potential legal effect; the contribution which debates in the Convention have made to the development of certain concepts in the EU debate, notably the idea of the European Union as a community of values; and the role of the Charter process as a model for EU institutional change. At all three levels the Charter experience marked significant change which, it is argued, has had an important effect on the EU's own attempts to legitimate itself. At the same time, the accords reached in all three domains during the Convention negotiations must be understood as temporary, because even though the rights in the Charter have now been included in the Draft Constitution and are unlikely to be renegotiated in the near future, the Charter's effect depends essentially on different interpretations given to the Charter experience in different contexts (political and legal). The debates about the Charter in the second Convention, and changes it introduced to the rights, already testify to differing and evolving interpretations of the results produced by the Charter Convention. Nevertheless the temporary solutions reached in the Charter Convention are significant because they moved the EU-level debate into a new arena and thus improved the chances of a more legitimate EU. This chapter addresses each level in turn to show how, by their interaction, the Charter can be understood to have been a genuine trial-run for the wider constitutional process for the European polity.

To capture the different dimensions of the Charter's impact, the first part of the chapter looks at the Charter's *legal role* both as a point of reference in the EU legal process, and as an element of (legal) constitutionalisation. Especially with regard to the legal effects of the Charter before the ECJ it is still early to judge what the situation is going to be after the Charter has become part of the Constitutional Treaty, which does, however, still have to be ratified at the time of writing. Thus, even though a full legal appraisal of the Charter's (potential) effect is not possible here, the present analysis shows how the wording of the Charter, even as a political declaration, has already become a point of reference for actors in the EU-level legal process.[5] Such references do suggest that the Charter represents now an important benchmark for the EU's fundamental rights debate and as such has had a crucial impact on the second Convention and its debates. In the broader framework of EU constitutionalism, the effect of the Charter was therefore a considerable broadening of the constitutional exchange itself, and a consolidation of the foundations on which this debate rested until it was taken up by the Constitutional Convention.

The next part of the chapter then looks at the effects of the Charter debates on the *discourses* about the EU's common values and identity. As discussed in Chapter 2, the identity dimension is an important part of all concepts of legitimacy, and has been addressed in a variety of ways by European actors in trying to endow the EC/EU with the bases for an independent legitimacy (Chapter 3). The debates in the Charter Convention raised the discursive interaction about rights and values as elements of a European identity to a new level. This has important repercussions for the public's expectations from the Union, and its capacity to meet them. Therefore the Charter statements on identity and values set the standards against which the legitimacy of the EU and/or its policies was measured in the Constitutional Convention. The Charter Convention was the first institutionalised debate at EU level which consolidated the relevant discourses bringing together the deliberations of a key élite and a broader public.

The following section explores how far the Charter Convention quali-fied as a 'deliberative setting' according to the criteria set out by the proponents of deliberative democracy as a way to enhance the legiti-macy of a political system. The analysis also looks at the role played by the individual Convention members in moving the debates towards a deliberative process. Finally it addresses the capacity of the Charter process to carry the political debate into a wider public arena by engag-ing actors beyond the Convention. These issues in turn had important implications for how the next steps of constitutional change were thought about in the European Union: the Charter Convention acted as a model for the second Convention, and even though some impor-tant changes were made to the design between the two instances, the basic evaluation remains the same: While far from an ideal-type delib-erative setting, the Charter Convention institutionalised important ele-ments of deliberation at the EU constitutional level which contributed positively to the EU's legitimacy. The Charter project thus constituted a significant step in the EU's ongoing constitutionalisation because it produced 'new' expressions of the dimensions of the political process at the European level and as such contributed to improving both the polity and the regime legitimacy of the Union.

The legitimacy challenge

As has been discussed in Chapter 2, the role of fundamental rights in the complex of legitimacy of a political system is ambiguous at times. Fundamental rights have to fulfil a dual function: they are limiting the power of the political organisation, and at the same time they are a core element of that organisation. The EU is in a particularly difficult posi-tion. As a new structure, the essential parameters of political activity (i.e. Richard Bellamy's dimensions of scope, subjects, sphere, and styles) are less defined, and more contested than in the traditional state context. Moreover, external factors (usually collectively labelled as 'globalisa-tion'), and the particular dynamics of the integration project put diver-gent, sometimes opposing, pressures on the four dimensions.[6] While economic internationalisation pushes the countries of the EU towards ever closer cooperation and towards enlargement of the Union itself, political pressures within (some) member states against further integra-tion indicate that the presumed self-evidence of the benefits of Europe-anisation has been exhausted as a basis for legitimation at this moment in time.[7] The actors in the integration process, that is the European institutions and member states individually and collectively, have reacted to these pressures by deploying traditional as well as innovative political means in trying to improve the legitimacy of the new order (see Chapter 3).

An assessment of the Charter's contribution to the EU's legitimacy in this context is made difficult by the lack of distinction in the EU debate, between those elements of legitimacy which are supposed to support the polity as a whole and those elements which are concerned with the legitimate organisation of how to run the polity. The conflation of these two dimensions reflects the dual function commonly assigned to rights as *constituting*, and simultaneously *limiting*, the polity.[8] The ensuing ambiguous understanding of the link between rights and legitimacy is clearly visible in the mandate that commissioned the Charter, and this ambiguity itself became an important part of the debate in the Charter Convention. The Cologne mandate seems to suggest that providing a list of Fundamental Rights which already exist could legitimate the existence of the EU polity *and* its functioning. Yet, the discussion in Chapter 2 has shown that although the safeguarding of certain fundamental rights is a necessary condition for the legitimacy of the polity, it is not a sufficient condition. Rather, it is the debate over *which* fundamental rights constitute the four dimensions of political organisation, about how they are to be protected, by whom and for whom, that creates the kind of process which contributes to the legitimation of both polity and regime.

Richard Bellamy and Dario Castiglione add a further perspective to the duality of polity and regime legitimacy. For them, legitimacy also 'possesses an internal and an external dimension, the one linked to the values of political actors, not least the European peoples, the other to the principles we employ to evaluate a political system', and both are bound up inseparably with the polity- and the regime-dimension because '[t]he internal and external legitimacy of a polity is shaped by, and shapes the internal legitimacy of the regime that governs it.'[9] The two authors therefore conclude that the EU suffers from a 'four-fold legitimacy deficit'.[10] These four levels of legitimacy must therefore inform the assessment of the Charter's overall impact. In the Charter process, the intricate relationship between these different levels became clearly visible, and despite the necessity to distinguish analytically between them, it is the complex of their interaction which will determine the Charter's failure or success, and the EU's legitimacy at large.

The Charter includes both elements which aim at improving the internal regime legitimacy by ensuring democratic participation (for example the basic right to freedom of expression (Art. 11), the rights to vote and stand in European elections (Art. 39), and the potentially far reaching new right to 'good administration' (Art. 41)); and attempts to define the (external) legitimacy of the regime towards the outsiders, as in the opening up of many of the citizenship articles to non-EU citizens (see pp. 91–8 in this volume). At the same time, the Charter addresses the challenge to the EU as a polity, both internally (for example in the references to the concept of subsidiarity in both the preamble and in Art. 51), and externally (in the statements about the presumed function of the Union as a means to 'contribute' to the development of certain common values). Furthermore, the act itself of ascribing its rights to certain groups of people, and anchoring them at EU level, makes the Charter a statement about the external legitimacy of the EU polity which goes beyond the pre-Charter state of affairs.

On another level of analysis, but closely connected, it has been argued that the *debates* about the rights in the Charter also had a two-fold impact: on the one hand, the Convention method has been heralded as a new tool of institutional development of the European Union, which supposedly improves the regime legitimacy of Treaty changes. At the same time, the debates themselves helped to shape the preferences, understandings and identities of the individuals involved, and to con-solidate and develop the discourse of the EU as a guarantor of funda-mental rights, which as such is increasingly part of the EU's claim to a polity legitimacy distinct from, and above, its member states. This view of the EU has been repeatedly confirmed during the debates in the Constitutional Convention where the inclusion of the Charter was cited by an overwhelming majority of Convention members as a cornerstone of the constitutionalisation of the EU.

This chapter therefore tries to do justice to these different aspects of the Charter's impact on the EU's legitimacy. In the assessment of the Charter as a legal instrument the focus is on its relevance as an *additional* source of EU specific rights. The Charter here contributes to the internal aspect of the EU's legitimacy as a polity which provides a high degree of individual rights protection. Yet, this aspect cannot be separated from the discursive construction in the Convention and the Charter text, of the EU as an independent guardian of fundamental rights, both within the member states and beyond. While the debate about the values underlying European integration seems to be primarily about the inter-nal justification for the polity as a whole, it is clear that the boundary between internal and external is blurred here – (certainly with regard to the use of the 'value argument' vis-à-vis former or current applicant countries, but also because of other forms of EU 'value export').[11] More-over, the case of the sanctions against the inclusion of the far-right FPÖ in the Austrian government in the year 2000 (which coincided with the drafting of the Charter), showed how the casting of the EU in the role of protecting member states' citizens against their own governments (and themselves), directly touched upon the legitimacy of the EU regime, both internally and externally. Finally, the evaluation of the deliberation that took place in the Convention is concerned mainly with the internal legitimacy of the EU regime, and in particular with the way in which the ground rules (i.e. the EU's constitutional arrangements) could be changed in a more legitimate way. The challenge in understanding the significance of the Charter project is therefore to take account of these different, and at times divergent, analytical perspectives while keeping a clear focus on their cumulative effect at the empirical level.

The Charter's impact from the legal perspective

The Charter's legal context

As discussed, the Cologne mandate consciously left the eventual legal status of the Charter to be decided by the Council, at a later point in time. Nevertheless, for some, particularly the German government, a legally binding document was the clear priority from the very beginning.[12] In that view, only a legally enforceable catalogue of fundamental rights providing 'at least as much' protection of fundamental rights as the German Basic Law, would finally close the legal lacuna spotted, and temporarily papered over, by the German Constitutional Court in its *'Solange'* decisions of 1974 and 1986.[13] There had been several initiatives by the EC institutions, notably the European Parliament, to move in the direction of a catalogue of fundamental rights for the Community, but these had not found the necessary support among the member states.[14] It was against this historical background that the commitment to a Charter of Fundamental Rights, based on earlier proposals by the German Bundestag in 1995–96, could become part of the coalition treaty between the Social Democratic Party (SPD) and the Green Party (Bündnis 90-die Grünen) after the German federal elections in October 1998,[15] and later on one of the priorities of the German EU presidency for the first half of 1999.[16] In the Charter Convention, however, it turned out to be impossible to reach consensus on a legally binding Charter.

In this situation, the Cologne mandate's 'non-provision' on the legal status of the document proved to be a useful 'gap' in the Convention's mandate which, combined with Roman Herzog's determination to draft the text 'as if' it was going to become legally binding, did allow for agreement to be reached on a draft. At the same time, however, concerns were voiced both by supporters and adversaries of a binding Charter, that the unclear nature of the mandate would exacerbate legal uncertainty. The observers from the Council of Europe and the European Court of Human Rights in the Convention frequently warned in the early stages of the debates that there would be an overlap (and potential clash), between the two different sets of Fundamental Rights in Europe because the Charter (if binding), would affect EU member states directly when they are implementing EU laws and thus could impinge on the system of human rights protection under the European Convention.[17] The Charter, therefore, had to be drafted in legal language fully conscious of the potential interaction between the ECHR and the new document. In the end, the Council of Europe observers appeared satisfied with the safeguards included in Articles 51–53 of the EUCFR, with regard to the interaction of the two systems of rights protection under the ECHR's and the ECJ's jurisdiction respectively.[18] Whether a clash between the two courts can be ruled out on the basis of these provisions is, however, a matter for continued legal argument, even after the Charter has been included in the EU Constitution alongside with a commitment for the EU to accede as a signatory to the European Convention on Human Rights.[19]

For both the question of the legal status of the Charter, and its interaction with the European Convention of Human Rights, the 2003 debates in the Constitutional Convention and the eventual agreement in the Intergovernmental Conference mark important further developments, the end-result of which is not yet clear. The inclusion of the Charter as part II of the Constitutional Treaty with some significant changes to the horizontal articles (see below), as well as the explicit commitment to the EU's accession to the ECHR mean that the problems of 'overlap' and potential conflict between the Charter and EU Treaty-provisions on the one hand,[20] and the Charter and the ECHR on the other hand,[21] have now been internalised within the EU's constitutional system. If and when the Constitutional Treaty enters into force, and the EU does become party to the ECHR, legal practice and the relevant jurisdictions will have to find the solutions to the problems which might arise.

A separate issue of great importance for the eventual legal impact of the EU Charter is the legal-technical question of direct individual access to the European Court of Justice in cases concerning fundamental rights.[22] Such a legal mechanism could significantly alter the role of the

ECJ in the balance of European Institutions, which in turn would have a profound effect on the legitimacy of the Union as a whole.[23] The changes made to the article regulating access to the ECJ in the Constitutional Treaty (Art. III-365) may point in that direction. Yet, the implications of creating a European-level 'fundamental rights complaint' mechanism for individuals are quite independent of the Charter itself. Already before the Charter was conceived, individuals could (albeit under strict conditions) challenge member state and Community acts before the Court with reference to the ECJ's own case law on fundamental rights, and the ECHR.[24] Thus, beyond the technical question of formalising such a procedure, what is important here is the greater clarity (and visibility) of the rights for their owners, which was supposed to have been provided by the Charter according to its drafting mandate. Time will tell whether the greater visibility of fundamental rights enshrined in the Charter and now included in the Constitutional Treaty will lead to an increased awareness of these rights among ordinary citizens, and to what extent this will mean an increase in challenges to legal acts by the Union or the member states which are seen to violate such rights.

The Charter before the ECJ

Even before the Charter was included in the project for a European Constitution it had already become an important point of reference for actors in the European Union legal process. By the time of the Laeken declaration which set out the question of the status of the Charter as to be discussed in the second Convention (i.e. by December 2001), five cases before the ECJ had already solicited citations of the Charter. These early references gave important indications as to the potential role of the Charter rights in future attempts to define the scope, sphere, subjects (and, to a more limited extent, the styles) of EU politics in the legal arena. In four of the five cases, advocates general cited rights in the Charter as clarifications of principles/rights found elsewhere in ECJ case law or the ECHR. In the case of the *UK Broadcasting, Entertainment, Cinematographic and Theatre Union (BECTU)* v. *the UK Secretary of State for Trade and Industry* about the application and interpretation of the 1993 Working Time directive (Dir. 93/104/EC), Advocate General (AG) Tizzano supported his finding that a right to annual paid leave was indeed a fundamental right in the EU context, by reference to article 31(2) of the Charter.[25] This was particularly significant because there had been heated debate in the Convention whether such a right was to be included in the Charter at all.[26] AG Tizzano concluded that 'in proceedings concerned with the nature and scope of fundamental rights, the relevant statements of the Charter cannot be ignored'.[27]

In the opinion of Advocate General Jacobs in a case of an employee of the European Parliament who appealed against disciplinary action taken against him by the EP, and whose appeal had been dismissed by the Court of First Instance, the reference made by the AG to the Charter is also telling, because it concerned one of the most innovative rights contained in the document: the right to good administration in Art. 41. The claimant based his appeal partly on the view that the disciplinary action had been taken too slowly, and thus constituted an act of 'bad administration'. The advocate general in his opinion agreed with the claimant because in his view paragraph 1) of Article 41 EUCFR, 'while itself not legally binding, proclaims a generally recognised principle in stating . . . that 'Every person has a right to have his or her affairs handled impartially, fairly and within a reasonable time.'[28] Thus the Charter was interpreted here as a statement of 'generally recognised principles' which, through ECJ decisions, could be turned into legal precedent.

An even further-reaching understanding of the rights in the Charter emerges from AG Jacobs' view in another case, where the Netherlands brought proceedings against the European Parliament and the Council, in order to annul a directive on biotechnology. The case rested on the claim that the directive violated certain fundamental rights, and that there was no sufficient legal basis for it in Community law. The presumed violation of fundamental rights was construed by the claimants on the basis of the principle of human dignity and integrity of the human person. There was also an argument about a fundamental right to information of patients who might be treated with genetically modified material.[29] In his opinion, AG Jacobs maintained that 'the rights invoked by the Netherlands are indeed fundamental rights, respect for which must be ensured in the Community legal order. The right to human dignity is perhaps the most fundamental right of all, and is now expressed in Article 1 of the Charter of Fundamental Rights of the European Union.'[30] He also referred to Article 3(2) of the Charter which 'requires in the fields of medicine and biology, respect for the "free and informed consent of the person concerned, according to the procedures laid down by law". It must be accepted that any Community instrument infringing those rights would be unlawful.'[31] Even though Jacobs subsequently concluded that the rights in question had not been violated by the directive in this particular case, it is important that their origin was acknowledged as being the Charter. Especially with regard to human dignity, which had been rejected by Lord Goldsmith in the Charter debates initially as an 'injusticiable' concept rather than a right, the Charter visibly introduced new standards for EU-level fundamental rights disputes (see Chapter 4).

A fourth early reference to the Charter, in the joined cases *Booker Aquaculture and Hydro Seafood GSP* v. *The Scottish Ministers*[32] by Advocate General Mischo cites the Charter in support of his view that, similar to the European Convention of Human Rights First Protocol, the Charter does not contain an automatic right to compensation as part of its protection of the right of property. The significance of this reference did not, however, lie so much in the meaning attributed to a particular right in the Charter (Art. 17 in this case), but in the justification given by the advocate general for his use of the Charter: 'I know that the Charter is not legally binding, but it is worthwhile referring to it given that it constitutes the expression, at the highest level, of a democratically established political consensus on what must today be considered as the catalogue of fundamental rights guaranteed by the Community legal order.'[33] This argument highlights the role the Charter is already playing in determining such vague concepts as the 'political will of the EU member states' or 'common constitutional traditions' on matters concerning fundamental rights. It is also significant that the advocate general specifically referred to the presumed democratic legitimacy of the Charter as an expression of political consensus, a notion which is essential for the Charter's growing influence independently of its legal status.

Since then, the Charter has been referred to in a great number of cases by advocates general,[34] and has been also cited in several judgements of the Court of First Instance and some national constitutional courts.[35] The European Court of Justice itself has so far avoided referring directly to the Charter, but the other institutions of the European Union early on declared themselves bound by the provisions of the Charter. Consequently a great number of acts of secondary law (EC directives, regulations and framework decisions) contain references to underline that they should be interpreted 'in conformity with the Charter'.[36] These examples show how quickly the Charter has become entrenched in the EU legal system both as an aid to interpretation, and as an additional source of fundamental rights, its status as a political declaration notwithstanding. With the further debates about the merits of the Charter in the working group in the second Convention, and the eventual agreement on its complete inclusion in the Constitutional Treaty, the Charter rights are now clearly part of the legal *acquis*.

Thus, the references to the EU Charter so far seem to bear out the predictions of early academic analysis. De Witte had concluded already in late 2000 that even 'a non-binding Charter is likely to have a significant impact on the existing EU legal framework of fundamental rights protection'.[37] More specifically, Lenaerts and de Smijter maintained in early 2001: 'In practice . . . the legal effect of the solemn proclamation of the Charter of Fundamental Rights of the European Union will tend to be similar to that of its inclusion into the Treaties . . . Indeed, to the extent that the Charter is to be regarded as an expression of the constitutional traditions common to the Member States, the Court will be required to enforce it by virtue of Article 6(2) *juncto* Article 46 (d) EU as "general principles of Community law".'[38] This reasoning is clearly visible in AG Jacobs statement in the Court of First Instance case of the EP employee.[39] Even though the ECJ has so far not gone down that path, it is clear that with the adoption of the Constitutional Treaty the Charter will acquire the necessary legal force to fulfil its role as a modern, forward-looking and fully developed fundamental rights order.[40]

The Charter in the process of constitutionalisation

The Charter's potential effect on the interpretation of fundamental rights by the EU's courts is thus clearly visible. There is, however, a second aspect to the legal impact of the Charter, which also had a crucial effect on the legitimacy of the EU polity: this is the role of the Charter in promoting the legal-political development of that complex of Treaties and legal provisions which make up the constitutional fabric of the EU.[41] Many saw the Charter itself already at the time as the 'nucleus' of a European constitution.[42] But even if a consolidated, written European Constitution did not have to follow automatically from the Charter, it is clear that the document and process of the Charter were important steps in the Union's constitutional evolution. The 'Declaration on the Future of the Union' attached to the Treaty of Nice made the future inclusion of the Charter into the EU's primary legal framework one of the issues for the next IGC.[43] This commitment, together with continuing pressure from various directions (notably from the European Parliament[44]), to use the Convention method as tested in drafting the Charter, to prepare the next treaty revision, suggested that the Charter would play an important role in both the legal and the political debate over the following years. Lenaerts and de Smijter concluded on this basis that '[t]he Charter of Fundamental Rights of the European Union clearly functions as a catalyst of exchanges of ideas on the constitutionalization of the founding Treaties. . . . The Charter . . . is an ideal incentive in that respect, since it evokes the foundational values which the EU Member States have in common, it is a legally enforceable text [*sic!*] which underlines the importance of the rule of law in the EU, and it is the ultimate proof of the focal role that EU citizens have come to play in the European integration process.'[45]

With regard to the legitimation role which the Charter and its process could play, all the elements in this positive assessment are important and they mirror the debates about the four dimensions of politics solicited by the question of fundamental rights. While it is difficult to determine how far the debates started in the Charter Convention and the positive example of an eventual agreement on the fundamental rights have directly influenced the subsequent dynamics of the constitutional process, it is clear that the Charter experience was an important point of reference for the Constitutional Convention. The formula for setting up the Convention of including the 'four' components of relevant political actors in an open process was repeated, and especially the debates about the values and objectives of the European Union made frequent references to the Charter as the benchmark of Europe's common values.

At the same time, these elements alone do not answer the question how the constitutionalising push which was contained in the Charter affected and affects the legitimacy debate. As presented in Chapter 3, the notion of constitutionalism encompasses both the legal understanding as the consolidation and fixation of a set of rules and principles in a legal document with special (superior) legal status; and the broader understanding of constitutionalism as an ongoing process of casting and recasting the balances between the different political and legal dynamics that constitute a polity. It is precisely from this perspective that some proponents of a flexible and ongoing constitutional process have criticised the Charter because it lacked 'the subtlety and flexibility of the current system of negotiation. Instead, it is a highly conservative document which gives rise to a status quo approach.'[46]

Joseph Weiler, in a critical editorial on the Charter in June 2000, also pointed to the danger of the Charter 'chilling the constitutional dialogue' and disappointing high hopes vested in its ability to introduce 'much needed innovation to our constitutional norms'. Weiler saw these problems in particular if the Charter 'sticks to the rusty and trusty formulae of yesteryear around which constitutional consensus already exists and thus avoids innovation – not an unlikely outcome given a body composed of representatives of governments and parliaments from fifteen different countries operating on the principle of consensus.'[47] This evaluation of the process, however, not only failed to mention the inclusion of European Parliamentarians and a representative from the Commission in the body, thus downplaying the supra-national and innovative European element in the debates, but it also did not accurately predict the outcome. Innovation was achieved in many areas in the Charter, and the often ambiguous formulae of the final compromise, while indeed presenting difficulties for a strict notion of 'legal certainty', also mean that the dialogue about the precise meaning of fundamental rights in the European Union is everything but 'chilled'. Moreover, the constitutional process itself was dynamised, rather than chilled, by the Charter Convention.

It is, however, true that the drafting of a new catalogue of fundamental rights, if understood narrowly as an exercise in legal codification, could contribute to a further 'juridification' of European politics.[48] If the 'debate' about fundamental rights, or that on other aspects of the four dimensions of the political process, was transferred permanently from the political arena to the more closed legal arena of the ECJ, this would ultimately be detrimental for the legitimacy of the EU polity.[49] The essence of a legitimate and democratic political process is the participation of all (or at least their representatives) in controlling collective decisions on an equal basis.[50] Thus, if political decisions are taken by judges who are unelected and by virtue of their office in a privileged position to take decisions, this exacerbates the problem of legitimacy, not only at the European level.[51] Yet, the Charter itself can also be seen as enforcing the democratic ' "right of rights", [that] is the right to participation' because it ensures the rights of citizens in their interaction with the new polity, and because 'it directs us to the deficiencies of the EU as a political order'.[52]

Nevertheless, Weiler has repeatedly criticised the Charter for 'distracting attention from . . . [t]he real problem of the Community [which] is the absence of a human rights policy, with everything this entails: a Commissioner, a Directorate General, a budget and a horizontal action plan'.[53] More recently he concluded in the context of the second Convention, however, that even though 'the single most important thing the next IGC can do for human rights is . . . the commitment to, and adoption of a human rights policy', it was clear that 'at this point continued rejection of the Charter would be, in and of itself, very damaging'.[54] Yet, while there is certainly room for much improvement and a fundamental institutional strengthening of the EU's human rights policy, it is not clear why the Charter would prevent, rather than add to, the political pressure building for such a development. Indeed, as argued here, the Charter provided the most 'political' forum to date to discuss the rights and their role in the polity and thus moved also the wider debate about the role of human rights in the EU beyond the legal conversation.

The Charter in the Constitutional Convention

The inclusion of the 'Charter question' in the Declaration on the Future of the Union and the ensuing debates highlighted once more that the drafting of the rights catalogue did not mean a closure of the political debate.[55] There was agreement by the time of the Laeken summit that one important task of the second Convention should be to determine the fate of the Charter. Unlike the first Convention, which decided to debate all issues in its plenary assembly because no division of the task into sub-sections could be agreed upon,[56] the second, larger Convention duly set up a number of working groups. Working group II was dedicated to the Charter-question and was chaired by EU Commissioner Antònio Vitorino, who had also been the Commission's representative in the Charter Convention. The mandate of the working group prepared by the chairman immediately made clear that he saw the purpose of the working group not as discussing 'the major political questions (whether the Charter should be incorporated)', but to find solutions to the question 'how' this could be achieved, and the question of how the EU could accede to the European Convention of Human Rights, a question which Vitorino introduced as 'complementary and not alternative'.[57]

Thus the tone was set for a rather focused debate on a number of legal-technical possibilities and details, despite the fact that some members of the Convention did try to reopen questions of substance and in particular the British government was adamant in pushing for a further limitation of the scope of application for the Charter because it was feared that otherwise the latter could be used as a tool in trying to extend the competencies of the Union. Consequently, the most substantial changes that were applied to the Charter text by the second Convention concern the so-called horizontal articles (Charter Arts 51 and 52): Article 51 of the Charter (Article II-111 of the Constitutional Treaty) now stresses even more firmly that the Charter is addressed to the EU institutions and to the member states only when they are implementing Union law, because it underlines that the Charter rights apply only within the 'limits of the powers of the Union as conferred on it in other parts of the Constitution' (Art. II-111.1), and that the Charter does not extend the field of application of Union law in any way (II-111.2). Article 52 (II-112) has been extended by four additional paragraphs to recognise explicitly the respect for the constitutional traditions of the member states (Art. II-112.4), the limitations of the Charter rights to the EU's institutions and acts (Art. II-112.5), and the importance of the references to national laws in certain articles of the Charter itself (Art. II-112.6).

Yet, even with these stringent limits, in particular the British government representative in the final phases of the second Convention pushed through that, as a further 'safeguard', a reference to the 'explanations' of the Charter Convention's presidium was included in Article II-112.7.[58] These explanations, which themselves were 'updated' by the second Convention, are somewhat curious because they had been drafted by the Charter presidium at the very end of the negotiations, without consulting the Convention as a whole. As noted above, several Charter Convention members were outraged and the explanations were published as 'prepared at the instigation of the presidium' and as having 'no legal value' at the time.[59] The fact that after the second Convention they are now referred to not only in Art. II-112.7, but also in a new sentence in the Charter preamble (paragraph 5) and that they have been published as Declaration 12 annexed to the Constitutional Treaty, clearly shows, that by now they have become an 'official' part of the Charter, but it is not quite clear what their effect will be, especially since they contain a number of 'inconsistencies' in their updated form.[60]

As for the actual integration of the Charter in the Constitutional Treaty, working group II of the Constitutional Convention actually proposed three different alternatives: by including the Charter's full text in the Constitution, by annexing it to the text, or through an 'indirect reference' in an article of the Constitutional Treaty. These options were proposed in a 'highly consensual report' by the working group where there was wide agreement that the Charter should become legally binding, and the overwhelming majority favoured a full-text inclusion of the Charter.[61] This option was confirmed by the plenary of the second Convention on 28/29 October 2002. Likewise, the working group recommended an accession of the European Union to the ECHR, and the Constitutional Treaty created the pre-conditions for such a step by granting the EU legal personality (Art. I-7) and making an explicit commitment that the Union 'shall accede to the European Convention for the Protection of Human Rights and Fundamental Freedoms' in Article I-9.

Nevertheless, a number of questions remain open with regard to the Charter, such as the precise meaning and scope of the limitations to Charter rights under article II-112 or, as mentioned, the interaction between the Charter rights and the ECHR system. Answers will have to be found through legal practice or through future changes to the

Constitution's provisions themselves.[62] The actual use of Charter rights by individual citizens will naturally affect the balance of competencies in the EU and consequently the legitimacy of the EU as an area of rights protection, despite the attempts to prevent precisely such changes.[63] In this sense, the political debate about the Charter and its rights is far from over. The challenge for the future is therefore indeed to keep the process of rights actualisation at European level open and to avoid it being exclusively relegated to the judicial arena. While the ECJ and its judicial activism have played an important role in balancing the EU's constitutional development so far, the Charter through its process and its very 'unfinishedness' holds the promise of political as well as legal constitutionalism. After all, the listing of fundamental rights by the Convention already produced a level of constitutional debate about the EU which had not taken place before the Charter process provided the inspiration for it. Moreover, one of the core constitutional contributions which the Charter process has made is to have established and tested a mechanism for amending the EU Treaties (including their fundamental rights contents) in a process which ensures more inclusion, participation, and democratic debate than the IGCs.

Yet, the legitimating potential of the debate about fundamental rights can only be used effectively as a political tool if it corresponds to an expectation that citizens harbour with regard to this particular aspect of the EU's sphere of politics.[64] In other words, EU citizens must feel that the EU *should* protect their fundamental rights in order to appreciate whether and how well it does. This is the internal legitimacy dimension of the improved rights protection argument. As has been argued in Chapter 3, discourses about a European identity, the European community of values, European citizenship, and the role of fundamental rights have been used over the past decades in the attempt to sustain the EC/EU's legitimacy, and they have created certain expectations on the part of the citizens.[65] The next section looks at the way in which the Charter process has expanded these discourses, and how this might change the expectations of Europe's people. With the Charter and the Constitutional Treaty, the debate about Europe as a rights-based polity reached new levels.

The discourses of legitimacy

Discursive construction of a rights protector

The significance of the EU's value and human rights discourse lies in its capacity to create and shape certain expectations on the part of the citizens, which the Union then seeks to fulfil in order to prove the legitimacy of its existence and operation.[66] Thus Thomas Diez notes in his proposal to include 'discourse analysis in the canon of approaches to European studies' that 'the various attempts to capture the Union's nature are not mere descriptions of an unknown polity, but [they] take part in the construction of the polity itself'.[67] In his argument, which needs to be seen in the wider context of recent growth in the application of 'constructivist' theoretical approaches to the process of European integration, Diez stresses the 'power of discourse' which is 'that it structures our conceptualizations of European governance'.[68] This section looks at the interaction between the Charter process, and the European discourses of human rights protection and a European community of values. It appears that there is a reciprocal link between the two discourses: the project to draft an EU catalogue of fundamental rights (which has been around for a long time)[69] came finally to fruition in 1999/2000 because the development of the EU-level human rights discourse had created certain expectations and opportunities. At the same time, the Charter debates themselves, as well as the Charter text that emerged, mark a further consolidation, and, in some areas, an expansion of the EU's human rights and value discourse (see Chapter 4).

The gradual development of European discourses, and its effect on policy, has been exemplified in particular with regard to the concept of European citizenship, where the discrepancy between the (initially) very limited legal consequences of the concept, and the much broader implications of the usage of the term 'citizen' have been particularly evident (see Chapter 3). Antje Wiener shows for the citizenship discourse that the initial use of the concept by some institutional actors led to a routinisation of the term, which then triggered the development of a political practice, and the eventual institutionalisation of the concept. Such an institutionalised policy in turn can re-enforce the discourse.[70] The example of the 'EU citizenship and rights discourse' also shows, however, that the development of a common discourse on these issues at European level, rather than being a cunningly master-minded undertaking to exert power through language, is often a haphazard and frequently ambiguous process, the results of which become visible only over time. Moreover, these developments are evolutionary rather than revolutionary. Nevertheless there are instances when a discourse that has been building up over time is suddenly thrust into the open by conscious act or accident, and becomes the focus of much intensified and pressurised interests. The Charter, and other instances of fundamental rights rhetoric at EU level at the turn of the twentieth century, are both products and parts of this phenomenon.

The EU rights discourse at work: Austria 2000

The 'proclamation' of the EU Charter of Fundamental Rights at the Nice summit (which in itself can be seen as a significant form of 'speech act'[71]), represented an important institutional consolidation of the EU rights discourse. This is especially interesting in conjunction with another discursive development that became visible at the same time: the progressive institutionalisation of the Union as a 'community of values' which achieved prominence with the action of fourteen EU governments against the new Austrian administration in early 2000. In their account of the reasons for the 'EU 14' to impose sanctions against the inclusion of the right-wing Freedom Party (FPÖ) in the coalition forming the Austrian government, Merlingen, Mudde and Sedelmeier stress that the explanation for this particular instance of political action must be seen in the 'interplay between value-based norms and self-interest [of individual political actors or whole member states]'.[72] For the first part of this dual explanation, the three authors employ the notion of '[d]iscursively constructed role conceptions' which 'endow actors with norms of appropriate behaviour, thereby shaping how they line up and act on issues'.[73] In the particular case, these were the norms of the EU as guarantor of fundamental rights and democratic standards which, as Merlingen, Mudde and Sedelmeier emphasise, had become, 'in the second half of the 1990s . . . a central part of the self-understanding of national and supra-national policy-makers in the EU'.[74] The three authors quote the drafting of the Charter as an additional example of this emerging self-understanding.

Thus, when the Austrian case arose, the political actors in other EU member states were presented with a limited set of possible reactions, which had been shaped by the fundamental rights and democracy discourse. While the limiting force of the discourse on a European value community should not be taken as the only explanation of the reaction of the fourteen,[75] it does seem to have played a significant part in shaping policy. Josef Melchior argues in a similar vein, that 'the "Austrian case" can be seen as the most spectacular, and most publicly visible, manifestation of the struggle for the realisation of a "European community of values"'.[76] He specifically links his analysis to the EU Charter, and in particular to the reference to common values in the Charter's preamble,[77] and concludes that, '[e]ven though the Charter of Fundamental Rights, according to its mandate, was only meant to summarise fundamental rights already existing in the EU, . . . [it] represents itself a milestone in the development of a common understanding of values, in so far as the Convention . . . succeeded in making explicit what it was prepared to accept as a common value basis of the integration process – cutting across deep national, party-political, ideological and religious divides.'[78]

As has been shown in the analysis of the preamble debates, the formulation of common values was at times a troubled endeavour. But the Charter Convention provided an institutionalised setting in which dialogue about the values underlying the integration process could flourish. It became possible to deepen and widen the EU-specific value discourse by providing new shared meanings for such concepts as 'fundamental rights' or 'solidarity', the latter eventually not only forming part of the list of values in the preamble, but also becoming one of the chapter headings of the Charter. At the same time, this definition and redefinition of shared meanings is an ongoing process. The meaning of 'solidarity' is clearly not exhausted by the rights which are grouped under this heading in the Charter (Arts. 27–38). The common values as they emerged from the Convention therefore provided the basis for the subsequent contestation and debate in the second Convention. Without going into the details of the value debate concerning the preamble and especially articles I-1 to I-3 of the EU Constitution, it is clear that the discourse of the EU as a community of values has achieved new prominence with the explicit statement of the Union's values in Article I-2 and the expansion of the list contained in this article.

With regard to the Charter's contribution to the legitimacy of the European Union, the value discourse in the Convention debates was an important element because it embodied what Vivien A. Schmidt calls the 'normative function' of the 'ideational dimension' of public discourse.[79] In her concept, discourse operates in two dimensions: the ideational and interactive. In each dimension, discourse fulfils two different functions: ideational discourse has the normative function of showing how particular policies are rooted in certain pre-existing values, and the cognitive function of providing a coherent narrative of political action. In the interactive dimension, discourse works by providing the élite with a means to coordinate its own activities, and to communicate with their public.[80]

In the Charter negotiations on supposedly common values, all four functions of rights discourse became visible. The four founding values (liberty, democracy, the rule of law, respect for human rights) were invoked to legitimate the policy of drafting a Charter, but in the process those values themselves were extended to include 'solidarity' and 'human dignity'. As mentioned, the Charter also saw the discursive recasting of Europe as a 'community of law', as an 'area of freedom, security and justice', and the gradual building of a 'European social model',[81] thus broadening the contents of the value discourse. The Cologne mandate's concern with the visibility of the rights (and by extension of the values which are expressed through those rights), reflects both the interactive dimension of the rights discourse (to communicate with the people), and the cognitive aspect of providing a coherent narrative to legitimate the EU polity.

The Charter debates provided a particularly well-suited, high-profile arena for the development of these European level discourses. With the underlying themes and many of the discursive elements already established (by the existing body of EC law, international fundamental rights, the EU's value and democracy discourse, and by the Cologne mandate), the Convention could clearly not revolutionise the concepts it dealt with. At the same time, however, with a Charter text as a final outcome and its 'solemn proclamation' as the declared aim of the process, the Convention was in a particularly strong position to consolidate and develop certain elements of its discourse, and to 'institutionalise' them at the same moment. For example the Charter's bold statement on the indivisibility of classical civic, political and human rights from economic and social rights, can be assumed to have changed the rights discourse within the EU, and probably globally, for good. Similarly, the value foundations of the Union moved from a more narrow basis with a strong emphasis on the procedures to ensure the permanence of these values (democracy, rule of law, respect of human rights), to include now also politically more contested values like 'solidarity' and 'human dignity'.

Given the legal and political structures in which it occurred, the Charter immediately became a discursive benchmark, behind which it would be difficult to retreat once it existed. The second Convention could build on these achievements. Whether as such they can improve the legitimacy of the European Union as a locus of political organisation depends on whether Europe's citizens recognise the values to which the Charter (and now the Constitution) lay claim, and whether they see the EU as being suited to deliver on them. In order to assess these elements of the Charter's legitimation role, it is of essential importance how the process of discourse formation in the Charter debates was extended and communicated to the wider public. It is here again that the process by which the Charter was drafted, and the style of how agreements were reached, become significant. In the next section the deliberative element of the Charter process will therefore be assessed.

The Convention process and its limitations

Deliberative decision-making

The legitimacy of collective decisions depends to a substantial degree on the procedures by which they are reached being recognised as legitimate.[82] In the deliberative democratic approach set out in Chapter 2, this means collective decision-making has to be seen to allow all voices to be heard as equals, and to be based on appropriate justification. It also presupposes the belief of those who ultimately disagree that their dissent will not lead to disproportionate sanctions against them. Legitimacy is thus increasingly understood, in modern democratic theory, 'in terms of the ability or opportunity to participate in effective deliberation on the part of those subject to collective decision', as John S. Dryzek notes.[83] This means that free and equal citizens must be able to engage in an exchange of reasons and try to persuade each other.

The need to reach decisions in a way which satisfies these requirements is even more prominent in an instance like the drafting of a catalogue of fundamental rights, than in day-to-day political argument. This is the case not only because one declared aim of the Charter project was to *improve* the EU's legitimacy, but also because the conflicts arising in this situation went to the very heart of political organisation. They concerned, as mentioned, the four dimensions of sphere, subjects, scope, and style of politics. A delicate balance had to be reached on these issues in order to sustain the legitimacy of the political order and its regime. According to Eriksen and Fossum, '[t]his calls attention to [deliberative] democracy as a legitimation principle because only the decision-making process in itself can lend legitimacy to outcomes when values, shared norms, and collective identities are lacking.'[84] While 'values, shared norms, and collective identities' are clearly no longer completely lacking in the EU case, they remain conflictual. The focus on deliberation is therefore useful in understanding the specific contribution of the Convention method to reaching agreement in a context where at least some values, norms, rights and identities were hotly contested.

The remainder of this section therefore investigates how far the Convention can be regarded as a 'deliberative setting' in Jon Elster's terms,[85] and to what degree the results it produced can be assumed to be deliberative outcomes. A deliberative setting, in this sense, is a decision-making arrangement in which the dominant form of social interaction is 'deliberation/persuasion', rather than 'coercion, diplomatic bargaining, . . . [or] copying/emulation'.[86] The focus of the investigation here is the question whether the *institutional conditions* for deliberation were there, because for a number of 'methodological' and 'epistemological' reasons it is quite difficult to ultimately judge whether or not 'real' deliberation takes place in a given situation.[87] Jeffrey Checkel for example points to the problem that accounts of deliberation at a micro-level (i.e. focused on the deliberation within a given institutional setting, like Checkel's own case-studies, or the Charter Convention) risk neglecting factors outside these settings (i.e. at the 'macro' level): '[i]n particular, social and material power receive insufficient attention'.[88] Secondly, the problem of 'getting into other people's minds' to find out *why* they may have changed their views, is an obvious limit to identifying 'real' deliberation. Nevertheless, 'being methodologically self-conscious and employing multiple data streams' in the analysis can help to reduce the impact of this problem. The account of the Charter Convention presented in the following tries to follow this advice to assess how far the Convention provided an environment in which deliberation could develop, and to which degree the members of the Convention were in a position to embark on such deliberation.

The Convention as a deliberative setting

In his comparative study of constitutional assemblies as deliberative fora, Jon Elster develops a number of criteria in order to assess the location of a dialogue within a particular institutional setting on the 'continuum between arguing and bargaining'.[89] The first of these criteria concerns the 'freedom' of the assembly to choose the subject of its own activity. Constitutional assemblies, in this account, '[b]y and large . . . refuse to be bound by upstream authorities', and they tend to 'assert the right to deliberate freely without any prior constraints on procedure or substance, ignoring mandates from their constituencies as well as instructions from the convening authority'.[90] It is clear that the Charter Convention did not fully qualify as a deliberative constituent assembly by this measure, because it had to follow the general lines of the Cologne mandate. But even though the Convention was not operating on a tabula rasa in this sense, the contestation of the mandate, and the ensuing debates about its scope (Chapter 4) show that the Convention used the windows of opportunity opened up by the ambiguities in the mandate.[91] The contents both of the Charter, and of the debates in the Convention, were clearly more than a list of existing rights. Thus, even if the original task of the body was meant to be about listing rights which had supposedly already gone through a process of justification and legitimation in their relevant national or international contexts, deliberation did take place in the event about the meaning and nature of such rights, which included challenges to substantial parts of the mandate itself.

In order to assess how deliberative a setting a given assembly is, Jon Elster then employs four more variables which determine the 'nature of the communication [i.e. its 'deliberativeness']'. These variables are *size* (small vs. large), *publicity* (open vs. closed proceedings), the presence or absence of *force*, and the importance of *interest* as a motivation of the actors.[92] From this theoretical perspective, a perfect deliberative setting would be a large, open body where the threat of force is absent and the interest of those deliberating is removed as far as possible from the outcome of their deliberation. At the same time, however, Elster acknowledges that these variables mitigate each other and can have opposite effects in different constellations: normally a large body is more likely to encourage arguing rather than bargaining, but at the same time 'debates [in large assemblies] tend to be dominated by a small number of skilled and charismatic speakers'.[93] Similarly, publicity can on the one hand be beneficial because it forces the delegates to substitute the 'language of interest by the language of reason and to replace impartial motives by passionate ones'.[94] On the other hand, a debate in public also means subjecting the delegates to external pressures, and makes persuasion more difficult because every change of position by an assembly member means a loss of face vis-à-vis the audience. How did the Charter Convention fare by these criteria?

With regard to its *size*, the EU Charter Convention, measured against Elster's comparative cases (the Frankfurt 1848 Assembly with 596 members, the 1787 Philadelphia Convention of 50, and the French 1789 *Constituante* of around 1,200 members), was medium-sized. Even including the substitute members who had a right to speak in the debates, and the observers from the Courts and the Economic and Social Committee, the Convention numbered less than 130 delegates. The attendance over the eighteen plenary meetings varied, but a rough estimate suggests that an average 60–80 members, deputy members and observers were present during the Convention's plenary sessions. The body was thus small enough for a feeling of belonging to a common endeavour to develop in the course of the process.[95] This is one of the conditions for 'normative learning' through persuasion to occur in a deliberative setting.[96] Thus, as the interviewed Convention members emphasised, a positive and increasingly familiar atmosphere prevailed on most occasions, which provided a positive backdrop to a constructive exchange of argument. Moreover, the assembly was not so big as to automatically break up into internal factions (in fact, the fluid nature of the internal cleavages was highlighted by most Convention members, despite the organisation into the four constituent delegations, see Chapter 4), but it was big enough to avoid pure bargaining.[97]

The element of *publicity*, as highlighted, was indeed one of the most important procedural innovations of the Charter process in the European context, and can be seen on balance as a positive element. The physically present 'audience' in the Convention itself was small, but grew as the process went on, from a few members of European institutions or interested NGO representatives in the earlier stages, to quite a sizeable, changing group of media representatives, NGO staff, visitors groups, and interested citizens in the second half of the Convention's existence. This public, however, never vocally intervened in the debates in the way that Elster describes for the deliberations of the French Assemblée, for example. Thus, it did not exert direct pressure on the delegates, but it also did not provide immediate feedback for them.

A second aspect of the Convention's publicity is of course the fact that the debate was taken beyond the chamber where the Convention met, and particularly the Convention website provided a novel forum which was used by a large number of organisations to express their views.[98] The precise impact of input from the public back to the deliberations themselves is difficult to measure, but the statements of various interests distributed via the website, or directed at individual Convention members, did influence the drafting of the Charter.[99] Moreover, the Convention members were keenly aware that one of the central aims of the Charter process was precisely to create a public interest in the rights debated, and therefore frequently referred to 'the public' (or the media as extensions of the public), as the real 'addressees' of the rights which were debated. At the same time, individual Convention members had differing degrees of freedom in their positions vis-à-vis their constituencies (see also below). Elizabeth Wicks shows for example that there was quite intense pressure from a (select) public in the UK on Lord Goldsmith, and due to this pressure the British government exercised direct control over its representative.[100] The Italian government representative Stefano Rodotà, in contrast, said that he had made his taking up the position in the Convention conditional on being free from government interference.[101] This was probably possible for the Italian government to concede because there was less public controversy over the issues in question in Italy.

These two examples show that the 'publicity' of the process was a double-edged sword and depended in part on the state of the debate in respective national contexts. Moreover, the involvement of civil society actors in particular through the website has been criticised as having been 'too open' because so many voices were invited to be heard that every individual contribution lost in weight.[102] Nevertheless, the knowledge on the part of Convention members, that the process was, and was supposed to be, open, had an important effect on the way the debates themselves were conducted. At the same time, it has to be noted that the public which actually did take an interest in the Charter drafting process in most EU member states was limited to a comparatively small section of the media, and groups with specific interests. A further limitation was, as in all European affairs, the absence of a genuinely European, trans-lingual media and public debate, which meant that coverage of the Charter debates was usually framed by national political sensitivities. Yet, the publicity which the Convention did receive over its ten-month existence, while falling far short of a general public awareness, was clearly more substantive than the extremely short-lived attention on IGCs and summit events.[103]

The *presence or absence of force* as a limiting factor on the debates was clearly not as direct an influence in the EU Charter debates as it was in Elster's historical examples, where constitutions were written at times under direct threat of violence from outside. The equivalent of these forces in the Charter process, however, was the threat to veto the entire process used by some governments on different occasions. As mentioned, the veto-threat was not used openly, but its existence did have an important impact on how the presidium conducted the debates on particular issues. It meant that the interaction on those occasions was based on 'coercion' rather than on persuasion or even bargaining,[104] which cast doubts on the equal standing of the Convention members and curtailed, if not the freedom to debate, at least the range of options ultimately available to the Convention. This observation overlaps in several respects with Elster's variable of *interest*, and with the question how much personal interest was mitigated in the 'real' deliberation by considerations of general interest and rational argument. Given the nature of the argument in the Convention (i.e. supposedly universal, already existing human rights), individual or even national interest was hardly to be expected to figure prominently among the reasons given openly in support of individual positions. All participants in the debates did in fact put great emphasis on the non-interest related, 'higher' nature of the rights discussed.

Thus, while it is difficult to 'measure' certain more concrete aspects of Elster's four variables in an actual political setting like the Charter Convention, and bearing the methodological and epistemological difficulties in mind, it still seems appropriate to consider the Convention as a setting in which deliberation was not only possible, but in which it was encouraged by the institutional arrangements. The findings with regard to the fluid nature of cleavages in the Convention, the agreement on the search for consensus (Chapter 4), and the participant observers' impression from the debates themselves, all suggest that the atmosphere was mostly conducive to a debate in which individual Convention members were free to deliberate and to be persuaded. Statements from members further support this overall assessment. Nevertheless, there are certain elements concerning the role of the individual Convention members in the process, which merit closer attention.

The members of the Convention

Beyond the insoluble problem of 'other minds' mentioned above, there are several factors which influence the likelihood of successful deliberation and persuasion at the individual level. As with the criteria used before in the institutional context, these factors do overlap, and require some balancing against each other, and they also interact with some of the institutional factors. Checkel lists the following criteria as 'key in promoting persuasion and deliberation': first a 'largely common educational and professional background'; second, a common sense of political pressure; third, the members' 'insulation from publicity and overt political pressure'; and fourth, 'perhaps most important, 'the individual powers of persuasion of particular members'.[105] It becomes immediately visible, especially with regard to the third criterion (insulation from publicity and political pressure), that this is as much a function of the institutional arrangements, as of the individual member's capacity to be independent. In the case of the Charter Convention, it is in fact clear that 'insulation from publicity' was certainly not wished for, because one of the aims formulated by many Convention members was to create a public debate in interaction with their own deliberations. With regards to the 'insulation from political pressure', this is very difficult to determine in the concrete case, because the boundary between 'political pressure' and the necessary accountability and responsiveness of democratic representatives is blurred. This also touches on a structural problem already hinted at, and linked closely with Checkel's fourth criterion, namely the legitimacy which each member brought to the deliberations by virtue of how they were selected. This clearly affects the individual's 'power of persuasion', and will be discussed in some greater detail below.

Thus in applying the first two criteria to the Charter Convention, a mixed picture emerges. On the question of the 'common educational background' of the members of the Convention, the legal bias is overwhelming. At least thirteen out of the fifteen titular representatives of national governments were professional lawyers or professors of law, and an estimated four-fifths of the representatives from national Parliaments also had a legal background.[106] The European Parliament delegation is once more the exception, with a ratio of eight lawyers to eight non-lawyers among the full Convention members. Given the subject to be debated, and the nature of the selection processes in national parliaments (see below), this composition of the Convention does not come as a surprise. In this situation, the legal experts did dominate the discussions, and those who were not experts felt sometimes that they could not contribute to these exchanges on an equal level.[107] Nevertheless, there was enough common ground among the members of the Convention to allow for dialogue to work, which certainly benefited from the high level of expertise on human rights in different contexts (both legal and political) within the Convention. At the same time, this expert bias is a severe limitation to the representativeness of the Convention's members.

As far as a 'common sense of the need to act' among the Convention members is concerned, the general picture that emerges is one of a broad agreement that a Charter would be a positive addition to the existing European-level structures. Though not seeing a Charter in all cases as a matter of urgency, the majority of Convention members interviewed expressed similar feelings that a Charter would improve the protection of fundamental rights in the European Union. Despite disagreement about the precise interpretation of the scope of the action, there was thus a sense of a common purpose. This underlying consensus on the need, or at least the usefulness to act, seems to have been sufficient to carry the process forward and, together with the institutional structure supporting it, to motivate a significant number of Convention members to travel to Brussels and participate in an intense programme of meetings.[108] Moreover, as one effect of deliberation in the Convention, this sense of common purpose probably grew during the ten months of the Convention's existence.

Representation in the Convention

With regard to the other factors which determine the individual standing of Convention members, i.e. the mandates from their constituencies, their 'insulation from political pressure', and their ensuing individual 'power of persuasion', the Charter Convention raises a number of intriguing questions. The composition of the body as determined by the Tampere mandate was an interesting novelty in the EU context in terms of the different kinds of legitimacy which Convention members from different institutional backgrounds brought to the table. The selection, and consequently the representativeness of individual members, differed widely between different institutions, which raises some doubts about the 'equality' of standing of the different categories of Convention members. It has been mentioned before that certain government representatives were much more prone than other Convention members, to think of themselves as having a veto power over individual proposals or even the Charter as a whole, because they knew that their governments would have veto power in the Council of ministers. There is little information on how government representatives (who were, after all, officially 'representatives of the Heads of State and Government'), were chosen, and whether they were accountable just to their direct 'masters', or to whole governments.[109]

The selection of parliamentary representatives to the Convention was also not clear in all cases. Several of them 'emerged' uncontested as appointees of the relevant European affairs committees of their Parliaments, or as nominees of their party groups, usually on the basis of previous European affairs and/or human rights interest and profile.[110] This fact can be read in three different ways: either it is evidence of a dubious, undemocratic form of indirect representation which still dominates the relationship between the different levels of EU governance where decisions are taken often by largely unaccountable 'delegates' from the national systems; secondly it can be seen as proof of a general lack of interest in the entire Charter process, which meant that in some national Parliaments not much effort was put into selecting representatives and endowing them with legitimate mandates by ensuring strong representational links; finally, however, the arrangements in some Parliaments can also be seen as attempts to ensure either non-partisan, or all-party selection of people with relevant expertise, in order to facilitate high-level deliberation on complex issues.

This final understanding is supported by the fact that in almost all cases the representatives of national governments and national parliaments did include government and opposition forces from the respective countries, and, in the case of bi-cameral parliaments, one member from each house. The multi-partisan approach was in most cases extended into the selection of 'substitute' Convention members, who did have the right to take full part in the deliberations. In this respect, the representation was as widespread as the limited size of the Convention permitted. Yet, different national arrangements for the accountability and information flows between the national level and the Convention members remain an important limitation to the overall transparency of the Charter process, and would validate further research.

In the European Parliament, the sixteen-strong delegation was composed of delegates chosen by the political groups on the basis of the overall composition of Parliament.[111] Eight of the sixteen full Convention members were also members of the EP's constitutional affairs committee, and it was this committee which, under the leadership of the two rapporteurs who were also members of the Convention (Andrew Duff and Johannes Voggenhuber) prepared the Parliamentary report on the Charter. This report was divided into two parts, the first of which (in March 2000), outlined the broad mandate of the EP members in the Convention.[112] Thus the European Parliament operated a comparatively transparent procedure to ensure the representativeness of its Convention members and their contribution to the debate.

In this sense, the process in the Charter Convention was an example of how different deliberative arenas with different internal logics could be combined at European level. Despite the problems in the procedures in some national parliaments, most of them held debates on the Charter,[113] some organised separate hearings with interested bodies from civil society,[114] or prepared extensive reports.[115] Thus the Charter process facilitated exchange between different parliamentary bodies, and certainly did raise the profile of national parliaments in the European context. The main problem, from this structural point of view, remains the intransparency of the selection and precise role of the representatives of national Heads of State and Government.

There is, however, another important criticism concerning the legitimacy of individual Convention members and the function of the Charter, which Richard Bellamy and Dario Castiglione raise. Taking issue with the central role which the Charter was supposed to play as the possible first step towards a fully grown constitution for the European Union, they argued in 2001 that the members drawn from pre-existing legal-political entities, would not have the legitimacy to establish a new balance of the four dimensions of politics in a new polity, because the legitimacy of such 'constitutional agents' would depend on the very constitutional process which they were embarking on.[116] A 'more direct relationship of communication and control', Bellamy and Castiglione argue, would therefore have had to be established between representatives and those represented in order to legitimate such a 'foundational moment'.[117]

This is a problem similar to that which has been referred to in Chapter 2 with regard to Habermas' understanding that the rules of the process (i.e. law) *and* the process itself (i.e. politics) constitute each other (being *'gleichursprünglich'*).[118] But while Habermas' concern is of a theoretical nature, Bellamy and Castiglione highlight the fact that in the 'real world' setup of the EU, national polities do exist as (more or less) legitimate structures. The question in the European context is, therefore, how to reconcile legitimacy claims old and new at different levels.[119] This question arose again with the second Convention drafting the Constitutional Treaty, and, as we know, a similar strategy of continuity rather than re-foundation of the European Union was adopted.

As for the Charter Convention, however, it has to be remembered that the body was created without a clear conception of how to ensure its representativeness because its very purpose was so vague. It is debateable if there is evidence of a clear understanding among the members of the European Council at Cologne, that the Convention was definitely *not supposed* to be a constitutional exercise. Yet, given the inbetweenness of the EU as a polity, and the evolving nature of Europe's constitutionalism, the peculiar mix of different kinds of representation in the Convention and the particular procedural setup chosen suggested more than a mere codification of existing rights. From the constitutionalist point of view it has therefore been noted that the Charter represented at the time a 'constitutional paradox' in that it reflected 'an emerging trend to agree on the use of the language of constitutionalism in European integration without agreeing on the conception of constitutionalism underlying such a language'.[120] The individual legitimacy of Convention members to make quasi-constitutional law at EU level could therefore be questioned, but the 'blame' for this problem cannot be put on the Convention itself. In the given circumstances, in any case, it can be argued that the deliberative process itself, as it unfolded in the Convention, 'created' the legitimacy to validate the end results.

An alternative option to legitimate the Charter *ex post*, i.e. a referendum on the Convention's product, was not discussed in great depth as long as the Charter remained a 'political declaration'. With the inclusion of the Charter in the Constitution, however, there will be referenda in a number of member states of the EU on the text, and in many countries the Charter is likely to be used as an argument in favour of ratifying the Constitutional Treaty.[121] The problem with these referenda remains, however, that a yes–no vote on something as complex as a catalogue of fundamental rights contained in a much larger constitutional text may not be an adequate way of giving the public a real say, because their decision will be based on oversimplified accounts of the numerous delicate (and temporary!) compromises achieved as a result of indepth debate.[122] Given these problems, the Convention process itself was aimed at broadening the exchanges beyond a limited élite, to reach a wider public. The next section therefore briefly looks at how the deliberation was carried beyond the Convention.

Deliberation beyond the Convention

The Cologne mandate had stipulated that 'social groups, as well as experts' should be invited to give their views before the body. As mentioned (see pp. 107–10 in this volume), the Tampere mandate widened this approach further by adding a commitment to 'transparency', by stating that an 'appropriate exchange of views with the applicant states should be held by the body', and that 'a complete language regime' should be applicable for sessions of the body.[123] The Council secretariat then decided to provide a website for contributions from a more general public which was subsequently kept open for four years. The quality, relevance, and the effect of these contributions on the debate varied greatly, as was to be expected in an open process. This new mechanism did, however, provide a very direct link for individuals and groups to the process of drafting the Charter.

As far as the NGOs were concerned, the Convention invited them to an official 'hearing' on 27 April 2000. There was criticism from several civil society organisations and NGOs who claimed that the hearings were held too early in the process, i.e. before a full draft of the Convention was available to comment on.[124] Moreover, Olivier de Schutter argues that the criteria for selecting NGOs to be invited for the hearings should be reviewed critically because as they were applied they lacked transparency and accountability.[125] This suggestion of course raises the wider issue of how to organise the interaction between the institutionalised political process and civil society, and the tricky question how to balance any kind of regulation of this interaction against the potential damage it might do to the freedom and spontaneity of civil society, to the detriment of its legitimation role in the political process.[126]

The Convention's Secretary, responsible for organising the hearings, insisted that the only criterion of selection employed in choosing the NGOs to be included, was that the groups had to be 'active at European level'. Jean-Paul Jacqué claimed that on this basis, 'virtually all the groups who had expressed an interest in being heard, could be invited'.[127] He also acknowledged, however, that the possibility of presenting points of view in five-minute statements in a marathon of more than sixty presentations, was probably not the best way to ensure a broad public involvement, and he emphasised that the main contributions of the NGOs to the Charter were therefore the written statements received by the Convention. Yet, even if the hearings were inadequate as a means to broaden substantive deliberation, the mere presence of the NGOs in the Convention was an important expression of the wider dimensions of the Charter. It created the backdrop to frequent reference by Convention members, in subsequent debates, to the wishes expressed by civil society.[128]

As for the involvement of the ten applicant countries who then acceded to the EU on 1 May 2004, plus Bulgaria, Romania and Turkey, it has to be noted that even more than in the case of the NGOs, the symbolic value of the invitation itself was significant, rather than a substantial involvement of the applicants' views. This was, however, partly due to the applicant countries' own reluctance to become more engaged. All thirteen countries participated in the hearing on 19 June, but the comments they made on the Charter project were in most cases of a very general nature.[129] This reflected the fact that the hearings were held *before* a complete draft Charter was available for them to comment on. Unsurprisingly, at this general level all applicants supported the idea of an additional document of fundamental rights.[130] While there was some disagreement on the legal status the applicants envisaged for the new Charter,[131] this hearing did not lead to any substantial debate either in the Convention, or in the domestic political arenas of the candidate countries themselves (see below). There was, however, a general expression of interest among all applicants for further consultation once a draft Charter would have emerged. It is unclear, why this second round of formal exchange of views did not take place. The Convention presidium apparently took the view that individual applicant countries could still express their views via the website, or through letters to the presidium, which they chose not to do. Generally, attempts by the author to clarify the applicant countries' position vis-à-vis the Charter at later stages revealed a very low interest in the process and its further implications for enlargement.[132]

This account of the involvement of the applicant countries in the Charter process reveals that here a clear opportunity to broaden deliberation in order to enhance the external legitimation basis of the European Union, especially in the applicant countries, was missed. From the EU side the involvement of the not-yet member states was dogged by the problem that it would have seemed excessive to involve them fully in decision-making about a Union of which they were not yet members.[133] Yet, as it stood, the inclusion of the applicants was too formalised and at too early a stage to generate a real feeling of involvement on their part. In their turn, the national administrations in the applicant countries seem to have judged the Charter process as marginal to their immediate strategic aim of early accession, and therefore limited their involvement to an expression of general subservience, with only very minor concerns for either the political or the legal substance of the project. Thus it is not surprising that in the applicant countries the whole process of drafting a Charter of Rights seems to have gone largely unnoticed. In reaction to this disappointing result, the Convention on the Future of Europe gave the candidate countries a much stronger role.

Fundamental deliberation

The results from the assessment of the deliberation in the Charter process are thus mixed. The Convention provided a deliberative setting in most respects, and this is supported by the Convention members' own account of the process. As far as Jeffrey Checkel's criteria for the individual qualities of effective deliberators are concerned, the Convention united a body of people who had, and further developed, a common sense of purpose during the debates. The quality of the exchanges was helped by their shared expertise in the area of human rights. Yet, the procedure by which Convention members were selected in their 'home' institutions to participate in the deliberations were not always clear. These shortcomings did not, however, limit the appeal of the Charter Convention as a model for the next deliberative exercise at EU constitutional level. Since any democratic structure has to strike internal balances between freedom and efficiency, between access to the debates by all, and the level of complexity and expertise required to address it, the Charter Convention did not do so badly and in many respects better than the larger, more diverse and more politically 'charged' Constitutional Convention.[134]

In a real world situation like the Convention there can be no 'pure' deliberation. Recognising this, Adam Przeworski for example criticises some theorists of deliberation (notably Joshua Cohen) for wishing 'away the vulgar fact that under democracy deliberation ends in voting'.[135] Even though the Convention did not formally 'vote', this criticism alerts us to the important problem that collective decision-making is subject to constraints of time, and the requirements of efficiency. In the concrete case of the deliberations on the Charter, on several occasions the presidium decided to end a debate when it deemed a sufficient consensus to have been reached. Since these decisions were not verified by votes, at various points criticism was expressed with regard to the 'arbitrary' decisions by the presidium, and the lack of transparency in its workings.[136] This is an issue that any deliberative arrangement must address if it wants to ensure the legitimacy of its decisions.

Nevertheless, even though the final consensus reached does 'cover' certain remaining differences, this consensus is a more substantial result than a mere aggregation of individual interests into a majority vote. It underlines that an exchange about fundamental rights provided a number of significant characteristics which favoured deliberation. Despite the insufficiencies of the process (such as those of the choice, accountability, and equality of its members, the constraints imposed by the time scale, and by practical limitations to the involvement of the wider public), the deliberative element of the Charter process was an important contribution to the legitimation of EU-level political organi- sation and has become an important precedent. Especially when one measures the Charter process against the classical method of constitutional-level decision-making in the EU, the Convention marks a significant advancement on the traditional settings such as the diplomatic, secretive, and power-game-ridden IGCs,[137] or purely advi- sory, non-accountable, and unrepresentative expert committees in the area of fundamental rights. Given that the deliberations about the Charter did not take place in a constitutional vacuum, but reflect the essential 'inbetweenness' of the EU, whose nature is determined by its duality of being a union of both states and people, the particular combination of different institutional backgrounds in the Convention seems very appropriate.

The Charter's role in legitimating the EU: what does it mean?

Regime legitimacy and polity legitimacy

This chapter has tried to assess the impact of the Charter on both aspects of the EU's legitimacy, the legitimacy of the Union as a new polity, and the legitimacy of its regime. Bellamy and Castiglione link two dimensions of the political process (i.e. the questions of its subjects and its sphere) to the legitimacy of a polity, and two (i.e. styles and scope of the political process) to the regime's legitimacy.[138] With this set of distinctions it becomes possible to evaluate the three levels of impact of the Charter project, with regard to their effect on the different aspects of legitimacy. Yet, as was argued in Chapter 2, the link between fundamental rights and the legitimacy of a political order is a complex one precisely because the two levels of legitimacy are often not clearly distinguishable. The ability of a political order to protect its members' fundamental rights is one of the main reasons for which individuals might decide to relinquish part of their individual freedom and form collective structures endowed with coercive power. As has been argued above, the EU increasingly invokes this function as one of the legitimation sources for its own existence. The problem is that this strategy of legitimation raises touchy questions of the legitimate subjects and spheres of EU politics – and thus has an ambiguous effect on the EU's legitimacy.[139]

At the same time, the respect of fundamental rights is also a necessary precondition for the legitimacy of a democratic regime: a political system that violates certain fundamental rights of its members cannot be legitimate. Yet, given the fact that fundamental rights, despite the rhetoric usually associated with them, are neither absolute nor universal, the problem of the political process is to establish a balance between different individual rights, and between rights and those collective powers which are necessary to enforce them.[140] Thus the supposed mere restatement of existing rights in a new catalogue in the EU's case turned as a matter of course into a reconfiguration of the scope and styles of politics in the Charter debates. This was inevitable because on the one hand the Charter contains important rights which organise the political process to achieve such a balance. On the other hand, the process of negotiating the Charter, with its capacity to bring the four dimensions of the political process into the open, and with its deliberative elements, itself had to strike a balance of this kind. This, however, brings us back to the criticism that the creation of a new 'solemnly proclaimed' document at that moment in time, rather than animating the necessary political debate, precluded (and precludes) more pragmatic, more concrete steps to improve the protection of fundamental rights.

'Genuine' human rights policy vs. Charter symbolism

On this basis, there are critical voices with regard to the Charter's capacity to improve the EU's overall legitimacy in a broader political process.

Admittedly, the codification of rights into a legal document, as in the case of the Charter, is just one way of balancing them, and even rights which have been codified need to be interpreted and balanced either in a political or in a legal process. It is for this reason that the mere invocation of fundamental rights as a 'founding principle' of a polity (the EU in this case) is not enough to 'prove' the polity's legitimacy. In this sense, Weiler's view that '[f]ar more important than any Charter for the effective vindication of human rights would be a simple Treaty amendment which made the active protection of human rights within the sphere of application of Community law one of the policies of the Community',[141] seems very much to the point.

Armin von Bogdandy, however, is very critical of Weiler's argument. Taking issue with the demand for a '"comprehensive and forward looking"' human rights policy' for the EU, articulated very clearly by Weiler and Alston in their report to the *Comité des Sages* in 1999,[142] von Bogdandy expresses the fear that such a policy could 'easily endanger the European constitutional setup between the Union and the Member states', especially '[g]iven the strong centralizing effects' such a policy would inevitably have.[143] In von Bogdandy's analysis, it would lead to an illegitimate expansion of the scope of EU politics, because it would only be effective if it encompassed a very broad range of economic and social rights, which are largely still exclusive national competencies.[144] Von Bogdandy, unfortunately, does not provide a final evaluation of how he thinks the Charter (which already contains, as he notes, 'something for almost every aspect of life') will ultimately affect the EU's human rights policy.[145] Instead, he proposes a restructuring of EU law which would make human rights the 'axis of the European legal system', and concludes: 'The core objectives [of the EU] should, for the moment at least, remain peace, wealth and an ever closer union among its peoples. Human rights, though important, should not be understood as the *raison d'être* of the Union.'[146]

The evidence gathered and analysed in this study suggests, however, that the Charter process holds at least the potential to pay more than mere lip-service to a dangerously misunderstood, or cynically reduced, notion of human rights. The Charter process was significant precisely because it showed the political means to avoid the danger perceived by von Bogdandy, by subjecting all dimensions of the political process to deliberative public debate. With regards to Weiler's criticism of the Charter as distracting from a 'real' human rights policy based on the EU's accession to the ECHR, it has to be noted that this addresses only the role of rights in legitimating the polity as a protector of rights.[147]

The legitimacy of the political regime within whose framework this occurs, however, requires a debate about the rights themselves in relation to this particular political structure. Simply taking an existing list of rights (such as the ECHR for example), and making it the focus of an EU rights protection policy, would not have generated the same kind of interaction between the normative principles underlying the polity, and the means by which they are supposed to be realised, as the debates in the Charter Convention did. Admittedly, the process was not perfect, and if it had stopped with the proclamation of the Charter it would indeed have had to be considered a dangerous instance of 'freezing' the rights debate. The subsequent events which led to the drafting of the European Constitution including the Charter as well as a commitment to accession to the ECHR show, however, that the constitutional dynamism which animated the Charter process continues to move the debate forward even within an enlarged Union.

Conclusion: the Charter and the future of Europe

In the face of the biggest enlargement to date of its membership, the EU had to assure itself, its current and prospective members, the world at large, and, above all, its people, that it is worth having an organisation of this kind. In order to do so, it needed to determine what it is there to achieve, for whom, and how it is doing it. Otherwise neither widening nor deepening of European integration can be legitimate. Therefore, the Union needed (and still needs) to define the sphere, scope, subjects, and styles of its political endeavour. The problem in doing so, which made the situation in 1999–2000 different from previous attempts to clarify one or the other of the four dimensions (see Chapter 3), was the fact that the EU needed to find one balance between the four dimensions then (i.e. prior to enlargement), knowing full well that with enlargement, this balance would be disturbed, and would have to be renegotiated. At a very basic level, an enlargement to include the ten new member countries which eventually joined in 2004 meant an increase in the 'subjects' of politics in the EU by more than 75 million people.

With this ongoing process of adding new *subjects* of integration, profound changes affect all other dimensions of politics. Contemporarily, the debate about the *spheres* of EU policy continues, in particular focusing on the fundamental question of Europe's role in the world and a further development of Europe's foreign and security policy capabilities (including the military option), and the contention about the distribution of competencies between the different levels, which in fact regard both scope and spheres. Moreover, the desperate need for a comprehensive reform of the financial system of the EU (including CAP) had already become clearly unavoidable before the 2004 enlargement. This and the continued problems of Europe's economy and competitiveness threw up questions over the right *scope* of redistributive politics at the EU level, and the debate continues. Finally, one important focus of this investigation has been the issue of the *style* of EU politics. With the rapid changes to the other three dimensions, the need to find styles which ensure that adjustments can be made continuously in a way which involves the citizens in the changes, and thus makes them acceptable, becomes ever more pressing.

Previous sections of this chapter have presented the Charter's legal repercussions as an extension of the rights with which the EU protects its citizens and have looked at the Convention as an important forum to debate the general constitutional framework of the EU polity. The Charter and its process therefore broadened the EU's polity legitimacy by discursively extending the sphere of integration in the area of the protection of fundamental rights. The debates also raised the question of how far the EU can be active in this sphere (i.e. the scope) of the EU's regime. By promoting a wider constitutional debate, the Charter exercise became a key stepping stone for the process in which the other elements of legitimacy could be and had to be addressed, and it thus set the parameters for the constitutional debates which followed. With their consolidation and extension of the EU discourses of common values and a common identity, the Charter debates advanced the common understanding of these bases, and thus improved the conceptual tools to define the subjects and the sphere of the EU polity, and the scope and style of its regime. The Convention also became a model for a more thorough and more inclusive debate about the EU's aims and functioning based on a deliberative mode of interaction and decision-making. The first Convention experience in this view improved the legitimacy of the EU regime by showing how a new style could be used to balance the other dimensions. Neither the Charter nor its process provided definite solutions to any of the problems of the EU in its development from an international cooperation arrangement into a new form of supra-, trans-, or intra-national governance, but they crucially showed how far we had come by the turn of the millennium and before the biggest enlargement in the Union's history.

The Charter and the Charter process therefore provide benchmarks against which to measure the legitimacy (or lack thereof) of the EU. On this basis the EU has to continue its search for new balances of legitimacy which can sustain the next steps in integration. The changes in response to enlargement and global development create a series of demands on the EU's political system. In responding to them, it has to find ways to allow individuals to participate in collective decision-making. To be able to do so, the participating individuals need to be informed and empowered. At the same time, the system must have the capacity to react effectively and efficiently to changing demands. It must itself be seen as legitimate in order to command the powers which are necessary to do so. The expectations of the individuals, their own political activity, the legitimacy of the political system, and its capacity to meet the expectations of the citizens are therefore locked into a circular link. Deficiencies in one lead to problems in the others. In the case of the European institutions, there is widespread and growing concern that this circle has been broken (or indeed, had never been closed), and is becoming a spiral of growing discontent of the people, leading to a diminished legitimacy of the institutions and other political means to act, which in turn further limits their ability to act in order to meet the expectations of the people.[148] As this analysis has shown, the way to break out of this spiral is a broader and continuous constitutional process which clarifies the expectations and the necessary political powers to fulfil them, and thus provides the basis to find a sustainable balance of legitimacy which takes account of the numerous facets of this concept, in the particular and changing setting of the EU.

6
Linking Rights, Process and Legitimacy

The Charter process as a legitimating exercise

In the year 2000, the European Union had reached a crossroads. New challenges were pressing on the Union, and change was inevitable – but this has always been the case since the integration project was embarked upon, and it continues to be the case even after a draft Constitution has been adopted. The dynamic ability of the process of integration to meet such challenges in the past is in fact its single most astonishing feature. This dynamic nature of the Union poses a great number of difficulties both for those who are trying to shape the process, and for those who are trying to describe and analyse it. The European Union remains a 'moving target'. Successive rounds of enlargement profoundly affect the nature of the EU as we believe to know it, and the underlying questions which were forced into the limelight by the prospect of a massive enlargement in 2004 remain topical: What is the EU? What should it do for whom? How can it act effectively and efficiently? How can it involve its people in the processes of decision-making? Satisfactory answers to all these questions at every given stage of integration are indispensable if the Union and its activities are to be acceptable to its people. They determine the Union's legitimacy.

Against this background, the heads of state and government of the fifteen EU member states decided in July 1999 that a Charter of Fundamental Rights should be drafted. The immediate aim of this exercise, as indicated in the Cologne mandate, was to make the fundamental rights that had developed in the fifteen member states, and in the Union itself, visible to Europe's people. The perceived need to do so was based on the notion that fundamental rights are simultaneously a founding principle of the European integration

162

project and a necessary pre-requisite for it to be legitimate. Departing from this understanding of the link between rights and legitimacy, this book has presented an analytical framework and empirical evidence to show what contribution the EU Charter of Fundamental Rights, and the process by which it was drafted, made and make to a more legitimate European Union. The short answer to this question is that the Charter project improved the EU's legitimacy because it provided for the first time a forum and a focus for clarifying and consolidating the four dimensions of the EU political process through democratic debate and thus enabled, and set the stage for, the constitutional debate which followed.

The main argument in support of this claim is that the Charter, even before it was included in the draft Constitution, already affected the EU's legitimacy in ways which went far beyond its narrow legal content. The Charter and the Charter process generated a debate about the four core dimensions of politics at the European level and thus contributed to the ongoing process of clarifying whom European integration is all about, which areas of politics should be treated as the spheres of European integration, how far integration can and should go in these areas, and by which means such integration may be achieved. These debates are essential elements in the wider political process which is necessary to constitute, and continuously to reconstitute, the legitimacy of the new political order that is the EU. The way these debates were framed in the context of drafting the EU Charter consequently provided a key point of reference for the wider discussions which followed on the EU Constitution.

By combining the empirical evidence collected during the working of the Charter Convention with the theoretical accounts of the role of fundamental rights in legitimating a political order, and the historical perspective on past attempts by European institutions to address the legitimacy problem, this analysis adds to the wider debate about the EU's legitimacy at two levels. On the one hand, it shows that a differentiated approach to the notion of legitimacy, combining the distinction between the legitimacy of a polity and the legitimacy of the regime, with a focus on the three core elements of input, output, and identity-related legitimacy,[1] is helpful in understanding the particular problems of EU legitimacy. On the other hand, the study shows how the concrete case of the EU Charter fits into the EU's ongoing efforts to legitimate itself, and what consequences can be drawn from the particular successes and failures in this case.

The Charter's significance

In order to assess its impact, the Charter of Fundamental Rights project had to be placed in the broader context of the ongoing, and intensifying debate about the EU's *'finalité'* (Chapter 1). Taking its inspiration from the text of the Cologne mandate, the link between the protection of fundamental rights and the legitimacy of any political order was established as the starting point for the analysis. The overall guiding question 'what effect does the EU Charter of Fundamental Rights, and the process by which it was drafted, have on the legitimacy of the European Union?' then had to be linked to the theoretical foundations of the EU's legitimacy problem.

This issue was pursued through the question 'What is the link between the legitimacy of a political order, and a body of fundamental rights which inform the organisation of this order?' (Chapter 2). The analysis brought out the role of rights as both limits to, and as essential elements of, the organisation of individuals into communities endowed with collective force. Two different notions of individual rights, as 'natural' and therefore pre-political facts on the one hand, and as inter-subjectively recognised and therefore political arrangements on the other, were identified as significant for the fundamental rights discourse at EU level. Accounts of legitimacy in the EU context usually do contain a rights-related element, as well as elements of identity, and of efficiency or effectiveness. The link between rights and legitimacy therefore has to be sensitive to the complexity of the concept of legitimacy.

Rights fulfil a dual function also with regard to legitimacy because they constitute a minimum standard for the polity, but at the same time rights and their realisation are a central element of the polity's operation (the regime). Following the idea of 'deliberative democracy' as formulated by Jürgen Habermas, it was maintained that in order to understand the link between them, rights and legitimacy need to be integrated with a process-based concept of democracy. The concept of legitimacy also needs to be refined by separating the legitimacy of the existence of a polity from the legitimacy of the regime operating in that polity. It then became possible to see the definition of a body of fundamental rights (as in the case of drafting the EU Charter), as an eminently political act which defined both core parts of the polity *and* the rules of its operation, and which also acted as a test-case for the legitimate functioning of the polity.

The third chapter presented the specific problems of legitimacy which beset the European Union, and the attempts which have been made by

European institutions to address them. The central challenge for the Union in this context was and is the EU's 'polity-problem', i.e. the question of what exactly the EU is, what it is there to do, and how. This problem directly affects the expectations that people have from the Union, and therefore its legitimacy. In reaction to the growing awareness of a problem in this area, different actors in the integration process over the years have attempted different strategies to provide the emerging new political order with a self-sustained legitimacy. Thus, the question 'What action has been taken in the past by actors in the European Union to improve the legitimacy of the Union?', was explored by presenting different EU 'strategies of legitimation', i.e. attempts to create a European identity; moves to improve the EC/EU's output efficiency/effectiveness; and changes aimed at improving the democratic input into the European political process.

These different initiatives were only partially successful, mainly because of the lack of a comprehensive framework for discussing and addressing the relationship between the EU polity and its constituent members, i.e. the citizens. The idea of creating a European citizenship was therefore examined in more detail because it was the most far-reaching attempt to tackle the EU's legitimacy problem up until the European Constitution was drafted. The analysis of the gradual construction of a notion of European citizenship is instructive in two respects with regard to the impact of the EU Charter. On the one hand, the Charter itself reiterates and thus politically strengthen the rights conferred upon Europeans under European citizenship. On the other hand, the development of EU citizenship over the years also provides a very useful case study of the discursive construction of the points of reference for the legitimacy debate.

Following ideas proposed by Antje Wiener on the 'routinisation' and eventual 'institutionalisation' of citizenship 'practices', the Charter drafting can be read as another instance in which important discursive elements of the citizenship and rights concepts were consolidated and expanded. Yet, in this the Convention was only one part of the wider development of the EU. The notions of EU constitutionalism and the Union's constitutional process provide the necessary analytical framework in which the Charter's implications become visible. Thus, the reply to the question 'How does the definition of a set of fundamental rights for a particular polity affect the legitimacy of that polity, in this case the EU?', is that the drafting of a Fundamental Rights Charter proved important because it was an important first step towards the institutionalisation of the constitutional process at European level.

To illustrate these claims, Chapter 4 focused on four key variables which determined the impact of the Charter project: the debate about the 'purpose' of the Charter, the role played by the concept of a 'European identity' in the debates, the discourse of Europe as a 'community of values', and the distinguishing features of the process in the Convention. These variables reflect at an empirical level the four dimensions of the political process which had been identified in Chapter 1. They throw light on the question 'What other elements contributed to the effect of the Charter project on the European Union's legitimacy?'

It emerged that the purpose of the undertaking was much less clear than the statement in the Cologne mandate had suggested. The mandate itself was seen as ambiguous by the Convention, and this very ambiguity was an important factor in broadening the dialogue about a limited number of fundamental rights into a general debate about the legitimate sphere of integration. Second, the look at the role of the European identity notion in the Charter process confirmed that the definition of fundamental rights did in fact raise the question of who these rights would be for, and what kind of polity an EU defined by such rights would be. Since the Cologne mandate had included rights pertaining only to EU citizens among those to be listed in the Charter, the new document was perceived by many members of the Convention as a way to give 'substance' to the notion of European citizenship. The Charter therefore had to find a new balance of inclusion and exclusion in defining the subjects of European integration.

Chapter 3 also showed how the notions of identity and common values had been explored by institutional actors in the past in order to find a firmer basis for defining the scope of European integration. By restating Europe's common values, the Charter moved this debate onto a new level. The controversies in the Charter Convention both about the precise purpose of the process (see above), and about the link of the new document to its historical and cultural context, revealed clearly the need to find a common understanding of the normative foundations of European integration. The issue became particularly visible in the exchanges about the Union's preamble. The disagreement over the reference to Europe's religious heritage and the subsequent compromise for a preamble show that a relatively broad basis of abstract common values existed. This set of values was expanded by the Charter debates to also include the concepts of 'human dignity', and a more pronounced commitment to 'solidarity' as a common value. Yet, the Charter process also showed that there were still widely diverging views with regard to the translation of these values into more concrete political action. The

Constitutional Convention could pick up the debate where the Charter Convention left off, but the resurfacing of the question of 'God' in the constitutional Convention has shown that on this question no 'consensus' has been built yet in the EU of now 25 member states.[2]

The final question was: 'What effect does the process by which a catalogue of fundamental rights was agreed upon, have on the EU's legitimacy?' It became clear early on that the process would be a significant part of the project's contribution to European integration both in the Convention, and in its public perception. The original provisions setting up the body allowed the Convention to develop its new approach, because they stipulated the special composition of the body of national and European parliamentarians (i.e. a majority of elected members), as well as government representatives and a member of the European Commission, but they also left some room for interpreting the rules on the functioning of the assembly. The Tampere mandate had charged the Convention with finding a 'consensus' and with working in public, thus encouraging a deliberative style of debate. At the same time, however, the instructions given by the Council had significant gaps (choice of Convention members, exact meaning of consensus, etc.). On the one hand, these ambiguities gave the body an opportunity to deliberate on its own functioning, but on the other hand they created problems which affected the legitimacy of the process itself. The most significant of these was the unclear role of the presidium in guiding the debates, and in deciding on their results. Despite these flaws, however, the process was successful in that it produced a document which was accepted nearly unanimously, in a comparatively short period of time.

Bringing these empirical findings together with the evidence from historical precedent and from the theoretical investigation of the link between rights, legitimacy and democratic process, Chapter 5 discussed how the Charter process, even if it produced at first a non-binding, non-justiciable document, could have a significant impact on the EU's legitimacy because it provided the model for a political process which is necessary to adjust the legitimacy balance of the developing EU polity. The Charter's impact became visible at three different levels: at the legal level, as a step in the development of European discourses on fundamental rights and the EU as a community of values, and as a trial-run instance for a deliberative setting for EU constitutional decision-making.

Even as a political declaration the Charter is already becoming legalised through the use which is made of it before the European Court of Justice as a point of reference for the interpretation of fundamental rights. With the inclusion of the Charter rights in the EU Constitution, the process which the Charter debates set in motion is bound to go on towards a more comprehensive EU human rights policy. At the second level of effect, the Charter debates enabled and encouraged the further discursive construction of certain concepts which became routinised in and through the Convention and now shape policy options and courses of reasoning or action for actors in the EU context. The example of the sanctions against a far-right party in the Austrian governing coalition by fourteen EU member states in 2000 illustrated how the discourse of a European community of values was already influencing political decision-making while the Convention was still debating the foundations of Europe's value system. The Charter debates, though not directly linked to the Austrian case, provided the most comprehensive expression at the time, of those values which were supposedly sustaining the European community of values. By discussion and ultimately agreeing on a set of fundamental values as common to Europe, the Charter debates responded to Europe's perceived need to strengthen its common value basis in order to legitimate integration before enlargement.

Finally, the Convention method itself was tested for the first time in drafting an EU Charter of Fundamental Rights. The process did show important structural features which encouraged open and generally free deliberation, and these elements of the process enhanced the legitimacy of the overall outcome. Even though the Convention was not a perfect 'deliberative setting' in Jon Elster's terms, in particular because of the problems of the selection of Convention members and their weak accountability, the process proved successful: agreement was reached in the end by nearly all members of the Convention as a result of mostly high-quality debate, on a range of issues which had looked at times as being very far from agreement indeed. The exchanges also reached a broader group of interested individuals (albeit this is mainly true for a still restricted EU-level élite) and opened up the constitutional questions to a wider public. The process was thus seen by most EU-level actors as such a useful addition to the more traditional styles of EU politics that they decided to use the Convention method again only two years later.

Defining the nature of the beast by the air it breathes

Puchala's famous analogy of the European Community as a 'beast', which is only inadequately defined by its constituent parts, continues to be a lucid description of the problems of the EU polity, despite the fact that not all people touching parts of the elephant may be 'blind', and an increasing number of them try their 'luck' at finding new definitions and descriptions.[3] As the process of integration goes on, however, it becomes increasingly clear that the beast itself has an identity crisis, especially at moments when the direction in which it is trotting, or even galloping, is unclear. The attempt to define the nature of the beast by investigating the conditions of its existence, the shape of its cage, the foodstuff it thrives on, the very air it breathes, therefore seems a valuable contribution to the overall understanding of the EU fauna. Researching the somewhat 'airy' subject of 'legitimacy' is precisely such an attempt to address a largely invisible, but at the same time indispensable, element of the survival of the EU.

A functioning balance of legitimacy is a *conditio sine qua non* of the continued existence and development of a European level of political organisation. Yet, as Philippe Schmitter notes, legitimacy 'usually enters the analytical picture when it is missing or deficient'.[4] As has been discussed, legitimacy is so difficult to define because of its subjective and often emotive nature, and because of the disagreement about which elements are important in constituting the legitimacy of a given political structure. At the same time, political actors, and everybody with common sense, seems to have certain notions of what legitimacy means. One such notion is that expressed in the Cologne mandate's proclamation that 'the protection of fundamental rights is a . . . prerequisite for its [the EU's] legitimacy'. This supposedly self-evident understanding of legitimacy then became the trigger and the justification for a major policy initiative: namely, the creation of a new body of fundamental rights for the European Union. The aim of this book was to critically examine the link between fundamental rights and legitimacy as it transpired from the Cologne mandate. By showing that, and how, fundamental rights and the process of defining them affected the legitimacy of the European Union, the concept of legitimacy itself becomes clearer: it is a label for an acceptable and credible balance achieved by the subjects of the political process (or their representatives) on the sphere, scope, and styles of the polity.

The drafting of the EU Charter of Fundamental Rights represented a particularly good opportunity to investigate this problem empirically, as well as theoretically, because the Charter Convention provided the first set of comprehensive, and easily accessible institutionalised debates on the issues concerned at the EU level. The Charter and the Convention brought the core legitimacy issues into the open in a concentrated form. Moreover, unlike the more general 'public-political debate', which also touches on the questions of scope, sphere, subjects, or styles of the political process in a more general fashion from time to time, the Charter project provided a context in which decisions had to be taken which then had to be cast in the comparative solidity of legal language. This made it easier to detect changes in perception or points of view within this process and thus allowed to test some of the theoretical assumptions about the normally evasive question of what constitutes the legitimacy of the European Union.

As we know well by now, many issues that achieved prominence in the Charter process could not be laid to rest with the answers found in the first Convention. The larger questions about the role of the European Union in the world, about how to bring the Union closer to its citizens, how to organise the institutional structure of an enlarged EU efficiently and effectively and what to do with the Charter of Fundamental Rights itself could not be 'solved' legitimately by the intergovernmental conference at Nice which followed the Charter Convention. Already one year later, at the European summit at Laeken in December 2001, the time was ripe to set up a new Convention to debate these questions and at least explore the possibility of a 'path towards a Constitution for the citizens of Europe'.[5] The story of this Convention, its debates and its product, the European Constitution, is told elsewhere.[6] With this second Convention the experience from the Charter Drafting process and especially the procedural innovations in order to improve the legitimacy of the EU through a deliberative process on fundamental questions, were validated. In order to place these individual instances of constitutional change on the continuum of the EU's constitutionalisation, it is useful to assess their specific contribution on form, substance, and perception of European integration. The concept of legitimacy is one possible prism through which such an analysis can be undertaken. The Charter-making experience is therefore an important piece in the fascinating jigsaw puzzle that is the European polity.

Appendix: Convention Members Interviewed

Name	Institution (nationality)	Party	Interview date
Berthu, Georges	MEP (F)	RPF/NI	15.09.2000
Bowness, Lord	Nat. Parl. (House of Lords) (GB)	Conservative	11.07.2000
Braibant, Guy	Nat. Gov. (F)		30.06.2000
Duff, Andrew	MEP (GB)	Liberal Democrats/ ELDR	25.05.2000
Einem, Caspar	Nat. Parl. (lower house) (A)	SPÖ	18.07.2000
Friedrich, Ingo	MEP (D)	CSU/EPP	02.05.2000
Goldsmith, Lord Peter	Nat. Gov. (GB)	Labour	17.07.2000
Griffith, Wyn	Nat. Parl. (House of Commons) (GB)	Labour	04.04.2000
Hirsch-Ballin, Ernst	Nat. Parl. (Senat) (NL)	CDA	26.09.2000
Jacque, Jean-Paul	Council Secretariat (F)		13.04.2000
Jansson, Gunnar	Nat. Parl. (FIN)	SFP	06.06.2000
Kaufmann, Sylvia	MEP (D)	PDS/GUE-NGL	20.09.2000
Korthals-Altes, Frederik	Nat. Gov. (NL)	VVD	18.07.2000
Magnusson, Jöran	Nat. Parl. (S)	SAP	25.09.2000
Melograni, Piero	Nat. Parl. (lower house) (I)	Forza Italia	30.06.2000
Méndez de Vigo, Iñigo	MEP (E)	PP/EPP	11.10.2000
Meyer, Jürgen	Nat. Parl. (lower house) (D)	SPD	10.07.2000
Mombaur, Peter	MEP (D)	CDU/EPP	14.09.2000
Neisser, Heinrich	Nat. Gov. (A)	ÖVP	06.06.2000
Pateijn, Michiel	Nat. Parl. (lower house) (NL)	VVD	18.07.2000
Rodotà, Stefano	Nat. Gov. (I)	DS	04.04.2000
Tarschys, Daniel	Nat. Gov. (S)	Liberal	11.05.2000
Vitorino, Antonio	Commission (P)	PSD	30.06.2000
Voggenhuber, Johannes	MEP (A)	Grüne/Verts-ALE	10.10.2000

Notes

1 The EU Charter of Fundamental Rights: Legitimating the European Union

1. The expression is taken from Gráinne de Búrca, 'The Quest for Legitimacy in the European Union', *Modern Law Review*, 59 (1996), 348–76.
2. The 2001 Commission White Paper on 'European Governance' substituted the term 'good governance' for 'legitimacy' but was concerned with many of the issues discussed below, see European Commission, *European Governance: a White Paper*, COM (2001) 428 final, Brussels (2001).
3. This literature is discussed below in Chs 2 and 3.
4. On composition and working method of the 'Convention' see also Ch. 4.
5. European Council meeting at Cologne, 3/4 June 1999, Conclusions of the Presidency, Annex IV.
6. Such scepticism was voiced more clearly during the debates of the Convention itself, but it has also been expressed since, see for example T. Kirkhope 'Charter of Fundamental Rights, the Enhancement of Humans and the Curtailment of Human Rights?', in K. Feus (ed.) *The EU Charter of Fundamental Rights: text and commentaries* (Federal Trust for Education and Research, London, 2000).
7. This is the criticism formulated by Richard Bellamy for example in 'The "Right to Have Rights": Citizenship Practice and the Political Constitution of the EU', in R. Bellamy & A. Warleigh (eds) *Citizenship and Governance in the European Union* (Continuum, London, 2001); and by Joseph Weiler 'Does the European Union Truly Need a Charter of Rights?', editorial in *European Law Journal*, 6 (2000), 95–7. See Ch. 5 for a more detailed discussion of these criticisms.
8. This problem is discussed at a general level in Ch. 2, and with regard to the EU in Ch. 3.
9. Most theories of legitimacy seem to follow this three-pronged approach, albeit differing on the three individual elements. See D. Beetham, *The Legitimation of Power* (Macmillan – now Palgrave Macmillan, Basingstoke, 1991).
10. This understanding is particularly influential in the international human rights discourse (discussed in Ch. 2), see F. E. Dowrick (ed.) *Human Rights: Problems, Perspectives, Texts* (Saxon House, Farnborough, 1979).
11. This distinction is developed by Bellamy and Castiglione in: 'Normative Theory and the European Union', in L. Trägårdh (ed.) *After National Democracy: Rights, Law and Power in America and the New Europe* (Hart, Oxford, 2002); see also Ch. 2 and pp. 156–7 in this volume.
12. This conceptualisation of the link between rights and the political process is based on works by Jürgen Habermas, see Ch. 2.
13. The notion of the four dimensions of the political process is based on Bellamy 'The "Right to have Rights"' op. cit.

14. J. H. H. Weiler 'European Democracy and the Principle of Constitutional Tolerance: the Soul of Europe', in F. Cerutti & E. Rudolf (eds) *A Soul for Europe: a Reader* (*Vol. 1*) (Peeters, Leuven, 2001).
15. European Commission, *European Governance*, p. 3.

2 Legitimacy and Fundamental Rights

1. Within the scope of this book, the notions of 'fundamental rights' and 'human rights' will be used interchangeably unless explicitly stated otherwise. This practice is common in the EU context and while in some cases the distinction is necessary because ' "fundamental rights" . . . includes a number of rights which can quite properly be invoked for the protection of legal as well as natural persons', in the general discussion this distinction is not of major relevance. See J. Shaw, *Law of the European Union*, 3rd edn (Macmillan – now Palgrave Macmillan, Basingstoke, 2000), p. 331.
2. P. Craig, 'Constitutions, Constitutionalism, and the European Union', *European Law Journal*, 7 (2001) 125–50, 141.
3. J. Habermas, 'Zur Legitimation durch Menschenrechte', in J. Habermas, *Die postnationale Konstellation: Politische Essays* (Suhrkamp, Frankfurt a. M., 1998), 170–92, 173.
4. J. Habermas, *Faktizität und Geltung* (esp. Ch. 7), (Suhrkamp, Frankfurt a. M., 1998).
5. E. O. Eriksen, J. E. Fossum & A. J. Menéndez, 'The Charter in Context', in E. O. Eriksen, J. E. Fossum & A. J. Menendez, *The Chartering of Europe* (Nomos Verlag, Baden-Baden, 2003).
6. A. Heywood, *Key Concepts in Politics* (Macmillan – now Palgrave Macmillan, Basingstoke, 2000), p. 29.
7. M. Weber, 'Legitimacy, Politics and the State', in W. Connolly, *Legitimacy and the State* (Blackwell, Oxford, 1984), p. 33 (emphasis added).
8. D. Beetham, *The Legitimation of Power* (Macmillan – now Palgrave Macmillan, Basingstoke, 1991), p. 8.
9. Ibid. p. 12 ff.
10. Heywood, *Key Concepts*, p. 29.
11. J. Finnis, *Natural Law and Natural Rights* (1980, p. 205), quoted in R. Bellamy 'The Constitution of Europe: Rights or Democracy?', in R. Bellamy, V. Bufacchi & D. Castiglione, *Democracy and Constitutional Culture in the Union of Europe* (Lothian Foundation Press, London, 1995), p. 154.
12. P. Jones, *Rights: Issues in Political Theory* (Macmillan – now Palgrave Macmillan, Basingstoke, 1994), p. 1.
13. Heading 'Naturrecht' (natural law) in *Kröner's Philosophisches Wörterbuch* (G. Schischkoff, ed.), (Krönerverlag, Stuttgart, 1991), p. 501.
14. J. Waldron, 'Rights' in R. E. Gordon & P. Pettit (eds) *A Companion to Contemporary Political Philosophy* (Blackwell, Oxford 1995), p. 575.
15. Jones, *Rights*, p. 81.
16. Jones, *Rights*, p. 3. With regard to the EU Charter of Fundamental Rights it is interesting to note, however, that the term 'Human Rights' is not used in the text (with the exception of the reference to the ECHR), but is replaced by the term 'fundamental rights'.

17. R. Bellamy & J. Schönlau, 'The Normality of Constitutional Politics: an Analysis of the Drafting of the EU Charter of Fundamental Rights', *Constellations*, 11, (2004), 412–33.
18. Jones, *Rights*, p. 3.
19. The term is taken from Bellamy, *Liberalism and Pluralism*.
20. Paul M. Sniderman et al., *The Clash of Rights: Liberty, Equality and Legitimacy in Pluralist Democracy* (Yale University Press, New Haven/London, 1996), p. 11.
21. C. Attucci, 'An Institutional Dialogue on Common Principles: Reflections on the Significance of the EU Charter of Fundamental Rights', in L. Dobson & A. Follesdal (eds) *Political Theory and the European Constitution* (Routledge, London, 2004).
22. Formula taken from the preamble to the 'Universal Declaration of Human Rights' (1948), to which the European Convention explicitly refers in its opening considerations.
23. F. E. Dowrick 'Introduction', in Dowrick (ed.) *Human Rights*, p. 15.
24. See for example F. Tulkens (Judge at the European Court of Human Rights, Strasbourg) 'Towards a Greater Normative Coherence in Europe/ the Implications of the Draft Charter of Fundamental Rights of the European Union', *Human Rights Law Journal*, 21 (2000), 329–32. With the inclusion of the Charter of Fundamental Rights (with some changes, see Ch. 5) in the draft Treaty establishing a European Constitution, the Charter rights will of course become legally binding once the Treaty enters into force.
25. Bellamy, 'The Constitution', p. 162.
26. A. Ingram, *A Political Theory of Rights* (Clarendon Press, Oxford, 1994), p. 3.
27. On this debate in the Charter Convention, see also J. Schönlau 'New Values for Europe? Deliberation, Compromise and Coercion in Drafting the Preamble to the EU Charter of Fundamental Rights', in E. O. Eriksen et al., *Chartering Europe*, op. cit. – on the debates in the Convention drafting the Constitution, see T. V. Olsen, 'Europe: United under God? Or not?', in Dobson & Follesdal, *Political Theory*.
28. Ingram, *A Political Theory*, p. 9.
29. E. O. Eriksen 'Deliberative Supranationalism in the EU', in E. O. Eriksen & J. E. Fossum (eds) *Democracy in the European Union: Integration through Deliberation?* (Routledge, London, 2000), p. 51.
30. Bellamy. 'The Constitution', p. 158.
31. Ingram, *A Political Theory*, p. 3.
32. Bellamy & Schönlau, 'The Normality . . .' op. cit.
33. Ingram, *A Political Theory*, p. 3.
34. Ibid. p. 4 (emphasis added).
35. Jürgen Habermas, 'Die postnationale Konstellation und die Zukunft der Demokratie', in Habermas, *Die postnationale Konstellation*.
36. See J. H. H. Weiler and his 'no-demos' argument in J. H. H. Weiler, U. Haltern & F. Mayer, 'European Democracy and its Critique: Five Uneasy Pieces', *EUI Working Paper* RSC 95/11, Florence (1995).
37. See R. Falk, *Human Rights Horizons: the Pursuit of Justice in a Globalizing World* (Routledge, London, 2000).

38. See for example the discussion about A. S. Milward's account of the *The European Rescue of the Nation-State* (2nd edn, Routledge, London, 2000) and the discussion of the democratic deficit of the EU (Ch. 3).
39. Ingram, *A Political Theory*, p. 12 (emphasis added).
40. See Habermas, 'Zur Legitimation durch Menschenrechte'.
41. Weber, 'Legitimacy, Politics and the State', pp. 32–62. David Beetham's critical attitude towards Weber's contribution has already been highlighted, but even Beetham himself proposes a concept of legitimacy based on 'three dimensions': 1) conformity to established rules; 2) justification based on reference to shared beliefs; 3) consent. See Beetham, *The Legitimation of Power*.
42. For a critical discussion of this link, see J. Habermas, 'Recht und Moral' (the Tanner Lectures 1986), in Habermas, *Faktizität und Geltung*, pp. 541–99.
43. D. Beetham & C. Lord, *Legitimacy and the European Union* (Longman, London/New York, 1998), pp. 3–4.
44. M. Höreth 'No Way Out for the Beast? The Unsolved Legitimacy Problem of European Governance', *Journal of European Public Policy*, 6 (1999) 249–68.
45. F. W. Scharpf, *Regieren in Europa: Effektiv und Demokratisch?* (Campus Verlag, Frankfurt a. M., 1999).
46. J. E. Fossum 'Constitution-making in the European Union', in Eriksen & Fossum (eds) *Democracy in the European Union?*
47. Ibid. pp. 119–20.
48. Ibid. p. 137.
49. Bellamy & Castiglione, 'Normative Theory', p. 3.
50. Höreth, 'No Way Out for the Beast?', p. 265.
51. Habermas, 'Zur Legitimation durch Menschenrechte', p. 173.
52. Jones, *Rights*, esp. Ch. 5 'Justifying Human Rights'.
53. Ibid. p. 3.
54. Ibid.
55. Bellamy, 'The Constitution' (citing C. Lefort, *Democracy and Political Theory*, Cambridge University Press, 1988), p. 167.
56. Conclusions of the Cologne summit, Annex IV, 3/4. June 1999.
57. See E. O. Eriksen & J. E. Fossum (eds) *Democracy in the European Union* or C. Closa & J. E Fossum (eds) *Deliberative Constitutional Politics in the EU*, ARENA Report No. 5/04, Oslo 2004.
58. Habermas, 'Zur Legitimation durch Menschenrechte', p. 171.
59. Habermas, *Faktizität und Geltung*, p. 169.
60. R. Bellamy, 'The Political Form of the Constitution: the Separation of Powers, Rights and Representative Democracy', in R. Bellamy & D. Castiglione (eds) *Constitutionalism in Transformation: European and Theoretical Perspectives* (Blackwell, Oxford, 1996), p. 25.
61. Habermas, *Faktizität und Geltung*, p. 166.
62. R. Bellamy, 'Citizenship Beyond the Nation-State: the Case of Europe', in N. O' Sullivan (ed.) *Political Theory in Transition* (Routledge, London, 2000).
63. UN Declaration preamble, as quoted in M. J. Perry, *The Idea of Human Rights: Four Inquiries* (Oxford University Press, Oxford, 1998).
64. Jones, *Rights*, esp. Ch. 5.

65. Habermas, 'Zur Legitimation durch Menschenrechte', p. 177.
66. Ibid. p. 178, with a reference to I. Maus, *'Volkssouveränität und das Prinzip der Nichtintervention in der Friedensphilosophie Immanuel Kants'.*
67. Whether, and if so how, the rights enshrined in these documents are protected is, of course, a different matter. The concern here is, however, whether a common 'understanding' of these rights can be reached or already exists as the basis for political dialogue.
68. Habermas, 'Zur Legitimation durch Menschenrechte', p. 181.
69. See for example T. W. Wilson (Jr.) 'A Bedrock of Consensus of Human Rights', in A. H. Henkin (ed.) *Human Dignity: the Internationalization of Human Rights* (Aspen Institute, New York, 1979).
70. Bellamy, 'The "Right to have Rights"', p. 7.
71. Jo Shaw, 'Process and Constitutional Discourse in the European Union', *Journal of Law and Society*, 27 (2000), 4–37, 7.
72. A. Weale, 'Democratic Legitimacy and the Constitution of Europe', in Bellamy et al., *Democracy and Constitutional Culture*, p. 93.
73. See J. Schönlau et al., *The Making and Unmaking of the European Constitution* (working title, Palgrave Macmillan, Basingstoke, 2006, forthcoming).
74. It has to be noted that there is widespread agreement that the European Union is in a process of constitutionalisation. See J. H. H. Weiler, 'The Reform of European Constitutionalism', *Journal of Common Market Studies*, 35 (1997) 97–131; or J. H. H. Weiler, 'European Neo-constitutionalism: in Search of Foundations for the European Constitutional Order', in R. Bellamy & D. Castiglione (eds) *Constitutionalism in Transformation: European and Theoretical Perspectives* (Blackwell, Oxford, 1996). The question, however, is if this process in its present form provides sufficient legitimation or if there is a 'legitimacy deficit'.
75. Habermas, *Faktizität und Geltung*, Ch. 7.
76. E. O. Eriksen, 'Deliberative Supranationalism in the EU', in Eriksen & Fossum (eds) *Democracy in the European Union*, p. 49 (referring to Habermas 1984: 392).
77. E. O. Eriksen & J. E. Fossum, 'Post-national Integration', in Eriksen & Fossum (eds) *Democracy in the European Union*, p. 16.
78. See Bellamy & Castiglione, 'Normative Theory'.
79. Fossum, 'Constitution-making in the EU', p. 119.

3 What Kind of Legitimacy for the EU?

1. J. Blondel, R. Sinnott & P. Svensson, *People and Parliament in the European Union: Participation, Democracy, and Legitimacy* (Clarendon Press, Oxford, 1998).
2. The questions of 'support for the European Union' and of 'trust in its institutions' form part of the Eurobarometer surveys, but their message as to the legitimacy of the EU, or lack thereof, is ambiguous because respondents probably know that they are not realistically faced with an 'either–or' option regarding European integration. Thus even those who state that they would not mind if the European Union was abolished tomorrow, can safely say so because they know that it will not happen. At the same time,

the degree of legitimacy perceived cannot be quantified, but can at best be compared to the legitimacy vested in other institutions (the nation-state for example). See Blondel et al., *People and Parliament*.

3. Even though most commentators on the legitimacy problem maintain that it became visible only with the Maastricht ratification crises in 1992, they also agree that its roots lie at least partly in the founding treaties of the European Communities themselves. See for example M. Shackleton, 'The Internal Legitimacy Crises of the European Union', in A. W. Cafruny & C. Lankowski (eds) *Europe's Ambiguous Unity: Conflict & Consensus in the Post-Maastricht Era* (Lynne Rienner, Boulder/London, 1997).

4. See Daniela Obradovic, 'Policy Legitimacy and the European Union', *Journal of Common Market Studies*, 34 (1996), 191–221.

5. D. Puchala, 'Of Blind Men, Elephants and International Integration', *Journal of Common Market Studies*, 10 (1972), 267–84.

6. Proponents in the predominantly intergovernmental nature of the EU still hold, of course, that there is no real problem of legitimacy because 'the current institutional form of the EU may well be democratically legitimate' because the EU as it exists today is 'far narrower and weaker a federation than any extant national federation', and therefore does not require state-type legitimacy. Andrew Moravcsik, 'European Federalism: Rhetoric and Reality', in R. Howse & K. Nicolaidis (eds) *The Federal Vision: Legitimacy and Levels of Governance in the US and the EU* (Oxford University Press, Oxford, 2001), p. 163.

7. de Búrca, 'The Quest for Legitimacy', p. 352.

8. See Jo Shaw, 'Postnational Constitutionalism in the European Union', *Journal of European Public Policy*, 6 (1999), 579–97.

9. See in particular the speeches on Europe's Future by German Foreign Minister Fischer (Berlin, 12.05.2000), French President Chirac (German Bundestag, 27.06.2000), British Prime Minister Tony Blair (Warsaw, 07.10.2000) and other European leaders in recent years.

10. See for example G. A. Bermann, editorial: 'The European Union as a Constitutional Experiment', *European Law Journal*, 10 (2004), 363–70.

11. See I. van den Burg, 'Die EU Grundrechtecharta aus der Sicht eines Sozialen Europa', in S. Y. Kaufmann (ed.) *Grundrechtecharta der Europäischen Union: Mitglieder und Beobachter des Konvents berichten* (Europa-Union Verlag, Bonn, 2001).

12. R. Bellamy & A. Warleigh (eds) *Citizenship and Governance in the European Union* (Continuum, London, 2001).

13. A. D. Smith, *National Identity* (Penguin, London, 1991).

14. D. Chryssochoou, *Democracy in the European Union* (Tauris Academic Studies, London/New York, 1998).

15. See for example T. A. Börzel, 'Policy Networks: a New Paradigm of European Governance', *EUI Working Paper* RSC 97/19, Florence, 1997, p. 2.

16. See M. S. Archer, *Culture and Agency* (Cambridge University Press, Cambridge, 1988).

17. See A. E. Wendt, 'The Agent–Structure Problem in International Relations Theory', *International Organization*, 41 (1987), 335–70.

18. See for example M. O' Neill, *The Politics of European Integration: a Reader* (Routledge, London, 1996, especially Ch. 1).

19. On the 'mechanics' of integration, see for example A. S. Sweet & W. Sandholtz, 'Integration, Supranational Governance and the Institutionalization of the European Polity', in W. Sandholtz & A. Stone Sweet (eds) *European Integration and Supranational Governance* (Oxford University Press, Oxford, 1998).

20. For an overview of theories of integration see B. Rosamond, *Theories of European Integration* (Palgrave – now Palgrave Macmillan, Basingstoke, 2000).

21. M. O'Neill, 'Theorising the European Union: Towards a Post-Foundational Discourse', *Current Politics and Economics of Europe*, 9 (2000), 121–41.

22. D. Chryssochoou, 'Meta Theory and the Study of the European Union: Capturing the Normative Turn', *European Integration*, 22 (2000), 123–44.

23. Beetham & Lord, *Legitimacy*.

24. J. Thomassen & H. Schmitt, 'Introduction: Political Representation and Legitimacy in the European Union', in Thomassen & Schmitt (eds) *Political Representation and Legitimacy in the European Union* (Oxford University Press, Oxford, 1999), p. 9.

25. Bellamy, 'The "Right to have Rights"'.

26. Thomassen & Schmitt, 'Introduction', p. 10, quoting Dahl, *Democracy and its Critics*, p. 204.

27. On the problem of inclusive/exclusive notions of community in the EU context, see the exchange between T. Kostakopoulou, 'Why a "Community of Europeans" Could be a Community of Exclusion: a Reply to Howe', and P. Howe 'Insiders and Outsiders in a Community of Europeans: a Reply to Kostakopoulou', both *Journal of Common Market Studies*, 35 (1997), 301–14.

28. L. Friis & A. Murphy, 'The European Union and Central and Eastern Europe: Governance and Boundaries', *Journal of Common Market Studies*, 37 (1999), 211–32.

29. Ibid., p. 213.

30. In the context of the constitutional process since 2000, however, there is now a growing awareness of the link between the 'constitutional' development of the EU and continuous enlargement, see N. Walker 'Constitutionalising Enlargement, Enlarging Constitutionalism', *European Law Journal*, 9 (2003), 365–85.

31. Weiler, Haltern & Mayer, 'European Democracy', p. 1.

32. Bellamy, 'The "Right to Have Rights"'.

33. The notion of the 'permissive consensus' is taken from L. N. Lindberg & S. A. Scheingold, *Europe's Would-Be Polity: Patterns of Change in the European Community* (Englewood Cliffs, Prentice Hall, 1970).

34. T. Banchoff & M. P. Smith (eds) *Legitimacy and the European Union: the Contested Polity* (Routledge, London, 1999) p. 219.

35. The positive answers to the question whether membership in the Union is 'overall' considered to be 'a good thing' saw a sharp decline from their peak of 72% in spring 1991 [quoted in M. Glaab, 'Die Bürger in Europa', in W. Weidenfeld (ed.) *Europahandbuch*, Verlag Bertelsmann Stiftung, Gütersloh, 1999, p. 605], but have remained relatively stable around the 50% mark in recent years: Eurobarometer (EB) 50 (Autumn 1998): 54%

positive answers, 49%, EB 52 (April 2000), 50% in February 2001 (EB 54) and EB 61 (spring 2004) 48%.

36. de Búrca, 'The Quest for Legitimacy', p. 351 and footnote 9, p. 351.
37. See for example the Final Report of the Reflection Group: 'The Long-Term Implications of EU Enlargement: the Nature of the New Border' (Chairman Giulio Amato, Rapporteur Judy Batt), (Robert Schuman Centre EUI Forward Studies Unit, Florence 1999).
38. The European Commission calls this 'a real paradox: On the one hand, Europeans want them [European leaders collectively] to find solutions to the major problems confronting our societies. On the other hand, people increasingly distrust institutions and politics', European Commission, *European Governance*, p. 3.
39. C. Attucci, 'An institutional dialogue . . .' p. 151.
40. Weiler, 'The Reform of European Constitutionalism'.
41. D. Dinan, *Ever Closer Union?* (1st edn, Macmillan – now Palgrave Macmillan, Basingstoke, 1994).
42. C. Lord, *Democracy in the European Union* (Sheffield Academic Press, Sheffield, 1998).
43. W. Wallace, 'Introduction: the Dynamics of European Integration', in W. Wallace (ed.) *The Dynamics of Integration* (Pinter, London, 1990), p. 9.
44. For an interesting exchange on this question in the national context, see A. D. Smith & E. Gellner, 'The Debate', *Nations and Nationalism*, 2 (1996), 358–70.
45. See contributions to *Journal of European Public Policy*, Special Issue on Constructivist Integration Theory, 6: 4 (1999).
46. E. B. Haas, *The Obsolescence of Regional Integration Theory* (University of California Press, Berkeley, 1975), p. 64.
47. Beetham & Lord, *Legitimacy*, esp. Ch. 4.
48. Weiler, Haltern & Mayer, 'European Democracy', p. 38.
49. See for example the debate in the Constitutional Convention on subsidiarity and the categorisation of competencies.
50. For a critical view on the contribution of subsidiarity to the problem of sovereignty and competencies in the EU, see L. Siedentop, *Democracy in Europe* (Penguin, London, 2000), esp. pp. 31–2.
51. Weiler, Haltern & Mayer, 'European Democracy', p. 40 ff.
52. Bellamy, 'The "Right to Have Rights"'.
53. Scharpf, *Regieren in Europa*.
54. Lord, *Democracy in the European Union*.
55. See R. G. Corbett, F. Jacobs & M. Shackleton (eds) *The European Parliament* (5th edn, John Harper, London, 2003).
56. Lord, *Democracy in the European Union*, esp. Ch. 2.
57. J. H. H. Weiler, *The Constitution of Europe: Do the New Clothes have an Emperor? and other Essays on European Integration* (Cambridge University Press, Cambridge, 1999), p. 350.
58. C. Lord, 'Assessing Democracy in a Contested Polity', *Journal of Common Market Studies*, 39 (2001), 641–61, 651.
59. The EU average turnout declined from 63% (1979) to 61% (1984), 58.5% (1989), 56.8% (1994), 49.8% (1999), 45.7% (2004).

60. A. McLaughlin & J. Greenwood, 'The Management of Interest Representation in the European Union', *Journal of Common Market Studies*, 33 (1995), 143–56.
61. M. Bond, 'Introduction', to A. Beresford Taylor: 'Is Civil Society heard in Brussels? Interest representation and the role of civil society in EU decision-making', *European Essay* No. 4, (Federal Trust, London, 2000).
62. European Commission, *European Governance*, p. 32.
63. N. Walker, 'The White Paper in Constitutional Context', in C. Joerges, Y. Meny & J. H. H. Weiler (eds) *Responding to the Commission White Paper* (EUI/Robert Schuman Centre, Florence, 2002).
64. Scharpf, *Regieren in Europa*, footnote 2, p. 18.
65. J. Habermas, 'Was ist ein Volk?', *Süddeutsche Zeitung*, München, 26.09.1996.
66. P. Howe, 'A Community of Europeans: the Requisite Underpinnings', *Journal of Common Market Studies,* 33 (1995), 27–46.
67. See A. Scheuer, 'A Political Community', in Schmitt & Thomassen, *Political Representation.*
68. Glaab, 'Die Bürger', p. 607.
69. EC 'Declaration on European Identity', *EC Bulletin*, EC 12/1973, 2501, pp. 118–22.
70. Ibid. p. 118.
71. Ian Manners adds to these 'core' norms also the 'centrality of peace found in key symbolic declarations such as that by Robert Schuman in 1950, as well as the preambles to the European Coal and Steel Treaty in 1951 and the Treaty establishing the European Communities (TEC) of 1957'. See I. Manners 'Normative Power Europe: the European Union between International and World Society', paper given at 6th Annual UACES Research Conference, Bristol, 04.09.2001, p. 7. While it is true, that 'preservation of peace' is paramount among the goals of European integration, it is not mentioned in the 1973 Declaration as a 'principle'.
72. EC 'Declaration on European Identity', p. 119.
73. Antje Wiener notes that Tindemans' report itself was based on ideas put forward earlier by European Commissioner Henri Davignon, see A. Wiener, *European Citizenship Practice: Building Institutions of a non-State* (Westview Press, Boulder, CO, 1998), Ch. 4.
74. European Commission, 'Towards Citizenship', *EC Bulletin*, Supplement 7/75.
75. L. Tindemans, 'Report on European Union,' *EC Bulletin*, Supplement 1/76.
76. EC 'Report on European Union', *EC Bulletin*, Supplement 5/75, p. 10.
77. Ibid., p. 26.
78. EC, 'Solemn Declaration on European Union', *EC Bulletin* 6/1983, pp. 24–9, 25.
79. Article 128 of the Treaty of Maastricht, now article 151. On the development of EU Cultural policy, see A. Ellmeier, 'EU Kulturpolitik: Europäische Kulturpolitik?' in A. Ellmeier & B. Rásky (eds) *Kulturpolitik in Europa: Europäische Kulturpolitik?: Von nationalstaatlichen und transnationalen Konzeptionen*, Internationales Archiv für Kulturanalysen, Wien (1997).
80. EC 'A People's Europe: Report from the ad hoc Committee' [chairman: Pietro Adonnino], to the European Council (part I 29/30.03.1985, Brussels;

part II 28/29.06.1985, Milan) in *EC Bulletin*, Supplement 7/85 (1985), pp. 7–32.
81. Ibid. p. 5.
82. Ibid.
83. Ibid. p. 9.
84. Ibid. p. 7.
85. Ibid. p. 21.
86. Ibid. p. 29.
87. The Treaty on European Union (TEU) of 1991 also refers to the concept of a European identity in its opening considerations, albeit only in the older context of an 'international' identity for the EU: 'Resolved to implement a common foreign and security policy . . . , thereby reinforcing the European identity and its independence', TEU, opening consideration No. 10.
88. One illustration of this development is the addition during the 1996 IGC, in reaction to the post-Maastricht debate, of a new article on respect for the national identities of the member states (Art. F.3, now Art. 6.3 TEU), as well as the addition of extra phrases to both the citizenship article (Art. 17.1, now stating 'citizenship of the Union shall complement and not replace national citizenship') and to the article on cultural policy, now explicitly referring to the EU's duty to 'respect and to promote the *diversity* of its cultures', (Art. 151, emphasis added).
89. While some (notably J. Weiler), argue that Europe's problems stem from the fact that it has 'no demos', it is clear that this statement refers to a particular, ethnic-culturally based understanding of 'demos'. (See Weiler, Haltern & Mayer, 'European Democracy'). Here I use 'demos' in the more neutral meaning of individuals constituting the democratic polity.
90. A. Warleigh, 'Frozen: Citizenship and European Unification', *Critical Review of International and Social Philosophy*, 1 (1998), 113–51.
91. See A. Wiener & V. Della Sala, 'Constitution-making and Citizenship Practice: Bridging the Democracy Gap in the EU', *Journal of Common Market Studies*, 35 (1997), 595–614.
92. S. O'Leary, *The Evolving Concept of Community Citizenship: From the Free Movement of Persons to Union Citizenship* (Kluwer Law International, London, 1996), p. 23.
93. One member of the Convention drafting the EU Charter, Georges Berthu (MEP, non-aligned), declared the concept of European citizenship 'meaningless' because citizenship could only apply to nation-states, but later on in the interview argued that European citizenship should contain special rights for European citizens because otherwise it would lose all meaning (interview Georges Berthu, 15.09.2000).
94. Wiener, *European Citizenship Practice*.
95. A. Wiener, 'The Embedded Acquis Communautaire: Transmission Belt And Prism of New Governance', in K. H. Neunreither & A. Wiener (eds) *European Integration After Amsterdam: Institutional Dynamics and Prospects for Democracy* (Oxford University Press, Oxford, 2000), p. 340.
96. R. Bellamy & A. Warleigh, 'Democracy and Messy Integration: Four Models of European Citizenship', in *First Report on European Citizenship Project*, Reading (1998), p. 2.

97. K. Nicolaidis, 'We, the Peoples of Europe . . .', *Foreign Affairs*, 83 (2004), 97–109.
98. P. Close, *Citizenship, Europe and Change* (Macmillan – now Palgrave Macmillan, Basingstoke, 1995), see Ch. 1 for the following.
99. Bellamy & Warleigh, 'Democracy and Messy Integration'.
100. Weiler, Haltern & Mayer, 'European Democracy'.
101. J. Habermas, 'Staatsbürgerschaft und nationale Identität', in Habermas, *Faktizität und Geltung*.
102. O'Leary, *The Evolving Concept*, p. 272.
103. Article B TEU (now Article 2 TEU).
104. O'Leary herself is well aware of this problem and argues for a wider definition of citizenship, see O'Leary, *The Evolving Concept*, Ch. 8.
105. At the same time, the legal provisions of European citizenship were incorporated into the EC, rather than into the EU treaty. Pechstein and Koenig observe that this was 'wrong' from the point of view of trying to create a 'Union-citizenship': M. Pechstein & C. Koenig, *Die Europäische Union: die Verträge von Maastricht und Amsterdam* (2nd edn, Mohr Siebeck, Tübingen, 1998), pp. 27–8.
106. Bull. EC 12/1974, Point 111.
107. Case 26/62 *Van Gend en Loos* v. *Nederlandse Administratie der Belastingen* [1963] ECR 1.
108. Case 29/69 *Stauder* v. *Stadt Ulm* [1969], ECR 419.
109. See Wiener, *European Citizenship Practice*, esp. Ch. 3.
110. Wiener, 'The Embedded Acquis Communautaire', p. 330.
111. Dinan, *Ever Closer Union?*, p. 89.
112. EC Commission, 'Towards European Citizenship'.
113. EC Commission, 'Report on European Union' (the Commission's contribution to the Tindemans report), *EC Bulletin*, Supplement 5/75, pp. 5–42.
114. As mentioned, the ECJ developed the notion of 'fundamental human rights [as] enshrined in the general principles of Community law and protected by the court' in its 1969 judgement in *Stauder* vs. *Stadt Ulm* (case 29/69 [1969] ECR 419), quoted in S. Weatherill & P. Beaumont, *EC Law* (Penguin, London, 1993) p. 220.
115. EC Commission, 'Report on European Union', p. 26.
116. Wiener, 'The Embedded Acquis Communautaire', p. 331.
117. EP Working Document 346/77 of 25.10.1977.
118. OJC 103 of 27.04.1977 (Fundamental rights in this one-page agreement are defined as those rights which are 'derived in particular from the constitutions of the Member States, and the European Convention on Human Rights and Fundamental Freedoms').
119. EC, 'Towards European citizenship', pp. 15–16.
120. Craig, 'Constitutions, Constitutionalism', pp. 145–6.
121. See Weiler, 'The Reform of EU Constitutionalism'.
122. OJC 120, 16.05.1989, p. 51.
123. EC, 'A People's Europe', p. 7.
124. EU, 'A People's Europe', pp. 19–21.
125. Delors speech at College of Europe, Bruges 20.10.1989, as quoted in Dinan, *Ever Closer Union?*, p. 158.
126. EP Docs. A3 47/ 90; A3 166/90, and A3 270/90.

127. Wiener, 'The Embedded Acquis Communautaire', p. 334.
128. Kohl and Mitterand letter to the Irish presidency, 19 April 1990.
129. Dinan, *Ever Closer Union?*, p. 166.
130. According to O' Leary, the idea of a formalised citizenship was first tabled by the Spanish government, see O' Leary, *The Evolving Concept*, p. 25.
131. Wiener, 'The Embedded Acquis Communautaire', p. 338.
132. The proceedings of the European Parliament in the runup to the 1996 IGC are collected in the 1996 *White Paper on the 1996 Intergovernmental Conference* (European Parliament, Luxembourg, 1996).
133. Wiener, 'The Embedded Acquis Communautaire', pp. 336–7.
134. Conclusion of the Presidency, Tampere European Council Meeting, 15/16.10.1999.
135. J. Leinen & J. Schönlau, 'Die Erarbeitung der EU-Grundrechtecharta im Konvent: nützliche Erfahrungen für die Zukunft Europas', *Integration*, 24 (2001), 26–33.
136. 'Declaration on the Future of the Union', Annex IV to Treaty of Nice, Document SN533/1/00, 2000.
137. European Council (2001) 'Declaration on the Future of the European Union', Annex I to the Conclusions of the Presidency, Laeken, 14/15.12.2001.
138. J. Elster, 'Deliberation and Constitution Making', in J. Elster (ed.) *Deliberative Democracy* (Cambridge University Press, Cambridge, 1998).
139. Weiler, 'The Reform of European Constitutionalism'.
140. Weatherill & Beaumont, *EC Law*, quoting from the *Van Gend en Loos* (case 26/62 [1963] ECR 1) judgement, p. 289.
141. Case 6/64 [1964] ECR 585.
142. Weiler, 'The Reform of European Constitutionalism', p. 113.
143. Ibid. p. 115.
144. Case 190/84 *Les Verts-Parti Ecologiste* v. *Parliament* [1988], ECR 1017.
145. J. H. H. Weiler, 'A Constitution for Europe? Some Hard Choices', *Journal of Common Market Studies*, 40 (2002), 563–80.
146. J. Shaw, 'Towards Postnational Constitutionalism in the European Union', Paper for the Panel on Governance and Constitutionalism in the EU, Socio-Legal Studies Association Annual Conference, Loughborough University, April 1999, p. 5.
147. Ibid. p. 6.
148. Weiler, 'The Reform of European Constitutionalism'.
149 Ibid., p. 124.
150. Shaw, 'Process and Constitutional Discourse', p. 12.
151. Ibid. p. 8.
152. Ibid. p. 11.
153. Ibid. p. 20.
154. See for example contributions to C. Closa & J. E. Fossum (eds) 'Deliberative Constitutional Politics in the EU', *Arena Report* No. 05/04, Oslo (2004).
155. Wiener & Della Sala, 'Constitution-making and Citizenship Practice', p. 597.
156. Ibid. pp. 598–9.
157. Ibid. p. 599.

158. Ibid. p. 601.
159. For an account of the Charter Convention in this perspective, see E. O. Eriksen, J. E. Fossum & A. J. Menendez (eds) *The Chartering of Europe* (Nomos, Baden-Baden, 2003); for an extension to the Constitutional Convention, see C. Closa & J. E. Fossum, 'Deliberative Constitutional Politics . . .'.
160. See for example Shaw, *Law of the European Union*, Ch. 9.
161. Greenland did leave the EU under special circumstances, in 1982.
162. R. Sinnott, 'Integration Theory, Subsidiarity and the Internationalisation of Issues: the Implications for Legitimacy', *EUI Working Paper* RSC No. 94/13, Florence (1994), p. 5.
163. Shaw, 'Process and Constitutional Discourse'; Fossum, 'Constitution-making in the EU'.
164. P. Craig acknowledges this aspect of the Charter, as part of a wider constitutional process, see Craig, 'Constitutions, Constitutionalism'.
165. Editorial Comment, *Common Market Law Review*, 38 (2001), 1–6, 1.

4 Drafting the Charter in the Convention

1. Bellamy, 'The "Right to have Rights"'.
2. Ibid., p. 43.
3. The phrase is taken from the Charter's preamble (emphasis added).
4. Bellamy & Castiglione, 'Normative Theory', pp. 4–5.
5. European Council, Conclusions of the Presidency, Cologne 3./4.06.1999.
6. John Elster argues that this is unusual for 'constituent assemblies' (see Elster, 'Deliberation and Constitution Making') – see also Ch. 5.
7. Interview with Lord Goldsmith, British Government Representative, 17.07.2000, reply to the question 'What do you see as the main task of the Charter?'
8. Interview with Jürgen Meyer, German Parliament representative, 10.01.2001.
9. On the basis of the sample structure of interviewees, this distribution should be roughly representative of the opinions among the 62 titular members of the Convention (see annex for a list). Elizabeth Wicks notes that 'the European Parliament and Commission's desire for a binding document . . . did not prevail because the governments of half of the states favoured a less binding declaration.' E. Wicks, '"Declaratory of Existing Rights" – the United Kingdom's Role in Drafting a European Bill of Rights, Mark II', *Public Law*, 51 (2001), 527–41, p. 529, see also Ch. 5.
10. See Convention Document 'Body 3' of 20.01.2000 for Herzog's 'as-if' approach.
11. O. de Schutter, 'La "Convention": un instrument au service de l'art de gouverner dans l'Union européenne?', background paper for the ARENA Workshop 'The Charter of Rights as a Constitution-Making Vehicle', Oslo (8/9.6.2001), footnote 3, p. 2.
12. For example Lord Bowness, British House of Lords representative, interview on 11.07.2000.
13. Final report of working group II, CONV 354/02, 22.10.2002.

14. For the concept of 'trimming' see R. Bellamy & J. Schönlau, 'The Normality . . .'.
15. Especially in the framework of the International Labour Organisation Convention, for example I. van den Burg (deputy member of the EP delegation, PSE), who also explored this issue in I. van den Burg, 'Die EU Grundrechtecharta'.
16. See A. J. Menéndez, 'The Sinews of Peace: Rights to Solidarity in the Charter of Fundamental Rights of the Union', *ARENA Report No. 8/2000 Chartering Europe: the Charter of Fundamental Rights in Context* (ARENA, Oslo, 2001), esp. pp. 208–10.
17. The European Court of Justice developed the notion of 'fundamental human rights enshrined in the general principles of Community law' in *Stauder* vs. *Stadt Ulm* (see Ch. 3) and the notion of the 'constitutional traditions common to the Member States' as a source for such rights in *Internationale Handelsgesellschaft* (case 11/70 [1970] ECR 1125).
18. See European Parliament, *Fundamental Social Rights in Europe*, DG Research Social Affairs, SOCI 104, Brussels, 2–2000.
19. See Document Charte 4473/00 (Convent 49, Oct 11.2000) for example on Art. 28 'Right of collective bargaining and action'; or Art. 34 (3) 'Social security and social assistance'. NB: Document Convent 49 'the Explanations' was prepared by the presidium without consulting the Convention – it was thus technically an 'unofficial' document, and several Convention members rejected the idea that this document which they had never debated, was part of the Convention's output (for example Jo Leinen MEP in the debate in EP delegation on 12.09.2000). Nevertheless the explanations were a crucial issue in the debates about the inclusion of the Charter in the Constitutional Treaty and even though they are not included themselves in the text, they are now explicitly referred to in Art. II-112.7 and have been annexed to the Constitutional Treaty in Declaration No. 12 (see also below).
20. There is for instance a well-established tradition in German constitutional law of '*Staatszielbestimmungen*' (determinations of the goals of the state) as constitutional principles – see Jutta Limbach: 'Das Bundesverfassungsgericht im Grenzbereich von Recht und Politik', lecture at Free University Berlin (5.2.1998). This stands in stark contrast with Lord Goldsmith's criticism in the early stages of the debate, of 'principles' as alien to the British constitutional tradition.
21. Document Convent 43 of 14.07.2000.
22. Debate on 19.07.2000.
23. Peter Mombaur (MEP-EPP (substitute Convention member)) in the Plenary debate of 19.07.2000.
24. It is this second reading which also transpires from the preamble to the Constitutional Treaty where the 'peoples of Europe are determined to transcend their former divisions and, united ever more closely, to forge a common destiny'.
25. Document Convent 45 of 28.07.2000.
26. For example Daniel Tarschys, Swedish government representative, interview on 11.05.2000.

27. From the introductory statements (which are not called 'preamble'!) to the EC Treaty (as amended by the TEU).
28. Preamble of the Charter of Fundamental Rights of the European Union.
29. Georges Berthu (MEP UEN), interview 15.09.2000.
30. Caspar Einem (Austrian Parliament Representative, Social Democrat), interview 18.07.2000; Michiel Pateijn (Dutch Parliament Representative, Liberal), interview 18.07.2000.
31. Guy Braibant, (French Government Representative), interview 30.06.2000.
32. Lord Bowness, interview 11.07.2000.
33. Georges Berthu, interview 15.09.2000.
34. Peter Mombaur, interview 14.09.2000.
35. Stefano Rodotà, interview 04.04.2000.
36. Art. E of Document Convent 17 of 20.03.2000.
37. Document Convent 45 of 28.07.2000.
38. J. Leinen & J. Schönlau, 'Auf dem Weg zur europäischen Demokratie-politische Parteien auf EU-Ebene', *Integration*, 26: 3 (2003), 218–27.
39. Document Convent 47 of 14.09.2000.
40. Document Convent 17 of 20.03.2000.
41. This opening towards rights of 'legal persons' is a characteristic of the Fundamental Rights doctrine as it evolved in the ECJ case law, and one possible reason, why the term 'fundamental rights' is preferred over 'human rights', see Shaw, *Law of the European Union*, pp. 363–4.
42. Document Convent 28 of 05.05.2000 phrased the right to asylum as 'Nationals of third countries shall have the right to asylum in the European Union'.
43. For a critical view, see J. Voggenhuber, 'Die Wahrheit ist bloss eine Behauptung', in Kaufmann (ed.) *Grundrechtecharta*.
44. Jo Leinen, in Convention plenary debate 19.07.2000.
45. Gabriel Cisneros, in Convention plenary debate 19.07.2000.
46. Andrew Duff, in Convention plenary debate 19.07.2000.
47. See for example Manners, 'Normative Power Europe'.
48. Merlingen, M., Mudde, C. & Sedelmeier, U., 'The Right and the Righteous? European Norms, Domestic Politics and the Sanctions against Austria', *Journal of Common Market Studies*, 39 (2001), 59–77, 62–3.
49. Case 29/69 [1969]/ Case 11/70 [1970], quoted in Weatherhill & Beaumont, *EC Law*, p. 220.
50. A. J. Menéndez, 'Finalité Through Rights', in Eriksen, Fossum & Menéndez, *The Chartering of Europe*.
51. Weatherill & Beaumont, *EC Law*, p. 221.
52. T. Bossi 'Die Grundrechtecharta – Wertekanon für die Europäische Union', in W. Weidenfeld (ed.) *Nizza in der Analyse* (Verlag Bertelsmann Stiftung, Gütersloh, 2001), p. 221 (my own translation).
53. Ibid. pp 221–2.
54. The fourth consideration reads 'DESIRING to deepen the solidarity between their peoples while respecting their history, their culture, and their traditions' TEU.
55. Bossi, 'Die Grundrechtecharta', footnote 26, p. 221.
56. Lord Goldsmith in the debates in the Convention on 04.04.2000 and 28.04.2000. For the British negotiating position, and especially the pressure

put on the British government on the social rights question by the Confederation of British Industries, see Wicks 'Declaratory of Existing Rights', p. 532.

57. Guy Braibant in plenary debate 28.04.2000.
58. The following is explored further in J. Schönlau, 'New Values for Europe?'
59. Especially Peter Altmaier (deputy representative of German Bundestag); Rijk van Dam (deputy EP delegation member, EDD).
60. Especially Ieke van den Burg, Johannes Voggenhuber.
61. Document Convent 17 of 20.03.2000.
62. Daniel Tarschys, Swedish Government representative, in Convention debate 28.03.2000.
63. Lord Goldsmith in Convention debate 28.03.2000.
64. Convention debate on 28.03.2000 – in favour of the proposal for example: Johannes Voggenhuber, Jürgen Meyer, Hannah Meij-Weggen (MEP-PSE).
65. The following account is based on the author's participant observation in the European Parliament delegation and the group of European Socialists in the Charter Convention. The complementary data which is available from the meetings of the delegation of national Parliamentarians (the national government representatives met behind closed doors for at least part of the debates on 11/25.09.2000) suggest that the question of the religious heritage was debated in the other delegations, but not as controversially as in the EP delegation. Three members of the national Parliamentarians' delegation, Barros Moura, Manzella, and Lallemand, are reported to have argued against a reference to the religious heritage, one member, Altmaier, spoke in favour, see Deutscher Bundestag (ed.) *Die Grundrechtecharta der Europäischen Union – Berichte und Dokumente*, Zur Sache, 1/2001 Berlin, pp. 380–2.
66. For a summary of the argument, see P. Berès, 'Die Charta – Ein Kampf für die Werte der Union', in Kaufmann (ed.) *Grundrechtecharta*, p. 22.
67. Elena Paciotti/Cathérine Lalumiere in EP Delegation debate on 21.09.2000.
68. Bellamy & Schönlau, 'The Normality . . .', p. 425.
69. T. Schmitz, 'Die Grundrechtecharta als Teil der Verfassung der Europäischen Union', *Zeitschrift Europarecht*, 39 (2004), 691–713.
70. Daniel Tarschys in a presentation given at the Workshop 'The Charter of Rights as a Constitution-Making Vehicle', (ARENA/University of Oslo, 08/09.06.2001)
71. Interview with Jürgen Meyer, 26.03.2004.
72. Interview with an official from the German Federal Ministry of Justice, by phone, 16.01.2001.
73. Reply to emailed questions by an official from the German Federal Ministry of Foreign Affairs, 09.08.2001.
74. Interview with H. Däubler-Gmelin 08.03.2004.
75. Interview with an official from the German Federal Ministry of Justice.
76. Merlingen, Mudde, & Sedelmeier, 'The Right and the Righteous?', p. 61.
77. J. March & J. P. Olsen, *Rediscovering Institutions: the Organizational Basis of Politics* (New York, Free Press, 1989), quoted in Merlingen, Mudde & Sedelmeier, p. 62.

78. Interview with H. Däubler-Gmelin.
79. Interview with Dittrich.
80. The following is largely based on the reply from H. Rotkirch, representative of the Finnish presidency in the COREPER Ad Hoc Working group on the Charter, to a list of the author's questions, by email of 07.02.2001.
81. H. Rotkirch.
82. H. Rotkirch.
83. http://ue.eu.int/DF/listall.asp?lang=en
84. The only exceptions to this rule were, as mentioned before, some of the delegation meetings in the later stages of the debates.
85. For a critical view see Voggenhuber, 'Die Wahrheit'; for a positive assessment of the role of the presidium, see P. Magnette, 'Le débat sur l'avenir de l'Union: processus et acteurs', *Contribution to the Colloquium of the Jean Monnet Action Group 'Europe 2004 – Le Grand Débat'*, European Commission, Brussels, 15/16.10.2001.
86. Interview with Convention Secretary Jean-Paul Jacqué on 13.04.2000 for this interpretation.
87. Georges Berthu and Jens Peter Bonde (EDD), both MEPs, did not 'support' the consensus communicated to the Council on 02.10.2000. Barriga on the other hand notes that only Hans-Peter Martin (MEP) 'showed rejection [of the Charter'] but this does not seem to have been 'registered' anywhere, see S. Barriga, *Die Entstehung der Charta der Grundrechte der Europäischen Union* (Nomos, Baden-Baden, 2003), footnote 7.
88. On the role of 'consensus' in the Constitutional Convention, see for example C. Closa, 'The Convention Method and the Transformation of EU Constitutional Politics', in Eriksen, E. O., Fossum, J. E. & Menéndez, A. J. (eds) *Developing a European Constitution* (Routledge, London, 2004).
89. Convention Plenary Debate of 06.06.2000.
90. Afterwards Roman Herzog himself called for an indicative vote once more, but without a clear result. See S. Barriga, 'Die Entstehung der Charta . . .', footnote 90.
91. Roman Herzog resigned from the presidency of the Convention after the death of his wife, with effect from 19.06.2000. He was then persuaded to continue as president of the Convention, but suffered a heart attack in September and was therefore not able to chair the Convention. Roman Herzog thus presided over 11 out of the 18 meetings of the Convention plenary.
92. F. Deloche-Gaudez, 'The Convention on a Charter of Fundamental Rights: a Method for the Future?', *Research and Policy Paper 15* (Notre Europe, Paris, 2001).
93. Lord Goldsmith, interview on 17.07.2000; Frederik Korthals-Altes, interview, 18.07.2000.
94. Ernst Hirsch Ballin, interview 26.09.2000.
95. Guy Braibant, interview 30.06.2000.
96. Peter Mombaur, interview 14.09.2000.
97. Stefano Rodotà, interview 04.04.2000.
98. Antonio Vitorino, interview 30.06.2000.
99. Georges Berthu, interview 15.09.2000.
100. Lord Goldsmith, interview 17.07.2000.

101. Michiel Pateijn, interview 18.07.2000.
102. Voggenhuber, 'Die Wahrheit', p. 113.
103. Jöran Magnusson, interview 25.09.2000; Johannes Voggenhuber, interview 10.10.2000.
104. Iñigo Méndez de Vigo, interview 11.10.2000.
105. Lord Bowness, interview 11.07.2000.
106. Guy Braibant, interview 30.06.2000.
107. Sylvia Yvonne Kaufmann, interview 20.09.2000.
108. Heinrich Neisser, interview 06.06.2000.
109. For example Ernst Hirsch Ballin, interview 26.09.2000; Gunnar Jansson, interview 06.06.2000.
110. The only member of the EP delegation in the sample who did not make this connection was Ingo Friedrich who put the emphasis on his contacts with 'NGOs and churches back home, and my party headquarters back in Munich', Ingo Friedrich, interview 02.05.2000.
111. Jürgen Meyer, interview 10.07.2000.
112. Together with Sylvia Kaufmann, Voggenhuber rejected the handling of compromise negotiations in the final stages by the EP delegation's president Méndez de Vigo during the debate in the EP delegation on 12.09.2000.
113. Caspar Einem, interview 18.07.2000.
114. See L. Hoffmann 'The Convention on the Future of Europe: Thoughts on the Convention-Model', *Jean Monnet Working Paper* 11/02 (2002), or D. Göler & A. Maurer, 'Die Konventsmethode in der Europäischen Union-Ausnahme oder Modell?', *SWP-Studie*, S 44 (2004).
115. Weiler, 'Does the European Union Truly Need . . .?', see also Ch. 5.

5 The Impact of the Charter

1. *ANSA-news bulletin* quoting the leader of Italy's Communist Refoundation Party: 'UE-Carta dei Diritti: Bertinotti: E' Aqua sul Marmo', 03.10.2000.
2. Commission President Prodi, quoted in *Berner Zeitung*, 'Ein "Herz" für die technokratische EU', 03.10.2000.
3. S. Alber of the European Court of Justice, quoted in *Financial Times*, 'Europe's Charter of rights given a smooth passage', 03.10.2000.
4. Two members objected to the Charter's final draft, G. Berthu and J. P. Bonde, and remained demonstratively seated when the European anthem was played.
5. For a list of legal references to the Charter as of 1 July 2003 see: S. Peers & A. Ward, *The European Union Charter of Fundamental Rights* (Hart Publishing, Oxford, 2004), Appendix 1.
6. P. Ziltener, *Strukturwandel in der europäischen Integration – die Europäische Union und die Veränderung von Staatlichkeit* (Verlag Westfälisches Dampfboot, Münster, 1999).
7. R. Bellamy & A. Warleigh, 'From an Ethics of Integration to an Ethics of Participation: Citizenship and the Future of the European Union', *Millennium: Journal of International Studies*, 27 (1998), 447–70.
8. See A. von Bogdandy, 'The European Union as a Human Rights Organization? Human Rights at the Core of the European Union', *Common Market Law Review*, 37 (2000), 1307–38, esp. pp. 1334–5.

9. Bellamy & Castiglione, 'Normative Theory', p. 3.
10. Ibid. For a discussion of the link between the commonly assumed 'democratic deficit' and the idea of a 'legitimacy deficit' see also C. Lord, *A Democratic Audit of the European Union* (Palgrave Macmillan, Basingstoke, 2004).
11. This problem took on new urgency in the debates surrounding the decision on opening accession negotiations with Turkey by the European Council in December 2004.
12. An official from the German Ministry of Foreign Affairs stated: 'The federal government declared (. . .) in Cologne, as well as in parallel with the workings of the Convention, time and again, that it was aiming in the long run at an inclusion of the Charter into the Treaties. . . . In this sense, one can indeed speak of a long-term strategy [for a legally binding document].' Email reply to author's question, my own translation, 09.08.2001.
13. BVerfGE 37, 271ff, of 1974 and BVerfGE 73, 339ff, of 1986.
14. S. Barriga, 'Die Entstehung der Charta', pp. 18–19.
15. 'Koalitionsvertrag' (coalition-agreement) between SPD and Bündnis 90/die Grünen of 20.10.1998.
16. Joschka Fischer included a reference to the Charter project in his speech outlining the priorities of the German presidency before the European Parliament on 12.01.1999. On the pre-history of the Charter Project in the German context, see J. Leinen & J. Schönlau, 'Charta der europäischen Grundrechte – Visitenkarte für Europa', in Kaufmann, *Grundrechtecharta*.
17. M. Fischbach, 'Kommentar zur Grundrechtecharta', in Kaufmann *Grundrechtecharta*.
18. Council of Europe observations on document Charte 4422/00, published as Contrib. 326 of 19.09.2000; also: Council of Europe Parliamentary Assembly, *Resolution 1228* (2000) (published as Contrib. 350 of 29.09.2000)).
19. See T. Schmitz, 'Die Grundrechtecharta als Teil'.
20. G. de Búrca, 'Human Rights: the Charter and Beyond', *Jean Monnet Working Paper* 10/01, New York (2001).
21. K. Lenaerts & M. Desomer, 'Bricks for a Constitutional Treaty of the European Union: Values, Objectives and Means', *European Law Review*, 27 (Aug. 2002), 377–407.
22. See G. Gaja, 'New Instruments and Institutions for Enhancing the Protection of Human Rights in Europe?' in Alston & Weiler (eds) *The EU and Human Rights*; for the pre-Charter situation see N. Reich, 'Zur Notwendigkeit einer Europäischen Grundrechtsbeschwerde', *Zeitschrift für Rechtspolitik*, 33 (2000), 375–9.
23. C. Engel, 'The European Charter of Rights: a Changed Political Opportunity Structure and its Normative Consequence', *European Law Journal*, 7 (2001), 151–70, 155/footnote 20.
24. Reich, 'Zur Notwendigkeit', p. 376.
25. Case C-173/99 *BECTU* v. *UK*, opinion of Advocate General Tizzano (08.02.2001), para. 26.
26. Charter Convention plenary debate on 04.04.2000.
27. Case C-173/99 *BECTU* v. *UK*, opinion of Advocate General Tizzano (08.02.2001), para. 28.

28. Case C-270/99P Z. v. *European Parliament*, opinion of Advocate General Jacobs (22.03.2001), para. 40.
29. Case C-377/98 *Kingdom of the Netherlands* v. *European Parliament and Council of the European Union*, opinion of Advocate General Jacobs (14.06.2001), para. 193.
30. Case C-377/98, opinion of Advocate General Jacobs (14.06.2001), para. 197.
31. Ibid.
32. Joined cases C-20/00 *Booker Aquaculture Ltd trading as Marine Harvest McConnell* and C-64/00 *Hydro Seafood GSP Ltd* v. *The Scottish Ministers*, opinion of Advocate General Mischo, 20.09.2001.
33. Cases 20/00 & 64/00, opinion of advocate general Mischo, 20.09.2001, para. 126.
34. Peers and Ward list more than 30 advocate-general references to the Charter by 1 July 2003, see Peers & Ward, *The European Union Charter*, Appendix 1.
35. A. Menéndez, '*Finalité* through Rights', in Eriksen, Fossum & Menéndez, *The Chartering of Europe*, pp. 42–6.
36. T. Schmitz, 'Die EU Grundrechtecharta', p. 694 (my own translation).
37. B. de Witte, 'The Legal Status of the Charter: Vital Question or non-Issue?', *Maastricht Journal of European and Comparative Law*, 8 (2001), 81–9, 89.
38. K. Lenaerts & E. de Smijter, 'A "Bill of Rights" for the European Union', *Common Market Law Review*, 38 (2001), 273–300, 298–9.
39. Case C-270/99 P, opinion of Advocate General Jacobs (22.03.2001).
40. T. Schmitz, 'Die Grundrechtecharta'.
41. As mentioned, the European Court referred to the EC Treaty as a 'constitutional charter' in the case 294/83 *Parti Ecologiste 'Les Verts'* v. *European Parliament* ECR 1339 [1987]; and as a 'constitutional charter of a Community based on the rule of law' in its opinion on the 'Draft Agreement on a European Economic Area' [1992], CMLR 245.
42. See H. Hohmann, 'Die Charta der Grundrechte der Europäischen Union-Ein wichtiger Beitrag zur Legitimation der EU', *Aus Politik und Zeitgeschichte*, B 52–3 (2000), 5–11.
43. See 'Declaration on the Future of the Union', Annex IV to Treaty of Nice, point 5.
44. European Parliament, 'Report on the Drafting of the EU Charter of Fundamental Rights' (rapporteurs: Andrew Duff & Johannes Voggenhuber), part II, *Document A5 00325/2000* (14.11.2000).
45. Lenaerts & de Smijter, 'A "Bill of Rights"', pp. 299–300.
46. R. Bellamy, 'The "Right to Have Rights"', p. 60.
47. Weiler, 'Does the European Union Truly Need', p. 96 (NB: published in June 2000!)
48. Engel, 'The European Charter of Fundamental Rights', p. 159.
49. Von Bogdandy, 'The European Union as a Human Rights Organization', esp. pp. 1324–5.
50. Beetham, *Democracy and Human Rights*.
51. For a discussion of this problem in the context of the German constitutional court, see J. Limbach, 'Das letzte Wort – Präsidentin Jutta Limbach

über die politische Macht des Bundesverfassungsgerichts', Spiegel-Gespräch, *Der Spiegel*, 40 (01.10.2001), 62–8.

52. E. O. Eriksen, 'Why a Constitutionalised Bill of Rights?' in Eriksen, Fossum & Menendez, *The Chartering of Europe*, pp. 68–9.
53. Weiler, 'IGC 2000: the Constitutional Agenda', in E. Best, M. Gray & A. Stubb (eds) *Rethinking the European Union*, p. 234.
54. J. H. H. Weiler, 'A Constitution for Europe?' p. 578.
55. See 'Declaration on the Future of the Union', Annex IV to Treaty of Nice; see also the documents of the Convention on the Future of Europe, working group on the Charter of Fundamental rights.
56. S. Barriga, 'Die Entstehung der Charta', p. 29.
57. Convention II Conv. 72/02, 31.05.2002, p. 2.
58. P. Norman, *The Accidental Constitution: the Story of the European Convention* (EuroComment, Brussels, 2003), p. 296.
59. Convention I Conv. 49, 11 October 2000.
60. T. Schmitz, 'Die Grundrechtecharta . . .', p. 693.
61. Convention II Conv. 354/02, 22 October, 2002 – Final report of working group II, p. 2.
62. T. Schmitz, 'Die Grundrechtecharta . . .', p. 713.
63. Ibid. pp. 695–6.
64. On the role of 'expectations' for legitimacy, see C. Lord & D. Beetham, 'Legitimizing the EU: is there a "Post-Parliamentary Basis" for its Legitimation?', *Journal of Common Market Studies*, 39 (2001), 443–62.
65. Eriksen and Fossum note that '[a]ppeals to values raise normative expectations . . .', see Eriksen & Fossum, 'Post-national integration', p. 14.
66. The Commission's White Paper on European Governance highlights the EU's problem with regard to its citizens' expectations: People 'still expect Europe-wide action in many domains, but they no longer trust the complex system to deliver what they want. In other words, people have disappointed expectations, but expectations nevertheless,' European Commission, *European Governance*, p. 7.
67. T. Diez, 'Speaking "Europe": the Politics of Integration Discourse', *Journal of European Public Policy*, 6 (1999), 598–613, p. 599.
68. Ibid. p. 605.
69. See Shaw, *Law of the European Union*, pp. 363–4.
70. Wiener, *European Citizenship Practice*.
71. P. Chilton & C. Schäffner, 'Discourse and Politics', in T. A. Van Dijk, *Discourse as Social Interaction* (Sage, London, 1997), p. 216.
72. Merlingen, Mudde & Sedelmeier, 'The Right and the Righteous?', p. 61.
73. Ibid. p. 62.
74. Ibid.
75. Merlingen, Mudde & Sedelmeier also stress the importance of domestic factors in different member states as well as individuals' strategic and tactical considerations, ibid.
76. J. Melchior, 'Die Europäische Wertegemeinschaft zwischen Rhetorik und Realität', in F. Karlhofer, J. Melchior & H. Sickinger (eds) *Anlassfall Österreich: Die Europäischen Union auf dem Weg zur Wertegemeinschaft* (Nomos Verlag, Baden-Baden, 2001) p. 1 (pagination referring to a pre-publication manuscript, my own translation).

77. It is, however, interesting that virtually all members of the Convention who were interviewed for this project denied a direct link between the Austrian case and the Charter (The 'link' understood, most likely, as the supposition that the Charter would be drafted in a particular way in order to legitimate the sanctions against the Austrian government *ex post*).

78. Melchior, 'Die Europäische Wertegemeinschaft', p. 4.

79. Despite the fact that Schmidt develops her categorisation of discourses on the basis of how *national* discourses are influenced by integration, it also holds for the European level itself. V. A. Schmidt, 'Democracy and Discourse in an Integrating Europe and a Globalising World', *European Law Journal*, 6 (2000), 277–300, p. 279.

80. Ibid.

81. Von Bogdandy remarks that 'putting solidarity on the same footing as human dignity, freedom and equality might provide the Charter with a specific European flavour, contrasting with the American understanding of fundamental rights', von Bogdandy, 'The European Union as a Human Rights Organization', p. 1314, footnote 37.

82. Eriksen & Fossum, 'Post-national integration', p. 17.

83. J. S. Dryzek, *Deliberative Democracy and Beyond: Liberals, Critics, Contestations* (Oxford University Press, Oxford, 2000), p. 1.

84. E. O. Eriksen & J. E. Fossum, 'The EU and Post-National Legitimacy', *ARENA Working Paper* 00/26, Oslo (2000).

85. J. Elster, 'Introduction', in Elster (ed.) *Deliberative Democracy*.

86. J. T. Checkel, 'Building New Identities? Debating Fundamental Rights in European Institutions', *ARENA Working Paper* 00/12, Oslo (2000), p. 8.

87. For an elaboration of these conditions, with reference to Elster's proposal, see J. Neyer, 'Discourse and Order in the EU', *Journal of Common Market Studies*, 41 (2003), 687–706.

88. J. T. Checkel, 'Taking Deliberation Seriously', *ARENA Working Paper* 01/14, Oslo (2001), p. 8.

89. Elster, 'Deliberation', p. 107. The question in how far both arguing and bargaining are forms of 'communicative interaction' or whether arguing is and bargaining is not, is discussed by Neyer in 'Discourse and Order in the EU'; the crucial question here is, however, rather which conditions the Convention provided for whichever form of communicative interaction.

90. Elster, 'Deliberation', pp. 105–6.

91. For a similar analysis of the role of the Constitutional Convention as a deliberative forum, see P. Magnette, 'Délibération vs. négotiation – Une premièr analyse de la Convention sur l'avenir de l'Union', *paper for the VIIe congrès de l'Association française de science politique* (Lille, 18–21.09.2002).

92. Elster, 'Deliberation', p. 107.

93. Elster, 'Deliberation', p. 109.

94. Ibid., p. 111.

95. For example, references to other speakers by name became more and more common as the acquaintance between Convention members grew, and the policy for speakers to introduce themselves before speaking was dropped very early in the proceedings.

96. Eriksen & Fossum, 'Post-national Integration', p. 16.

97. Elster, 'Deliberation', p. 107.

98. The website received more than 1,200 documents (including communications from the Charter Secretariat and multiple language versions), and the total number of contributions submitted to the presidium in different forms stands at around 900 (figures quoted by a member of the Convention Secretariat).

99. The author worked as a researcher for a Convention member from Oct. 1999–Oct. 2000. One important task in this capacity was to process large numbers of submissions sent directly to all, or to targeted Convention members. On several occasions, such interventions had a direct impact on the proposals made by the Member in the debates.

100. Wicks, 'Declaratory of Existing Rights'.

101. S. Rodotà during the conference 'The EU Charter of Fundamental Rights', University of Florence (Florence, 17.02.2001).

102. O. de Schutter, 'Europe in Search of its Civil Society', *European Law Journal*, 8 (2002), 198–217.

103. The dossier of presscuttings on the Charter assembled by the European Parliament DG Information (mentioned above) testifies to a comparatively close following of the Charter process by a number of major European newspapers.

104. One prominent exception in the Charter debates was the clear statement of the French government and its representative that a reference to Europe's religious heritage in the preamble would be 'unacceptable' to a secular country like France, see also J. Meyer (ed) *Kommentar zur Charta der Grundrechte der Europäischen Union* (Nomos Verlag, Baden-Baden, 2003), p. 22.

105. Checkel, 'Building New Institutions?', p. 9.

106. The information on the list of members of the Convention as published by the Convention secretariat as Document Charte 4158/00 (Convent 16), 15.03.00, is not complete, and does not take account of later changes in the Convention membership.

107. Piero Melograni, Professor of History, expressed this feeling, interview 30.06.2000; and Lord Bowness mentioned that he thought the lack of independent legal advice, especially for the non-experts, was one of the great shortcomings of the Convention, interview 11.07.2000.

108. The Convention met eighteen times between December 1999 and October 2000, usually for two days.

109. Information only available on the two cases of Stefano Rodatà and Lord Goldsmith. The latter stated: 'I am the British government's representative and therefore I am concerned with putting forward propositions which coincide with the British government's view of what would be acceptable,' interview 17.07.2000.

110. Caspar Einem, Austrian National Parliament (Social Democrat) representative said: 'Fundamentally there was an agreement in Austria that every party in Parliament should also be represented in the Convention . . . it was the right of nomination of the party group. When the government changed in Austria, an ÖVP (Conservative) member became the government representative, and I moved in as a social democrat representative of the Parliament', interview 18.07. 2000; Ernst Hirsch-Ballin, representative of the Dutch Senate, said 'The decision was taken by the presidium of our first Chamber, the

Senate, and I am a chairman of the committee of justice in our House, and I am supposed to know something about European law and so on' interview 26.09.2000; Jürgen Meyer 'I was elected by the Bundestag – I had no contestant. That is probably to do with the fact that I was the first German Parliamentarian to have addressed the topic in the Bundestag . . . So I was elected unanimously, with some abstentions', interview 10.07.2000.

111. That meant that the sixteen titular members included five from the EPP group, five from the PSE group, two from the ELDR group, and one each from the groups the United European Left/Nordic Green left (GUE/NGL), the Green/European Alliance group (Verts/ALE), the group for Europe of the Nations (UEN), and from the Group Europe of Democracy and Differences (EDD).

112. Duff/Voggenhuber report (quoted above). The European Parliament then voted on a resolution based on part II of the report (A5-0325/2000), endorsing the Charter by a majority of 410 votes to 93 (27 abstentions), 14.11.2000.

113. One interesting example is the German Bundestag which has recently all three debates held about the Charter, alongside with minutes from the Convention meetings and other relevant documents. Deutscher Bundestag, *Die Charta der Grundrechte*.

114. For example debate in the French Senate, Session 11.05.2000.

115. For example House of Lords, Select Committee on European Affairs, *Eighth Report*, on the Charter of Fundamental Rights, London, 16.05.2000.

116. R. Bellamy & D. Castiglione, 'Tra retorica e simbolismo: la Carta dei Diritti dell' Unione Europea', *Quaderni Forum*, 2 (2001).

117. Ibid., p. 4.

118. Habermas, *Faktizität und Geltung*.

119. Habermas recognises that the constitution of a new (supra-)national entity in addition to an existing one, with a new public arena and public deliberation to sustain it, is a circular process. See J. Habermas, 'Sì, voglio una Costituzione per L'Europa Federale', interview in *Caffè Europa online journal*, 14.12.00 (www.caffeeuropa.it/attualita/112habermas).

120. M. P. Maduro, 'The Double Constitutional Life of the Charter of Fundamental Rights', in Eriksen, Fossum & Menéndez, *The Chartering of Europe*.

121. M. Incerti, S. Kurpas & J. Schönlau, 'What Prospects for the Ratification of the Constitutional Treaty', *EPIN Working Paper* No. 12 (2005).

122. For a development of this argument in the context of the drafting of a Bill of Rights for Northern Ireland, see C. Harvey, 'The Politics of Rights and Deliberative Democracy: the Process of Drafting a Northern Irish Bill of Rights', *European Human Rights Law Review*, 1 (2001), 48–70.

123. Conclusions of the Tampere Council (15/16.10.2000).

124. See Hohmann, 'Die Charta der Grundrechte', footnote 18, p. 7.

125. de Schutter, 'La "Convention"', pp. 5ff.

126. For the general debate on this issue, see McLaughlin & Greenwood, 'Management of Interest Representation'.

127. Jean-Paul Jacqué, interview 13.04.2000.

128. The summary minutes compiled for the German Bundestag remark on the hearings: 'Clearly less than half of the Convention members were present.

Hardly any comments were made [by Convention members during the hearings]. The following day, however, frequent references were made to the hearings in support of a comprehensive catalogue of economic and social rights.' Deutscher Bundestag, *Die Charta der Grundrechte*, p. 262 (my own translation).

129. The following is mainly based on the statements made by representatives of the applicant countries during the hearings on 19 June, most of which were subsequently published in written form on the Charter website.

130. See Agènce Europe, 21.06.2000.

131. Those countries of Central Europe which were at the time more advanced in the application process (Czech Republic, Estonia, Hungary, Poland, and Slovenia), argued for a mere political declaration, while Cyprus and Malta, together with Romania, advocated a binding Charter. Most of the second-wave applicant countries (here especially Bulgaria, Latvia, Turkey, and to a certain extend Slovakia which had just been 'promoted' to the more advanced group), were reluctant to express a clear preference for or against a binding Charter. It is also interesting that among a general concern that the Charter rights should not produce new hurdles for applicant countries, the Estonian representative before the Convention explicitly stated that his country did not support the idea of social and economic rights as fundamental rights (interview with an official of the Estonian representation in Brussels on 15.09.2000).

132. Written answers to the author's questionnaire were received only from two countries (Hungary and Romania), while interviews could be arranged with officials from the EU Missions of two other countries (Estonia and Turkey). In all cases the respondents underlined the low profile of the Charter as a political issue in their respective countries, both for the national administrations and the general public, and reiterated the main concern that the Charter should not interfere with the protection systems under the ECHR which were seen as the main point of reference on human rights.

133. See also Magnette, 'Le débat', in particular with a view how the applicant countries could be involved in the Constitutional Convention, pp. 7–8.

134. See R. Bellamy & J. Schönlau, 'The Good, the Bad and the Ugly: the need for constitutional compromise and the drafting of the EU Constitution', in Dobson & Follesdal, *Political Theory*.

135. A. Przeworski, 'Deliberation and Ideological Domination', in Elster (ed.) *Deliberative Democracy*, p. 141.

136. See Voggenhuber, 'Die Wahrheit'.

137. For a comparision between the two methods based on the Constitutional Convention (but still in many respects applicable to the Charter Convention) see J. Pollack & P. Slominiski, 'The Representative Quality of EU Treaty Reform: a Comparison between the IGC and the Convention', *European Integration*, 26 (2004), 201–26.

138. Bellamy & Castiglione, 'Normative Theory', pp. 4–5.

139. While the projection of the EU's values towards the outside seems to have had little effect on the legitimacy debate so far, mainly because EU policy in this area is still in the early stages of its development (see for example J. Zielonka (ed.) *Paradoxes of European Foreign Policy* (Kluwer Law Interna-

tional, The Hague, 1998)), in the internal context the Austrian case for example suggests that the effects on legitimacy are negative.

140. See von Bogdandy, 'The European Union as a Human Rights Organization', esp. pp. 1324–30.
141. Weiler, 'Does the European Union Truly Need', p. 96.
142. P. Alston & J. H. H. Weiler, 'An "Ever Closer Union" in Need of a Human Rights Policy: the European Union and Human Rights', in Alston & Weiler (eds) *The EU and Human Rights*.
143. von Bogdandy, 'The European Union as a Human Rights Organization', p. 1337.
144. Ibid., p. 1311.
145. Ibid.
146. Ibid., p. 1338.
147. Weiler, 'Does the European Union Truely Need'.
148. European Commission, *European Governance*, p. 3.

6 Linking Rights, Process and Legitimacy

1. Bellamy & Castiglione, 'Normative Theory'.
2. See for example T. V. Olsen, 'Europe: United under God? Or not?' in Dobson & Follesdal, *Political Theory*.
3. Puchala, 'Of Blind Men, Elephants, and International Integration'.
4. Schmitter, 'What is There to Legitimize', p. 7.
5. European Council, Laeken, 14/15 December 2001, 'Declaration on the Future of Europe'.
6. See for example J. Schönlau, D. Castiglione et al., *The Making and Unmaking of the European Constitution* (working title, Palgrave Macmillan, Basingstoke, forthcoming, 2006).

Select Bibliography

Alston, P. & Weiler, J. H. H., 'An "Ever Closer Union" in Need of a Human Rights Policy: the European Union and Human Rights', in P. Alston & J. H. H. Weiler (eds) *The EU and Human Rights* (Oxford University Press, Oxford, 1999).

Archer, M. S., *Culture and Agency* (Cambridge University Press, Cambridge, 1988).

Attucci, C., 'An Institutional Dialogue on Common Principles – Reflections on the significance of the EU Charter of Fundamental Rights', in L. Dobson & A. Follesdal (eds) *Political Theory and the European Constitution* (Routledge, London, 2004).

Banchoff, T. & Smith, M. P. (eds) *Legitimacy and the European Union: the Contested Polity* (Routledge, London, 1999).

Barriga, S., *Die Entstehung der Charta der Grundrechte der Europäischen Union* (Nomos, Baden-Baden, 2003).

Beetham, D., *The Legitimation of Power* (Macmillan – now Palgrave Macmillan, Basingstoke, 1991).

Beetham, D. & Lord, C., *Legitimacy and the European Union* (Longman, London/ New York, 1998).

Bellamy, R., 'The Political Form of the Constitution: the Separation of Powers, Rights and Representative Democracy', in R. Bellamy & D. Castiglione (eds) *Constitutionalism in Transformation: European and Theoretical Perspectives* (Blackwell, Oxford, 1996).

Bellamy, R., *Liberalison and Pluralism: Towards a Politics of Compromise* (Routledge, London, 1999).

Bellamy, R.,'Citizenship Beyond the Nation State: the Case of Europe', in N. O'Sullivan (ed.) *Political Theory in Transition* (Routledge, London, 2000).

Bellamy, R. & Castiglione, D., 'Tra retorica e simbolismo: La Carta europea dei diritti fondamentali', *Quaderni Forum*, 2 (2001).

Bellamy, R. & Castiglione, D., 'Normative Theory and the European Union: Legitimising the Euro-Polity and its Regime', in: L. Trägårdh (ed.) *After National Democracy: Rights, Law and Power in America and the New Europe* (Hart, Oxford, 2002).

Bellamy, R., Bufacchi, V. & Castiglione, D. (eds) *Democracy and Constitutional Culture in the Union of Europe* (Lothian Press, London, 1995).

Bellamy, R. & Schönlau, J., 'The Normality of Constitutional Politics: an Analysis of the Drafting of the EU Charter of Fundamental Rights', in *Constellations*, 11: 3 (2004), 412–33.

Bellamy, R. & Warleigh, A., 'From an Ethics of Integration to an Ethics of Participation: Citizenship and the Future of the European Union', *Millennium: Journal of International Studies*, 27: 3 (1998), 447–70.

Bellamy, R. & Warleigh, A., 'Democracy and Messy Integration: Four Models of European Citizenship', in *First Report on European Citizenship Project* (Reading, 1998).

Bellamy, R. & Warleigh, A., (eds) *Citizenship and Governance in the European Union* (Continuum, London, 2001).

Beresford Taylor, A., 'Is Civil Society heard in Brussels?: Interest representation and the role of civil society in EU decision-making', *European Essay* No. 4, Federal Trust, London (2000).

Bermann, G. A., 'Editorial, "The European Union as a Constitutional Experiment"', *European Law Journal*, 10: 4 (July 2004), 363–70.

Best, E., Gray, M., & Stubb, A. (eds) *Rethinking the European Union: IGC 2000 and Beyond* (European Institute of Public Administration, Maastricht, 2000).

Blondel, J., Sinnott, R., & Svensson, P., *People and Parliament in the European Union: Participation, Democracy, and Legitimacy* (Clarendon Press, Oxford, 1998).

Börzel, T. A., 'Policy Networks: a New Paradigm of European Governance', *EUI Working Paper* RSC 97/19, Florence (1997).

Bossi, T., 'Die Grundrechtecharta: Wertekanon für die Europäische Union', in W. Weidenfeld (ed.) *Nizza in der Analyse* (Verlag Bertelsmann Stiftung, Gütersloh, 2001).

Checkel, J. T., 'Building New Identities? Debating Fundamental Rights in European Institutions', *ARENA Working Paper* No. 00/12, Oslo (2000).

Checkel, J. T., 'Taking Deliberation Seriously', *ARENA Working Paper* No. 01/14, Oslo (2001).

Chilton, P. & Schäffner, C., 'Discourse and Politics', in T. A. Van Dijk, *Discourse as Social Interaction* (Sage, London, 1997).

Chryssochoou, Dimitris, *Democracy in the European Union* (Tauris Academic Studies, London/New York, 1998).

Chryssochoou, Dimitris, 'Meta-theory and the Study of the European Union: Capturing the Normative Turn', *European Integration*, 22: 2 (2000), 123–44.

Closa, C., 'The Convention Method and the Transformation of EU Constitutional Politics', in E. O. Eriksen, J. E. Fossum & A. J. Menéndez (eds) *Developing a European Constitution* (Routledge, London, 2004).

Closa, C., & Fossum, J. E. (eds) *Deliberative Constitutional Politics in the EU*, ARENA Report No. 5/04, Oslo 2004.

Close, P., *Citizenship, Europe and Change* (Macmillan – now Palgrave Macmillan, Basingstoke, 1995).

Corbett, R. G., Jacobs, F. & Shackleton, M. (eds) *The European Parliament* (5th edn, John Harper Publishing, London, 2003).

Craig, P., 'Constitutions, Constitutionalism, and the European Union', *European Law Journal*, 7: 2 (2001), 125–50.

de Búrca, G., 'The Quest for Legitimacy in the European Union', *Modern Law Review*, 59: 2 (1996), 348–76.

de Búrca, G., 'Human Rights: the Charter and Beyond', *Jean Monnet Working Paper* 10/01, New York (2001).

de Búrca, G., 'The Drafting of the EU Charter of Fundamental Rights', *European Law Review*, 26: 2 (2001), 126–38.

Deloche-Gaudez, F., 'The Convention on a Charter of Fundamental Rights: a Method for the Future?', *Notre Europe Research and Policy Paper 15*, Paris (2001).

de Schutter, O., 'Europe in Search of its Civil Society', *European Law Journal*, 8: 2 (2002), 198–217.

Deutscher Bundestag (ed.) *Die Charta der Grundrechte der Europäischen Union – Berichte und Dokumente* (Refereat Öffentlichkeitsarbeit, Zur Sache 01/01, Berlin, 2001).

de Witte, B., 'The Legal Status of the Charter: Vital Question or non-Issue?', *Maastricht Journal of European and Comparative Law*, 8: 1 (2001), 81–9.

Diez, T., 'Speaking "Europe": the politics of integration discourse', *Journal of European Public Policy*, 6: 4 (Special Issue, 1999), 598–613.

Dinan, D., *Ever Closer Union?* (1st edn, Macmillan – now Palgrave Macmillan, Basingstoke, 1994).

Dobson, L. & Follesdal, A., *Political Theory and the European Constitution* (Routledge, London, 2004).

Dowrick, F. E., (ed.) *Human Rights: Problems, Perspectives, Texts* (Saxon House, Farnborough, 1979).

Dryzek, J. S., *Deliberative Democracy and Beyond: Liberals, Critics, Contestations*, (Oxford University Press, Oxford, 2000).

Ellmeier, A. & Rásky, B. (eds) *Kulturpolitik in Europa – Europäische Kulturpolitik?: Von nationalstaatlichen und transnationalen Konzeptionen* (Internationales Archiv füe Kulturanalysen, Wien, 1997).

Elster, J., (ed.) *Deliberative Democracy* (Cambridge University Press, Cambridge, 1998).

Engel, C., 'The European Charter of Rights: a Changed Political Opportunity Structure and its Normative Consequence', *European Law Journal*, 7: 2 (2001), 151–70.

Eriksen, E. O. & Fossum, J. E. (eds) *Democracy in the European Union: Integration through Deliberation?* (Routledge, London, 2000).

Eriksen, E. O. & Fossum, J. E. 'The EU and Post-National Legitimacy', *ARENA Working Paper* No. 00/26, Oslo (2000).

Eriksen, E. O., Fossum, J. E. & Menéndez, A. J. (eds) *The Chartering of Europe* (Nomos, Baden-Baden, 2003).

Eriksen, E. O., Fossum, J. E. & Menéndez, A. J. (eds) *Developing a European Constitution* (Routledge, London, 2004).

European Commission, *European Governance: a White Paper*, COM (2001) 428, Brussels, 25.07.2001.

European Commission, 'Report on European Union' (the Commission's contribution to the Tindemans report), *EC Bulletin*, Supplement 5/75, pp. 5–42.

European Commission, 'Towards European citizenship', *EC Bulletin*, Supplement 7/75.

European Council, 'Declaration on European Identity', *EC Bulletin*, EC 12/1973.

European Council, 'Solemn Declaration on European Union', *EC Bulletin*, 6/1983.

European Council, 'Report from the ad hoc Committee on a People's Europe to the European Council (part one March 29/30th 1985 Brussels, part two June 28/29th Milan), *EC Bulletin*, Supplement 7/85 (1985).

European Council, 'Declaration on the Future of the Union', Annex IV to the Nice Treaty, Nice, 10.12.2000.

European Council, 'Declaration on the Future of the EU', Annex to the Conclusions of the presidency, Laeken, 14/15.12.2001.

European Parliament, 'Report on the Drafting of the EU Charter of Fundamental Rights' (rapporteurs: Andrew Duff & Johannes Voggenhuber), part I Document

A5 0064/2000 of 16.03.2000; part II, Document A5 00325/2000 of 14.11.2000.

European University Institute: Reflection Group on 'The Long-Term Implications of EU Enlargement: the Nature of the New Border', Chairman Giulio Amato, Rapporteur Judy Batt, *Final Report* (The Robert Schumann Centre-EUI/European Commission Forward Studies Unit, Florence, 1999).

Falk, R., *Human Rights Horizons: the Pursuit of Justice in a Globalizing World* (Routledge, London, 2000).

Feus, K. (ed.) *The EU Charter of Fundamental Rights: text and commentaries* (Federal Trust, London, 2001).

Friis, L. & Murphy, A., 'The European Union and Central and Eastern Europe: Governance and Boundaries', *Journal of Common Market Studies*, 37: 2 (1999), 211–32.

Gaja, G., 'New Instruments and Institutions for Enhancing the Protection of Human Rights in Europe?', in P. Alston & J. H. H. Weiler (eds) *The EU and Human Rights* (Oxford University Press, Oxford, 1999).

Glaab, M., 'Die Bürger in Europa', in W. Weidenfeld (ed.) *Europahandbuch* (Verlag Bertelsmannstiftung, Gütersloh, 1999).

Göler, D. & Maurer, A., 'Die Konventsmethode in der Europäischen Union-Ausnahme oder Modell?', *SWP-Studie*, S 44, (2004).

Haas, E. B., *The Obsolescence of Regional Integration Theory* (University of California Press, Berkeley, 1975).

Habermas, J., 'Sì, voglio una Costituzione per l'Europa federale', interview with the *Caffè Europa online journal*, 14.12.00 (www.caffeeuropa.it/attualita/112habermas).

Habermas, Jürgen, 'Was ist ein Volk?', Süddeutsche Zeitung, München (26.09.1996).

Habermas, J., *Faktizität und Geltung* (Suhrkamp, Frankfurt a. M., 1998).

Habermas, J., *Die postnationale Konstellation: Politische Essays* (Suhrkamp, Frankfurt a. M., 1998).

Habermas, J., *Die Einbeziehung des Anderen – Studien zur politischen Theorie* (Suhrkamp, Frankfurt a. M., 1999).

Heywood, A., *Key Concepts in Politics*, Macmillan Study Guides (Macmillan – now Palgrave Macmillan, Basingstoke, 2000).

Hoffmann, L., 'The Convention on the Future of Europe: Thoughts on the Convention-Model', *Jean Monnet Working Paper 11/02* (2002).

Hohmann, H., 'Die Charta der Grundrechte der Europäischen Union- Ein wichtiger Beitrag zur Legitimation der EU', *Aus Politik und Zeitgeschichte*, B 52–53/2000, 5–11.

Höreth, M., 'No Way Out for the Beast? The Unsolved Legitimacy Problem of European Governance', *Journal of European Public Policy*, 6: 2 (1999), 249–68.

Howe, P., 'A Community of Europeans: the Requisite Underpinnings', *Journal of Common Market Studies*, 33: 1 (1995), 27–46.

Howe, P., 'Insiders and Outsiders in a Community of Europeans: a Reply to Kostakopoulou', *Journal of Common Market Studies*, 35: 2 (1997), 308–14.

Incerti, M., Kurpas, S. & Schönlau, J. 'What Prospects for the Ratification of the Constitutional Treaty?', *EPIN-Working Paper* No. 12, Brussels (2005).

Ingram, Attracta, *A Political Theory of Rights* (Clarendon Press, Oxford, 1994).

Jones, P., *Rights: Issues in Political Theory* (Macmillan – now Palgrave Macmillan, Basingstoke, 1994).

Kaufmann, S. Y., *Grundrechtecharta der Europäischen Union* (Europa Union Verlag, Bonn, 2001).

Kostakopoulou, T., 'Why a "Community of Europeans" could be a Community of Exclusion: a Reply to Howe', *Journal of Common Market Studies*, 35: 2 (1997), 301–07.

Kröner's *Philosophisches Wörterbuch* (G. Schischkoff, ed.), (Kröner, Stuttgart, 1991).

Kumm, M., 'The Revolt of National Courts: an Assessment of the New Challenges to the Supremacy of the European Legal Order', in *The Changing Face of Europe*, Proceedings of the 16th Annual Graduate Student Conference, Institute on Western Europe, Columbia University, New York (25–27.03.1999).

Leinen, J & Schönlau, J., 'Die Erarbeitung der EU-Grundrechtecharta im Konvent: nützliche Erfahrungen für die Zukunft Europas', *Integration*, 24: 1 (2001), 26–33.

Leinen, J. & Schönlau, J., 'Auf dem Weg zur europäischen Demokratie-politische Parteien auf EU-Ebene', *Integration*, 26: 3 (2003), 218–27.

Lenaerts, K. & Desomer, M., 'Bricks for a Constitutional Treaty of the European Union: Values, Objectives and Means', *European Law Review*, 27 (Aug. 2002), 377–407.

Lenaerts, K. & de Smijter, E., 'A "Bill of Rights" for the European Union', *Common Market Law Review*, 38: 2 (2001), 273–300.

Limbach, J., 'Das letzte Wort – Präsidentin Jutta Limbach über die politische Macht des Bundesverfassungsgerichts', Spiegel-Gespräch, *Der Spiegel*, 40 (01.10.2001), 62–8.

Lindberg, L. N. & Scheingold, S. A., *Europe's Would-Be Polity: Patterns of Change in the European Community* (Englewood Cliffs, Prentice Hall, 1970).

Lord, C., *Democracy in the European Union* (Sheffield Academic Press, Sheffield, 1998).

Lord, C., 'Assessing Democracy in a Contested Polity', *Journal of Common Market Studies*, 39: 4 (2001), 641–61.

Lord, C., *A Democratic Audit of the European Union* (Palgrave Macmillan, Basingstoke, 2004).

Lord, C. & Beetham, D., 'Legitimizing the EU: Is there a "Post-parliamentary Basis" for its Legitimation?', *Journal of Common Market Studies*, 39: 3 (2001), 443–62.

Magnette, P., 'Le débat sur l'avenir de l'Union: processus et acteurs', *Contribution to the Colloquium of the Jean Monnet Action group Europe 2004 – Le Grand Débat* (European Commission, Brussels, 2001).

Magnette, P., 'Délibération vs. négotiation – Une premièr analyse de la Convention sur l'avenir de l'Union', *paper for the VIIe congrès de l' Association française de science politique* (Lille, 18–21.09.2002).

Magnette, P., 'La Convention Européenne: Argumenter et Négotier dans une Assemblée Constituente', *Revue française de science politique*, 54 (2004), 5–24.

McLaughlin, A. & Greenwood, J., 'The Management of Interest Representation in the European Union', *Journal of Common Market Studies*, 33: 1 (1995), 143–56.

Melchior, J., 'Die Europäische Wertegemeinschaft zwischen Rhetorik und Realität', in F. Karlhofer, J. Melchior & H. Sickinger (eds) *Anlassfall Österreich:*

Die Europäischen Union auf dem Weg zur Wertegemeinschaft (Nomos Verlag, Baden-Baden, 2001).

Menéndez, A. J., 'The Sinews of Peace: Rights to Solidarity in the Charter of Fundamental Rights of the Union', in E. O. Eriksen, J. E. Fossumand and A. J. Menéndez (eds) *The Chartering of Europe: the Charter of Fundamental Rights in Context* ARENA Report No. 8/2001, ARENA, Oslo (2001).

Merlingen, M., Mudde, C. & Sedelmeier, U., 'The Right and the Righteous? European Norms, Domestic Politics and the Sanctions against Austria', *Journal of Common Market Studies*, 39: 1 (2001), 59–77.

Meyer, J. (ed.), *Kommentar zur Charta der Grundrechte der Europäischen Union* (Nomos Verlag, Baden-Baden, 2003).

Milward, A., *The European Rescue of the Nation-State* (2nd edn, Routledge, London, 2000).

Moravcsik, A., 'European Federalism: Rhetoric and Reality', in R. Howse & K. Nicolaidis (eds) *The Federal Vision: Legitimacy and Levels of Governance in the US and the EU* (Oxford University Press, Oxford, 2001).

Müller-Graff, P. C., 'Europäische Verfassung und Grundrechtscharta: die Europäische Union als transnationales Gemeinwesen', *Integration*, 23: 1 (2000), 34–48.

Neyer, J., 'Discourse and Order in the EU', *Journal of Common Market Studies*, 41: 4 (2003), 687–706.

Nicolaidis, K., 'We, the Peoples of Europe . . . ', *Foreign Affairs*, 83: 6 (2004), 97–109.

Norman, P., *The Accidental Constitution: the Story of the European Convention* (Euro-Comment, Brussels, 2003).

Obradovic, D., 'Policy Legitimacy and the European Union', *Journal of Common Market Studies*, 34: 2 (1996), 191–221.

O'Leary, S., *The Evolving Concept of Community Citizenship: From the Free Movement of Persons to Union Citizenship* (Kluwer Law International, London, 1996).

O'Neill, M., 'Theorising the European Union: Towards a Post-Foundational Discourse', *Current Politics and Economics of Europe*, 9: 2 (2000), 121–41.

Pechstein, M. & Koenig, C., *Die Europäische Union – die Verträge von Maastricht und Amsterdam* (2nd edn, Mohr Siebeck, Tübingen, 1998).

Peers, S. & Ward, A., *The European Union Charter of Fundamental Rights* (Hart Publishing, Oxford, 2004).

Perry, M. J., *The Idea of Human Rights: Four Inquiries* (Oxford University Press, Oxford, 1998).

Pollack, J. & Slominiski, P.,'The Representative Quality of EU Treaty Reform: a Comparison between the IGC and the Convention', *European Integration*, 26: 3 (2004), 201–26.

Puchala, D. J., 'Of Blind Men, Elephants and International Integration', *Journal of Common Market Studies*, 10: 3 (1972), 267–84.

Reich, N., 'Zur Notwendigkeit einer Europäischen Grundrechtsbeschwerde', *Zeitschrift für Rechtspolitik*, 33: 9 (2000), 375–9.

Risse-Kappen, T., 'Exploring the Nature of the Beast: International Relations Theory and Comparative Policy Analysis meet the European Union', *Journal of Common Market Studies*, 34: 1 (1996), 53–80.

Rosamond, B., *Theories of European Integration* (Palgrave – now Palgrave Macmillan, Basingstoke, 2000).

Sandholtz, W. & Stone Sweet, A., (eds) *European Integration and Supranational Governance* (Oxford University Press, Oxford, 1998).

Scharpf, F. W., *Regieren in Europa: Effektiv und Demokratisch?* (Campus Verlag, Frankfurt a. M., 1999).

Scheuer, A., 'A Political Community', in H. Schmitt & J. Thomassen, *Political Representation and Legitimacy in the European Union* (Oxford University Press, Oxford, 1999).

Schimmelfennig, F., 'Legitimate Rule in the European Union: the Academic Debate', *Tübinger Arbeitspapier zur Internationalen Politik und Friedensforschung*, Nr 27, Tübingen (1996).

Schmidt, V. A., 'Democracy and Discourse in an Integrating Europe and a Globalising World', *European Law Journal*, 6: 3 (2000), 277–300.

Schmitter, P. C., 'What is There to Legitimize in the European Union . . . and How Might this be Accomplished?', *Institut für Höhere Studien Working Paper*, No. 75, Wien (2001).

Schmitz, T., 'Die Grundrechtecharta als Teil der Verfassung der Europäischen Union', *Zeitschrift Europarecht*, 39: 5 (2004), 691–713.

Schmuck, O., 'Die Ausarbeitung der Europäischen Grundrechtecharta als Element der Verfassungsentwicklung', *Integration*, 23: 1 (2000), 48–56.

Schönlau, J. & Castiglione, D., *The Making and Unmaking of the European Constitution* (working title, Palgrave Macmillan, Basingstoke, forthcoming 2006).

Shackleton, M., 'The Internal Legitimacy Crises of the European Union', in A. W. Cafruny & C. Lankowski (eds) *Europe's Ambiguous Unity: Conflict & Consensus in the Post-Maastricht Era* (Lynne Rienner, Boulder/London, 1997).

Shaw, J., 'Postnational Constitutionalism in the European Union', *Journal of European Public Policy*, 6: 4 (1999), 579–97.

Shaw, J., 'Process and Constitutional Discourse in the European Union', *Journal of Law and Society*, 27: 1 (2000), 4–37.

Shaw, J., *Law of the European Union* (3rd edn, Palgrave – now Palgrave Macmillan, Basingstoke, 2000).

Shaw, J. & Wiener, A., 'The Paradox of the "European Polity"', *Harvard Jean Monnet Working Paper*, WP 10/00, Cambridge, MA, (1999).

Siedentop, L., *Democracy in Europe* (Penguin, London, 2000).

Sinnott, R., 'Integration Theory, Subsidiarity and the Internationalisation of Issues: the Implications for Legitimacy', *EUI Working Paper* RSC No. 94/13, Florence (1994).

Smith, A. D., *National Identity* (Penguin, London, 1991).

Smith, A. D. & Gellner, E., 'The Debate', *Nations and Nationalism*, 2: 3 (1996), 358–70.

Sniderman, P. M., Fletcher, J. F., Russell, P. H. & Tetlock, P. E., *The Clash of Rights: Liberty, Equality, and Legitimacy in Pluralist Democracy* (Yale University Press, New Haven/London, 1996).

Thomassen, J. & Schmitt, H. (eds) *Political Representation and Legitimacy in the European Union* (Oxford University Press, Oxford, 1999).

Tindemans, L., 'Report on European Union', *EC Bulletin*, Supplement 1/76.

Tulkens, F., 'Towards a Greater Normative Coherence in Europe/the Implications of the Draft Charter of Fundamental Rights of the European Union', *Human Rights Law Journal*, 21: 8 (2000), 329–32.

von Bogdandy, A., 'The European Union as a Human Rights Organization? Human Rights at the Core of the European Union', *Common Market Law Review*, 37: 2 (2000), 1307–38.

Waldron, J., 'Rights', in R. E. Gordon & P. Pettit (eds) *A Companion to Contemporary Philosophical Philosophy.* (Blackwell, Oxford, 1995).

Walker, N., 'The White Paper in Constitutional Context', in C. Joerges, Y. Meny & J. H. H. Weiler, *Responding to the Commission White Paper* (EUI/Robert Schumann Centre, Florence, 2002).

Walker, N., 'Constitutionalising Enlargement, Enlarging Constitutionalism', *European Law Journal*, 9 (2003), 365–85.

Wallace, W. (ed.) *The Dynamics of Integration* (Pinter, London, 1990).

Warleigh, A., 'Frozen: Citizenship and European Unification', *Critical Review of International and Social Political Philosophy*, 1: 4 (1998), 113–51.

Warleigh, A., 'Better the Devil You Know? Synthetic and Confederal Understandings of European Unification', *West European Politics*, 21: 3 (1998), 1–18.

Warleigh, A., 'History Repeating? Framework Theory and Europe's Multi-Level Confederation', *European Integration*, 22: 2 (2000), 173–200.

Weatherill, S. & Beaumont, P., *EC Law* (Penguin, London, 1993).

Weber, Max, 'Legitimacy, Politics and the State', in W. Connolly (ed.) *Legitimacy and the State* (Blackwell, Oxford, 1984).

Weiler, J. H. H., 'European Neo-constitutionalism: in Search of Foundations for the European Constitutional Order', in R. Bellamy & D. Castiglione (eds) *Constitutionalism in Transformation: European and Theoretical Perspectives* (Blackwell, Oxford, 1996).

Weiler, J. H. H., 'The Reform of European Constitutionalism', *Journal of Common Market Studies*, 35: 1 (1997), 97–131.

Weiler, J. H. H., *The Constitution of Europe: Do the New Clothes have an Emperor? and other Essays on European Integration* (Cambridge University Press, Cambridge, 1999).

Weiler, J. H. H., 'Does the European Union Truly Need a Charter of Rights?', editorial in *European Law Journal*, 6: 2 (2000), 95–7.

Weiler, J. H. H., 'European Democracy and the Principle of Constitutional Tolerance: the Soul of Europe', in F. Cerutti & E. Rudolf (eds) *A Soul for Europe: a Reader (Vol. I)*, (Peeters, Leuven, 2001).

Weiler, J. H. H., 'A Constitution for Europe? Some Hard Choices', *Journal of Common Market Studies*, 40: 4 (2002), 563–80.

Weiler, J. H. H., Haltern, U. & Mayer, F., 'European Democracy and its Critique: Five Uneasy Pieces', *EUI Working Paper* RSC 95/11, Florence (1995).

Wendt, A. E., 'The Agent–Structure Problem in International Relations Theory', *International Organization*, 41: 3 (1987), 335–70.

Wicks, E., '"Declaratory of Existing Rights" – the United Kingdom's Role in Drafting a European Bill of Rights, Mark II', *Public Law*, 51: 3 (2001), 527–41.

Wiener, A. & Della Sala, V., 'Constitution-making and Citizenship Practice: Bridging the Democracy Gap in the EU', *Journal of Common Market Studies*, 35: 4 (1997), 595–614.

Wiener, A., *European Citizenship Practice: Building Institutions of the non-State* (Westview Press, Boulder, CO, 1998).

Wiener, A., 'The Embedded Acquis Communautaire: Transmission Belt And Prism of New Governance', in K. Neunreither & A. Wiener, *European Integration After Amsterdam: Institutional Dynamics and Prospects for Democracy* (Oxford University Press, Oxford, 2000).
Ziltener, P., *Strukturwandel in der europäischen Integration – die Europäische Union und die Veränderung von Staatlichkeit* (Verlag Westfälisches Dampfboot, Münster, 1999).

European Court of Justice Cases

Case 26/62 *Van Gend en Loos* v. *Nederlandse Administratie der Belastingen* [1963] ECR 1.
Case 6/64 [1964] ECR 585.
Case 29/69 *Stauder* v. *Stadt Ulm* [1969] ECR 419.
Case 11/70 *Internationale Handelsgesellschaft* v. *Einfuhr- und Vorratsstelle Getreide* [1970] ECR 1125.
Case 4/73 *Nold* v. *Commission* [1974], ECR 491.
Case 294/83 *Parti Ecologiste 'Les Verts'* v. *European Parliament* ECR 1339 [1987].
Case 190/84 *Les Verts-Parti Ecologiste* v. *Parliament* [1988] ECR 1017.
Case C-173/99 *BECTU* v. *UK*, opinion of Advocate General Tizzano (08.02.2001).
Case C-270/99 P, *Z* v. *European Parliament*, opinion of Advocate General Jacobs (22.03.2001).
Case C-377/98 *Netherlands* v. *European Parliament and Council*, opinion of Advocate General Jacobs (14.06.2001).
Case T-112/98, Court of First Instance, Judgement (20.02.2001).
Joined Cases C-20/00 *Booker Aquaculture Ltd trading as Marine Harvest McConnell* and C-64/00 *Hydro Seafood GSP Ltd* v. *The Scottish Ministers*, opinion of Advocate General Mischo, 20.09.2001.

Index

accountability, 72, 122, 148, 151, 153, 156, 168
acquis communautaire, 67, 75, 121, 132
added value (of the Charter), 52, 57, 64, 92, 94, 101
Adonnino report (on a 'Citizens' Europe), 56–7, 65–6
advocates general, 130–2
  see also European Court of Justice
applicant countries *see* candidate countries
'as-if' approach (on drafting the Charter), 84, 129
  see also Herzog, Roman
authority (political) 6, 13, 15, 18–19, 22, 24, 26–7, 70, 102, 109
autonomy, 6, 19, 23, 28, 35

belief (as element of legitimacy), 15, 22, 24, 29, 34, 43, 143
belonging, feeling of, 38, 52, 61, 68–9, 72–4, 94–5
  see also identity
boundaries (of the EU polity), 37, 44–5, 72
Bulgaria *see* candidate countries
Bundesverfassungsgericht *see* German constitutional court

candidate countries (also: applicant countries), 109, 122, 127
  role in the Convention, 153–4
citizens' Europe, 65
  see Adonnino report
citizens' initiative, 52
citizenship
  citizenship and identity 40, 51
  citizenship practice, 56, 60, 64, 67, 72, 75
  citizenship rights, 92–8

European citizenship, 8, 23, 40, 51, 56–69, 73, 77–9, 86, 91–5, 120–1, 138–9, 166
  see also demos, identity, routinisation
civil society, 9, 122, 147, 151, 153–4
cleavages within the Convention, 103, 114–15, 148
codification of rights, 4, 7, 26, 135, 152, 158
collectivity, 6, 8, 13, 15–16, 28, 42, 49, 61, 68, 103
Cologne mandate, 3, 12, 26, 34–5, 46, 66, 77, 81–92, 99–102, 107, 111, 119, 126, 142, 153, 162–3, 166, 169
  see also summits
Commission (European), 3, 10, 43, 51–2, 55, 64–5, 81, 109–10, 134, 136, 166
Committee of Permanent Representatives (COREPER), 108–9
Committee of the Regions, 81, 109
common currency, 46, 94
community
  of rights, 27
  of values, 9, 55, 78–80, 98, 101, 119, 138–41, 166–8
Community Charter of Fundamental Social Rights of Workers, 81, 86
competencies of the EU, 49, 78, 86–8, 136, 159
components of the Convention, 134
  see also delegations
compossibility of different rights, (Bellamy), 19
consent (as element of legitimacy), 6, 15, 22, 34, 39, 131
consensus, 4, 20–1, 29, 36, 45–6, 74–5, 79, 84, 110, 113–18, 132–5, 148, 156, 167
constituent assembly, 32, 144

Index of Names